M000111461

Hiking Washington's William O. Douglas Wilderness

A Guide to the Area's Greatest Hiking Adventures

Fred Barstad

FALCON GUIDE ®

GUILFORD, CONNECTICUT
HELENA, MONTANA

AN IMPRINT OF THE GLOBE PEQUOT PRESS

A **FALCON**GUIDE ®

Text design by Nancy Freeborn
Maps by Mapping Specialists © Morris Book
Publishing, LLC
Spine photo © 2004 Michael DeYoung
All photos by author Fred Barstad

Library of Congress Cataloging-in-Publication Data
Barstad, Fred.
  Hiking Washington's William O. Douglas wilderness :
a guide to the area's greatest hiking adventures /
Fred Barstad.
      p. cm.
  ISBN-13: 978-0-7627-3659-1
  ISBN-10: 0-7627-3659-3
  1. Hiking–Washington (State)–William O. Douglas
Wilderness–Guidebooks. 2. Trails–Washington (State–
William O. Douglas Wilderness–Guidebooks. [1.
William O. Douglas Wilderness
(Wash.)–Guidebooks.] I. Title.
  GV199.42.W2B27 2006
  796.5209797–dc22
                                    2006009211
Manufactured in the United States of America
First Edition/First Printing

Contents

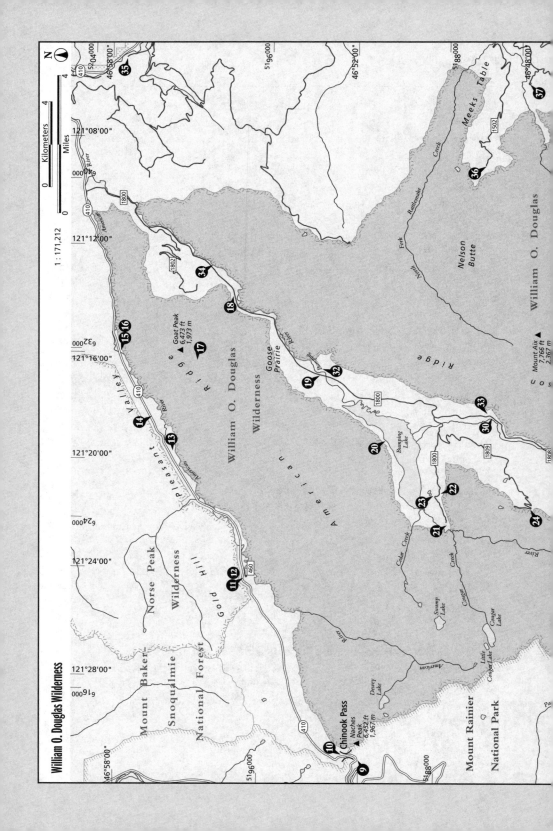

William O. Douglas Wilderness

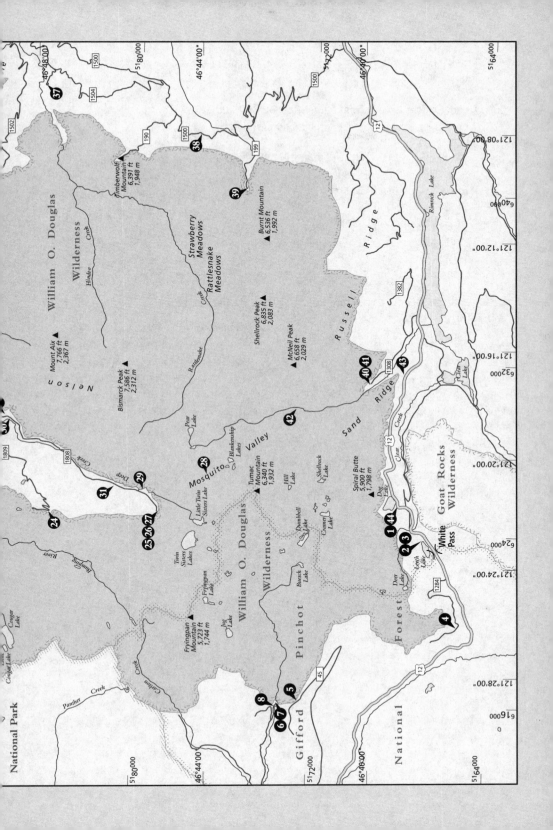

Acknowledgments

Thanks to the employees of the USDA Forest Service at Naches Ranger District for providing valuable information. Thanks to Denny and Darlene Sveen for providing trail information and cooking meals for tired hikers. Thanks to Bob and Gina Barstad for climbing to the summit of Mount Aix with me and to Jeanette Sams for hiking and camping with me. Thanks to the many people who camped close to me in the campgrounds around the perimeter of the wilderness and made the evenings much more pleasant. Most of all, thanks to my wife, Sue Barstad, for spending much of her summer hiking and camping with me and editing my raw text.

Every effort has been made by the author and editors to make this guide as accurate and useful as possible. However, many things can change after a guide is published—trails are rerouted, regulations change, techniques evolve, facilities come under new management, etc.

We would love to hear from you concerning your experiences with this guide and how you feel it could be improved and kept up to date. While we may not be able to respond to all comments and suggestions, we'll take them to heart, and we'll also make certain to share them with the author. Please send your comments and suggestions to the following address:

> The Globe Pequot Press
> Reader Response/Editorial Department
> P.O. Box 480
> Guilford, CT 06437

Or you may e-mail us at:

> editorial@GlobePequot.com

Thanks for your input, and happy trails!

Lily Lake (Hike 23)

Introduction

History of the William O. Douglas Wilderness

Before the time of European exploration, Native Americans hunted and fished in the territory that was to become the William O. Douglas Wilderness. As early as the 1860s, Cowlitz Pass was studied as a possible route for a road across the Cascade Mountains. By 1880 cattlemen were using many parts of the area. Starting a few years later and continuing until about 1940, sheepherders grazed huge bands of sheep on the meadows and subalpine slopes.

Around 1890, mining claims were filed near the site of Copper City. If it were not for the narrow strip of nonwilderness along the Bumping River and Deep Creek, Copper City would be in the very heart of the William O. Douglas Wilderness. After the claims were filed, a small mining boom took place. It was rumored that a railroad was to be built up the Naches and Bumping River Canyons to access coal deposits near Fish Lake, which is now within the wilderness. The idea of close railroad access only fueled the fires of development at Copper City. The mines never really became a paying operation, and the railroad was never built. In the 1940s mining ceased at Copper City.

The Bumping Lake Dam was built about 1910 by the U.S. Bureau of Reclamation to store water for agricultural use in the Yakima Valley. Shortly before the completion of the dam, a road was constructed from the dam site to Copper City. Today the roads up the Bumping River and Deep Creek provide access to the heart of the William O. Douglas Wilderness, as well as for the campers and anglers along the Bumping River and at Bumping Lake.

In 1946 a 90,000-acre portion of the present William O. Douglas Wilderness was designated as "Cougar Lakes Limited Area." There was a proposal in 1963 to split the area into the Cougar Lakes Scenic Area and the Mount Aix Wild Area. This started a series of proposals that eventually ended with the Washington Wilderness Bill of 1984, which created the present William O. Douglas Wilderness. The wilderness was named for U.S. Supreme Court justice William Orville Douglas, who grew up in Yakima. President Franklin D. Roosevelt appointed Douglas to the Supreme Court in 1939, and he served until 1975.

Cascades Geology

From central Washington to Northern California, the Cascade Range is mostly composed of uplifted sedimentary and ancient lava rock. These uplifted mountains are known as the Old Cascades. Built atop this foundation, and in some cases slightly to the east of it, are a string of huge, lofty strato-volcanoes, as well as lesser cones, vents, and subsequent lava flows. These peaks, called the High Cascades, are part of what is known as the "Ring of Fire" that encircles the Pacific Ocean. On a clear day

1

Glacial scratches on rock near Blankenship Lake.

one or more of these strato-volcanoes are visible from almost any elevated spot in the range. In the area east of Mount Rainier where the William O. Douglas Wilderness lies, ridges made up mostly of volcanic rock extend east from the crest of the range for many miles. Just beneath the forest duff in most places, there is a layer of light gray volcanic ash from the 1980 eruption of Mount St. Helens. This ash was spread over the entire William O. Douglas Wilderness, and where it hasn't been washed away, it is still present.

Geography of the William O. Douglas Wilderness

The 166,000-acre William O. Douglas Wilderness is an area of widely diverse geography. Most of the wilderness lies east of the summit of the Cascade Range, southeast of and bordering Mount Rainier National Park. The wilderness is generally bordered on the south by U.S. Highway 12 and on the north by State Route 410. On the east, Forest Road 1500 generally parallels the wilderness boundary between US 12 and SR 410.

Climbing north from US 12 at White Pass on the Sand Lake, Pacific Crest, or Cramer Lake Trails, you soon gain a plateau. This broad, relatively flat area extends north to Twin Lakes, about 6 miles from the pass. An ice sheet once covered the plateau, which is dotted with literally hundreds of small to medium-size lakes, ponds, and marshes. The ice smoothed the landscape to a great extent but also gored out many shallow depressions. These depressions combined with the generally poor drainage of much of the plateau account for the large number of lakes and ponds. Some of the smoothed bedrock of the area shows parallel scratches on its surface, further evidence of glacial movement. Near the center of the plateau stands the volcanic cone of 6,340-foot-high Tumac Mountain. To the west a row of small, generally rounded peaks marks the edge of the plateau. Several streams cut between these peaks to descend into the Cowlitz River drainage.

Along the western edge of the wilderness, across Carlton Pass, north of the plateau and extending to Chinook Pass, the Cascade Crest is far more rugged and well defined. Steeply sloping alpine meadows mingle with rocky peaks and cliffs and stands of alpine timber. These flower-covered meadows provide a kaleidoscope of color starting shortly after the snow melts.

American Ridge rises above the American River Canyon east of Chinook Pass. Close to its western end, the flora on American Ridge is nearly the same as that along the Cascade Crest. As you get farther east along the rugged ridgeline, the country becomes drier and the terrain begins to resemble the ridges and canyons of the eastern portion of the wilderness.

East of the Bumping River, Deep Creek, and Indian Creek, the William O. Douglas Wilderness takes on a completely different character than is found farther to the west. In this drier climate, most of the higher ridges are bare rock. The highest peaks in the wilderness, 7,766-foot-high Mount Aix and 7,586-foot-high Bismarck Peak, are along the ridges east of Deep Creek. A few patches of snow cling to the sheltered slopes of these peaks throughout the summer. Farther to the east, below the high ridges, the forks of Rattlesnake Creek have cut deep, precipitous canyons as they flow north toward the Naches River. Much of the eastern boundary of the wilderness is along the high and comparatively dry rims east of the Rattlesnake drainage.

Climate

The ridgeline of the Cascade Range, rising a mile or more above the Pacific Ocean in most places along the western boundary of the William O. Douglas Wilderness, creates a barrier to moisture-laden storms coming from the west. The moist marine air is forced to rise and therefore cool as it climbs over the western slope of the range. Cooler air can hold less moisture so it precipitates in the form of rain or snow—in some spots there is up to 150 inches of rainfall per year. At times, low clouds (sometimes called a "marine deck") may fill the western canyons and valleys while the higher ridges and peaks are basking in sunshine. Because of this damp, maritime climate, the western side of the mountains, except where logging or fires have disturbed it, is covered with dense forest.

Along the crest, clouds sometimes get stuck and continue to drop precipitation even after the main storm has passed. Snowstorms and freezing temperatures can occur any time of the year. These conditions cause a very heavy snowpack to accumulate along the crest. This snowpack lingers well into the early summer and provides moisture for the expansive flower gardens that cover nearly every unforested slope. The heavy snowpack along the crest also protects the flowers and ground-hugging shrubs from the intense cold, allowing them to prosper in this harsh environment.

The higher peaks and ridgelines at times make their own weather. Cloud caps can appear from an otherwise clear sky. In these caps, heavy wind, fog, and rain or snow can combine to make hiking miserable, difficult, and dangerous, if not impossible.

As the air passes the crest and begins to drop, it warms by compression (sometimes called the "Chinook effect"). Since this warmer air is able to hold more water, there is much less rainfall, and in some cases the clouds just evaporate. Because of the drier climate, the forest gradually thins out and the flower displays, while still abundant, usually cannot match the ones close to the crest of the range. Much of the William O. Douglas Wilderness lies within this drier zone.

The range is also a temperature barrier. On the western slopes the ocean moderates the climate. It is rarely very hot in the summer, and the cold continental air from the interior only occasionally spills over the crest in the winter. East of the crest, including most of the William O. Douglas Wilderness, the winters are colder and the summers hotter than they are on the western slopes of the range.

Big Watchable Wildlife

Deer

Blacktail deer are the most commonly seen large animal in the Washington Cascades west of the Cascade summit. Blacktails *(Odocoileus hemionus columbianus)*, a slightly smaller and darker subspecies of mule deer *(Odocoileus hemionus hemionus)*, inhabit the damp western slopes of the Cascades as well as the Coast Range. Typical of a forest-loving animal, the antlers of a blacktail are much smaller than those of a mule deer. The namesake of a blacktail, its tail, is wider than that of a mule deer and completely black on its upper side. When alarmed, a blacktail will generally run with its tail carried horizontally, but they occasionally flag (hold their tail straight up). In the William O. Douglas Wilderness, blacktail deer are common only along the very far-western edge.

East of the Cascades is the range of the larger-antlered mule deer. The mule deer is easily distinguished from the blacktail by its white ropelike tail, which is tipped in black and generally hangs straight down even when alarmed. A mule deer's much larger ears (hence its name) appear to be fuzzy on the edges and inside because of a thin covering of longer hair. The farther east you get in the William O. Douglas Wilderness, the more likely it is that the deer you will see are mule deer.

Over most of the William O. Douglas Wilderness, you may see deer that you can't identify as either a blacktail or a mule deer. This animal's tail is nearly as wide as a

Pika.

blacktail's, but it's white with a black tip and a black stripe running up the center of its top. Many of the characteristics of this deer appear to be in between those of mule deer and blacktails because they are cross-breeds. Nearly all the deer in some areas are these "cross deer," sometimes called "cross bucks."

You can expect to see deer or at least their tracks along all the hikes described in this book. In fact, unfortunately some people get too close a look when they hit them with their cars.

Elk

Two subspecies of elk (aka wapiti) roam the William O. Douglas Wilderness. The wetter western slope, which constitutes only a small part of the western edge of the wilderness, is the home of the slightly larger and darker Roosevelt elk *(Cervus elaphus rooseveliti)*. Roosevelt bulls, which may weigh more than 1,000 pounds, are the largest animals to inhabit the Cascades. Roosevelts are common and may be expected almost anywhere on the west slopes and along the crest of the mountains. Roosevelt elk normally have calves every other year whereas Rocky Mountain elk have them yearly.

Mountain goat.

On the eastern slopes of the range, where a large part of the William O. Douglas Wilderness lies, live the Rocky Mountain elk *(Cervus elaphus nelsoni)*. In 1913 a group of landowners, sportsmen, and county officials introduced Rocky Mountain elk from Yellowstone National Park into the Yakima area of central Washington. Now the herd numbers 8,000 or more. During the winter elk feed at the Oak Creek State Wildlife Area west of Naches, making this an excellent viewing site. A herd of California bighorn sheep also winters on the Oak Creek State Wildlife Area, providing an excellent viewing opportunity.

With only a couple of exceptions, elk sightings are possible along all the trails described in this book. A note of caution: When driving west of Naches along US 12 or SR 410, especially in the winter and spring, keep a lookout for these huge animals. Hitting one could easily total your car.

Mountain goats

Mountain goats *(Oreamnos americanus)* reside on most of the more rugged peaks and ridges of the William O. Douglas Wilderness. Bands of these agile climbers occupy the precipitous slopes of Nelson Ridge and around Mount Aix. Many of the smaller peaks and ridges in the region have resident herds as well. Mountain goats are pure white except for their eyes, horns, and hooves and are almost never found far from the cliffs. Unlike deer and elk, which seek shelter at lower elevations, goats tend to stay on the high ridges throughout the winter. On these exposed ridgelines, hurricane-force winds blow away most of the snow cover, exposing the rocks that are covered with lichen and also uncovering other tiny alpine plants. The goats exist on this seemingly meager diet through the long winter months.

Bears

Black Bears *(Ursus americanus)* are found throughout the Cascade Range. See "Be Bear Aware" under "Backcountry Safety and Hazards," below, for more information about hiking and camping in bear country. Better yet, pick up a copy of the pocket-size book *Bear Aware,* by Bill Schneider, another FalconGuide.

Cougars

Cougars *(Felis concolor),* also known as mountain lions, though seldom seen by hikers, are also found throughout the region. See "Be Cougar Alert" under "Backcountry Safety and Hazards" for more information.

Backcountry Safety and Hazards

Being Prepared

There are a few simple things you can do that will improve your chances of staying healthy while you are hiking.

Being very careful about your drinking-water supply is one of the most important things you can do to keep yourself healthy on the trail. Filter, chemically treat, or boil all surface water before drinking, washing utensils, or brushing your teeth with it. The water may look clean and pure, and it may be, but you can never be sure. In a few cases there is no water along the trail, so you need to take along all that you will need. If you use a filter, be sure it has a fairly new cartridge or has been recently cleaned before you leave on your hike. Many of the trailheads do not have potable water.

Before heading into the mountains, check the weather report. Stormy weather with wind, rain, or even snow is possible at any time of year. If you are using an altimeter, check it when you are at camp or anyplace where you'll be staying for a few hours. If your altimeter reads higher than it did a few hours ago, the air pressure is falling and there may be a storm approaching.

Hot sunny weather on the exposed slopes can cause quick dehydration. Keep yourself well fed and drink plenty of liquids. Also at these times, a broad-brimmed hat, light-colored, loose-fitting clothes, and lots of sunscreen are what is needed.

Inform friends or relatives of your plans and when you plan to return. If you are planning a long or difficult hike, be sure to get into shape ahead of time. This will make your trip much more pleasant as well as safer. Of all the safety tips, the most important is to take your brain with you when you go into the wilderness. Without it, no tips will help, and with it almost any obstacle can be avoided or overcome. Think about what you are doing, be safe, and have a great time in the outdoors.

You Might Never Know What Hit You

Thunderstorms are not particularly common in the William O. Douglas Wilderness, but they do occur. On the high ridges and peaks, it is relatively easy to see and hear a thunderstorm before it reaches your location. But in the valleys and canyons, a storm can be on you with very little advance warning. If a lightning storm catches you, take special precautions.

Remember:

- Lightning can travel far ahead of the storm, so try to take cover well before the storm hits.
- If you are on a peak or ridgeline, get off of it as fast as you safely can.
- Don't try to get back to your vehicle. It isn't worth the risk. Instead, seek the best shelter you can find. Lightning storms usually last only a short time, and from a safe spot you might even enjoy watching the storm.
- Generally the best place to wait out a lightning storm is in an area of evenly sized, preferably smaller, timber, well away from individual large trees.
- Stay away from anything that might attract lightning, such as metal tent poles, graphite fishing rods, and metal-frame backpacks.

Meeting Stock on the Trail

Meeting stock traffic is a fairly common occurrence in the William O. Douglas Wilderness, so it's a good idea to know how to pass stock with the least possible disturbance or danger. If you meet parties with stock, try to get as far off the trail as possible. Horsemen prefer that you stand on the downhill side of the trail, but there is some question as to whether this is the safest place for a hiker. If possible, I like to get well off the trail on the uphill side. It is often a good idea to talk quietly to the horses and their riders, as this often seems to calm the horses. If you have the family dog with you, be sure to keep it restrained and quiet. Dogs cause many horse wrecks.

Following a Faint Trail

A few of the trails described in this book are faint, so good map-reading and route-finding skills are required to find your way. There are a few things you can do to make your route-finding task easier.

Before you start your hike, read the entire hike description for the hike you are about to take. Try to keep track of your position on your map at all times while hiking. Learn to use your compass. Remember that a compass points toward magnetic north, which is not necessarily true north. In the William O. Douglas Wilderness, the declination is about 18 degrees east. That means that the compass points that much east of true north. The USGS quad maps show the magnetic declination for that particular map.

When properly used, an altimeter can be very helpful for tracking your progress. Altimeters run on air pressure, which is always changing, so they must be set often. Any time you reach a point where you are sure of the elevation, set your altimeter, even if you previously set it only 2 or 3 hours ago.

GPS coordinates for the trailheads and most major trail junctions are given at the end of most hike descriptions. If you are proficient in the use of a GPS receiver, these can be very helpful, but remember that the government scrambles GPS signals. This may cause the readings to be a little off. Usually the reading you will get on your receiver will be within 30 yards of your actual location, but at times they may be much farther off than that. In a few spots, especially down in a canyon in deep forest, GPS signals may be hard to get. Some GPS units use the GPS signal to plot your altitude, while others have a built-in altimeter. The ones that use the GPS signal will often be off by 150 feet or more, which is too far to be very helpful in finding your location. Don't rely on your GPS unit or your altimeter as your only means of navigation—they are very useful tools but don't take the place of knowing how to use a map and compass effectively.

While you're hiking, watch for blazes cut into the bark of trees and rock cairns on the ground. Logs that have been sawed off may also be an indicator of the trail's route. Trees with the branches missing on one side may show that the trail passes on that side of the tree. Through thick woods, look for strips where the trees are much smaller or nonexistent; this could be the route that was once cleared for the trail.

All these things are not positive signs that you are going the right way, but when used together with good compass and map skills, they make it much easier to follow a faint trail.

Be Bear Aware

The first step of any hike in bear country is an attitude adjustment. Being prepared for bears means having the right information as well as the right equipment. Unlike national-park bears, the black bears in the part of the Washington Cascades covered in this book are lightly hunted each year. This hunting doesn't seem to have much effect on the overall population of bears, but it does make them warier of people and less likely to become a problem. Bears in this area rarely approach humans, but they may pose a danger if you handle food improperly. At the very least, letting a bear get human food is like contributing—directly—to the eventual destruction of the bear. Think of proper bear etiquette as protecting the bears as much as yourself. Black bears may be found on any hike covered in this book.

Camping in bear country. Staying overnight in bear country is not terribly dangerous, but it adds an additional risk to your trip. The main problems are the presence of food, cooking, and garbage. Following a few basic rules greatly minimizes the risk to you and the bears.

Storing food and garbage. Be sure to finalize your food-storage plans before it gets dark. It's not only difficult to store food in the dark, it's easier to forget some juicy morsel you may have dropped on the ground. Also, be sure to store food in air-tight, waterproof bags to prevent food odors from circulating through the forest. Store your garbage just as if it were food: It is food to a bear.

Take a special bag for storing food. The bag must be sturdy and waterproof. You can get dry bags at most outdoor-specialty stores, but you can get by with a trash-compactor bag. Regular garbage bags break and leave your food spread on the ground. You also need 100 feet of nylon cord. Parachute cord will usually suffice. The classic method of hanging food and gear smelling of food is to tie a rock or piece of wood to the end of your cord and toss it over a branch. And, of course, don't let the rock or stick come down and hit you or someone else on the head. Attach the bag and hoist it up 10 feet or more and well away from the trunk of any tree.

What to hang. To be as safe as possible, hang anything that has any food smell. If you spilled something on your clothes, change before sleeping and hang the soiled garments with the food and garbage.

What to keep in your tent. You can't be too careful in keeping food smells out of the tent. Just in case a bear has become accustomed to coming into that campsite looking for food, it's vital to keep all food smells out of the tent. This usually includes your pack, which is hard to keep odor-free. Only take valuables (like cameras, binoculars, clothing, and sleeping gear) into the tent.

Types of food. What food you have along is much less critical than how you handle it, cook it, and store it. Consider, however, that the fewer dishes and/or less packaging the better.

Hanging food at night is not the only storage issue. Also make sure you place food correctly in your pack. Use airtight packages as much as possible. Store food in the containers it came in or, if open, in ziplock bags. This keeps food smells out of your pack and off your camping gear and clothes.

Don't cook so much food that you have to deal with leftovers. If you do end up with extra food, however, you only have two choices. Carry it out or burn it. Don't bury it, throw it in a lake, or leave it anywhere in bear country. A bear will most likely find and dig up any food or garbage buried in the backcountry.

If you end up with lots of food scraps in the dishwater, strain out the scraps and store them in ziplock bags with the other garbage or burn them. You can bring a lightweight screen to filter the food scraps from the dishwater, but be sure to store the screen with the food and garbage. If you have a campfire, pour the dishwater around the edge of the fire. If you don't have a campfire, take the dishwater at least 100 yards downwind and downhill from camp and pour it on the ground or in a small hole. Don't put dishwater or food scraps in a lake or stream. Wash dishes immediately after eating so a minimum of food odors linger in the area.

Be Cougar Alert

If you have done much hiking in cougar country, you have almost surely been watched by a cougar and never even known it. Many people consider themselves very lucky to see this furtive animal in the wild, but the big cats, nature's perfect predators, are potentially dangerous. Attacks on humans are exceedingly rare, but it is wise to educate yourself before entering mountain lion country.

To stay as safe as possible in cougar habitat, follow this advice:

- Travel with a friend or group. There is safety in numbers.
- Don't let small children wander away by themselves. Small adults and children are more likely to be attacked than are larger adults.
- Don't let pets run unleashed.
- Know how to behave if you meet a cougar.

What to Do if You Encounter a Cougar

In the vast majority of mountain lion encounters, these animals exhibit avoidance, curiosity, or even indifference that never results in human injury, but it is natural to be alarmed if you have an encounter of any kind. Try to keep cool and consider the following:

Recognize threatening cougar behavior. A few clues may gauge the risk of attack. If a mountain lion is 50 yards or more away and directs its attention toward you, it might just be curious. This situation represents only a slight risk to adults but a more serious risk to unaccompanied children. At this point you should move away, while keeping the animal in your peripheral vision. Also look for rocks, sticks, or something to use as a weapon, just in case.

If the cougar is crouched and staring at you from less than 50 yards away, it may be assessing the chances of a successful attack. If this behavior continues, your risk may be high.

Do not approach a cougar. Instead, give the animal an opportunity to move on. Slowly back away, but maintain eye contact if close. Cougars are not known to attack humans to defend their young or a kill, but they have been reported to "charge" in rare instances and may want to remain in the area. If you come upon a cougar on a kill, it is best to take another route.

Do not run from a cougar. Running may stimulate the animal's predatory response, and you may get chased.

Make lots of noise. If you encounter a cougar, be vocal, talk loudly and constantly, and yell to make others in the area aware of the situation. Try not to panic.

Maintain eye contact. Eye contact shows the cougar that you are aware of his presence. However, if the lion's behavior is not threatening (for example, grooming or periodically looking away), maintain visual contact with your peripheral vision and move away.

Appear larger than you are. Raise your arms above your head and make steady waving motions. Raise your jacket or other object above your head. Do not bend over, as this will make you look smaller and more "preylike."

If you are with small children, pick them up. Bring the children close to you without bending over, maintaining eye contact with the cougar. If you are with other children or adults, band together.

Defend yourself. If attacked, fight back. Try to remain standing. Do not feign death. Pick up a branch or rock; pull out a knife, pepper spray, or other deterrent device. Everything is a potential weapon; individuals have fended off cougar attacks with rocks, branches, and even cameras.

Defend others. In past attacks on children, adults have successfully stopped the attacks. Defend your partners, but don't physically defend your pet.

Respect any warning signs posted by agencies. For the most part these signs alert the public to recent cougar sightings near campgrounds or trailheads.

Spread the word. Before leaving on your hike, discuss lions and teach others in your group how to behave in case of a cougar encounter.

Report encounters. If you have an encounter, record the location and details of the encounter, and notify the landowner or land management agency. In areas like the southern Washington Cascades, where cougars are fairly common, a sighting doesn't constitute an encounter and may not warrant any action.

If physical injury occurs, it is important to not disturb the site of the attack any more than is necessary to rescue the victim. Cougars that have attacked people must be killed, and an undisturbed site may be critical in locating the dangerous cat.

See the FalconGuide *Lion Sense* for more details and tips for safe outdoor recreation in cougar country.

Be Rattlesnake Alert

Once you hear a rattlesnake buzz, it's a sound you will never forget. Forty-five of the fifty states are home to at least one species of rattlesnake. Unless you will be hiking only in Alaska, Hawaii, Rhode Island, Delaware, or Maine, you need to be aware of the possibility of encountering one. Within these rattlesnake states, some areas have only a very small population of these poisonous reptiles, and other areas have none at all. Local inquiry is the best way to assess your chances of meeting a rattler on the trail. Rattlesnakes are not common on any of the hikes covered in this book—in fact, on most of these hikes, there is almost no chance that you will encounter one. The exception is the lower parts of the Rattlesnake Creek drainage close to the eastern boundary of the wilderness, where there are a few rattlers.

Rattlesnakes are members of the pit viper family. Pit vipers have heat-sensing organs (pits) in their faces that are used to detect heat. This heat-detection system is probably integrated with the snakes' visual senses, allowing the snake to *see* heat. This allows rattlers to easily strike in the dark.

Rattlesnakes inhabit a wide range of climatic zones. They are found from below sea level up to subalpine zones in the mountains of the western United States. However, they are seldom common above the transition (ponderosa pine) zone. Most people don't realize that rattlers may be out during cooler temperatures and are occasionally seen sunning themselves on warm rocks when the air temperature is only a few degrees above freezing. Conversely, the snakes seek shade and/or burrows when it is very hot. For a rattlesnake the perfect temperature is about 80 degrees Fahrenheit.

Of the approximately 8,000 venomous snakebites in the United States each year, only ten to twenty are fatal, and in many cases these fatalities can be at least partly attributed to other preexisting medical problems. Of these fatal bites, the diamond-back rattlesnake, which ranges generally south of a line from Southern California to North Carolina, causes 95 percent. This is not to say that other species of rattlers do not cause much pain and an occasional death, but your chances of being killed by a snake diminish greatly as you travel north. Of the people who are bitten, about 35 percent are not injected with poison. These "dry bites" lead some people to wrongly believe that they are immune to rattlesnake venom.

Preventing Bites

Don't count on rattlesnakes to rattle at your approach: They are generally shy creatures in their encounters with humans. In most cases they will do their best to escape or lie quietly and let people pass without noticing them. In my personal experience only about half of the snakes have rattled before I saw them. Rattlers will sometimes strike before rattling.

Don't place your hands or feet in places that you can't see clearly. About 65 percent of snakebites are on the hands or forearms, and another 24 percent are on the feet, ankles, and lower legs.

In areas where there is a good chance of encountering a rattler, it may be advisable to wear protective clothing such as snake-proof gaiters or chaps and sturdy hiking boots.

During hot weather be especially alert during the morning, evening, and night as the snakes are most active at those times.

Don't handle any snake unless you can positively identify it as being nonpoisonous. Many people have been bitten by snakes that were believed to be dead when encountered.

Inquisitive children have a higher than average chance of being bitten by a rattlesnake. Because of their smaller bodies, they are also more susceptible to the toxins in the venom. Warn your children of the danger and watch them closely when you're in snake country.

First Aid for Snakebites

The best first-aid treatment for a snakebite is to get medical help as soon as possible, so that an injection of antivenom can be administered. Antivenom is the only proven treatment for snakebites. If you are within 45 minutes of medical assistance, just get there as quickly as safety allows, and don't bother with any other type of treatment.

If you are more than 45 minutes from medical help, first-aid treatment may be of some advantage. If there are three or more people in your party, you may want to send someone for help while you are starting the first-aid treatment, but don't leave the victim alone at this point.

A snakebite kit is necessary to adequately perform the treatment. There are two main types of snakebite kits available on the market. The most common ones include two or three rubber suction cups and a razor blade. The more advanced kits include a two-stage suction pump. The pump is capable of applying much more suction and is the preferred kit to carry. In addition to a snakebite kit, an elastic bandage is helpful in most treatments. If there is no disinfectant already in your snakebite or general first-aid kit, you should get some. If there is no safety razor included in your kit, one should be purchased. *Before putting your snakebite kit in your pack or pocket, open it, read the instructions, and familiarize yourself with its proper use.*

Forest Roads

Most of the roads leading to the trailheads described in this book are either paved or consist of a reasonably good gravel surface. Rough roads requiring a high-clearance vehicle are noted in the "Finding the trailhead" section at the beginning of each hike description.

Some of the paved roads are only one lane, with turnouts. Be very careful on these roads: Because of their smooth paved surfaces, many drivers drive much too fast on them. Brush grows up to the pavement edge on some of these roads, and sometimes this brush hangs out over part of the lane, severely limiting your sight line.

Wilderness Regulations

The maximum size of a group traveling together in the William O. Douglas Wilderness is twelve. This includes any combination of stock and people. Dogs, however, are not considered stock and are excluded from this regulation.

Motorized vehicles and equipment are prohibited in the wilderness, as are all wheeled vehicles including bicycles, wagons, and carts. The exception to this rule is that wheelchairs are permitted if they are that person's only means of transportation. Landing of aircraft or air drops, hang gliders, and parasails are also not allowed.

Camping and Campfires

Camping is allowed as long as you are at least 100 feet away from any lake and the Pacific Crest National Scenic Trail 2000. Camping and entry are prohibited in any area set aside for restoration. These areas are generally close to lakes and are marked with small signs.

Campfires are generally allowed within the William O. Douglas Wilderness except during periods of high fire danger. Because of the wilderness's location on the drier eastern slopes of the Cascade Range, this period often begins earlier in the summer and extends longer than it does in the wetter parts of the range. From late June through October, be sure to check with the Forest Service at either Packwood Ranger Station or Naches Ranger Station before lighting a campfire.

Artifacts
The collecting of artifacts, including anything left by Native Americans or the miners or settlers that came after them, is strictly prohibited. Enjoy the artifacts but leave them where you find them.

Northwest Forest Pass–Wilderness Permits
A Northwest Forest Pass is required to park at many of the trailheads. These passes are available at any Gifford Pinchot or Wenatchee National Forest office and many retail outlets. A wilderness permit is necessary to enter the William O. Douglas Wilderness. Wilderness permits are self-issuing and can be obtained at most trailheads near the wilderness boundary.

How to Use This Guide

Trail Descriptions
Most of the trails in this book interconnect either in the hike descriptions or in the hike options described at the end of the hikes. Most of the routes are described to lead from the edge of the wilderness into the more remote places deep inside. If you read the descriptions for several trails in the same general area, you will find that many longer hikes are possible. Some of these longer hikes will require a car shuttle from one side of the wilderness to the other.

Difficulty Ratings
The trails in this book are rated easy, moderate, or strenuous, with the length or time involved not taken into account. Only the roughness of the trail, elevation change, and difficulty of following the route are considered.

The trails that are rated "easy" will generally have gentle grades and are easy to follow; however, there may be short sections that are rocky or eroded. Anyone in reasonable condition can hike the easy trails described herein if enough time is allotted.

Trails rated as "moderate" will climb or descend more steeply than easy trails. They may climb 500 or 600 feet per mile and have fairly long sections that are rough or eroded. Some route-finding skills may be required to follow these trails. If route finding is required for a particular hike, the hike description will so state. A person in good physical condition can hike these trails with no problem. However, people in poor condition and small children may find them grueling.

Trails rated as "strenuous" are best left to expert backpackers and mountaineers. These trails may climb or descend 1,000 feet or more per mile and be very rough. Sections of these trails may be very vague or nonexistent, so excellent route-finding skills are a requirement for safe travel. In some cases there may be considerable exposure; falling from the trail or route can cause serious injury or even death. Many of these trails are not usable by parties with stock.

Trail Mileage

I have personally hiked all of the trails described in this book, many of them in both directions. The mileage was very difficult to gauge precisely. Mileage from Forest Service signs and maps was taken into account whenever possible. Times were kept while hiking. The mileage was calculated by knowing the approximate hiking speed used on various types of trail. The mileage printed in each hike description was figured by combining these means and in some cases by pacing off the distance.

For loop and shuttle hikes, distances are described as one-way, so this will be the entire distance you will hike. Out-and-back hikes are described as round-trip, so you will hike the stated distance to make the complete trip. The additional hiking options are not taken into consideration when stating the total. Internal-connector hikes are described as one-way.

How to Use the Maps

The USDA Forest Service William O. Douglas and Norse Peak Wilderness topo map is adequate for most of the hikes described in this book. This map is generally very accurate and up to date; however, its small scale of 1:63,360 (1 inch to the mile) and its fine print make it a bit difficult for some of us to read.

The United States Geological Survey (USGS) 7.5-minute quad maps mentioned near the beginning of each hike description are a much larger scale, 1:24,000 (about 2.7 inches to the mile). These topo maps are easier to read and very accurate as far as the topography goes. Some of them are, however, somewhat out of date as far as the exact location of the trails. Some trails have been rerouted since some of these

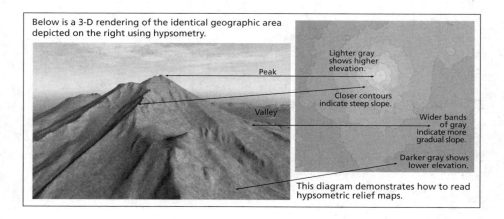

Below is a 3-D rendering of the identical geographic area depicted on the right using hypsometry.

Peak

Valley

Lighter gray shows higher elevation.

Closer contours indicate steep slope.

Wider bands of gray indicate more gradual slope.

Darker gray shows lower elevation.

This diagram demonstrates how to read hypsometric relief maps.

maps have been updated. Near the lower right corner of the USGS maps, you will find the year that it was last updated.

The USDA Forest Service Wenatchee and Gifford Pinchot National Forest maps can be very helpful in finding the trailheads, but their small scale makes them of little value as trail maps.

The maps in this book that depict a detailed close-up of an area use elevation tints, called hypsometry, to portray relief. Each gray tone represents a range of equal elevation, as shown in the scale key with the map. These maps will give you a good idea of elevation gain and loss. The darker tones are lower elevations and the lighter grays are higher elevations. The lighter the tone, the higher the elevation. Narrow bands of different gray tones spaced closely together indicate steep terrain, whereas wider bands indicate areas of more gradual slope.

Maps that show larger geographic areas use shaded, or shadow, relief. Shadow relief does not represent elevation; it demonstrates slope or relative steepness. This gives an almost 3-D perspective of the physiography of a region and will help you see where ranges and valleys are.

Trail Finder

	Hike	Streams Easy	Streams Moderate	Streams Difficult	Ridgetop trails Easy	Ridgetop trails Moderate	Ridgetop trails Difficult	Alpine country Easy	Alpine country Moderate	Alpine country Difficult	Overnight backpacking Easy	Overnight backpacking Moderate	Overnight backpacking Difficult	Lakes Easy	Lakes Moderate	Lakes Difficult	Historical features Easy	Historical features Moderate	Historical features Difficult	Old-growth forest Easy	Old-growth forest Moderate	Old-growth forest Difficult	Mountain peaks Easy	Mountain peaks Moderate	Mountain peaks Difficult	Wilderness isolation Easy	Wilderness isolation Moderate	Wilderness isolation Difficult	Geologic features Easy	Geologic features Moderate	Geologic features Difficult
1	Cramer Lake–Dumbbell Lake Trails 1106 and 56														●																
2	Dark Meadow Trails, 2000, 1107, and 1106																			●											
3	Pacific Crest National Scenic Trail 2000, Leech Lake Trailhead to Fish Lake								●			●			●																
4	Sand Lake Trail 60											●			●																
5	Cortright Trail 57																										●				
6	Cowlitz Trail 44														●																
7	Jug Lake–Chain Lakes Trails 44, 43, and 47												●			●															
8	Soda Springs																												●		
9	Naches Peak Loop National Park Trail and Trail 2000								●																						
10	Cougar Lake Trails 2000, 958, and 958a								●			●			●																
11	Mesatchee Creek Trail 969		●																												
12	Dewey Lake Trails 969 and 968		●									●			●						●										
13	Pleasant Valley Nature Loop																			●											
14	Pleasant Valley Lake Trail 958b																											●			
15	Pleasant Valley Loop Trail 999	●									●																				
16	Goat Peak Trails 958c and 958						●			●															●						
17	American Ridge Trail 958, Goat Creek Trail to American Ridge Trailhead								●																						
18	Goat Peak via Goat Creek Trails 959 and 958								●															●							
19	Goose Prairie Trail 972																														
20	Bumping Lake Trail 971													●																	
21	Swamp Lake Trail 970		●									●			●																
22	Fish Lake Trails 971a, 971, and 2000														●						●										

Trail Finder

#	Hike	Streams			Ridgetop trails			Alpine country			Overnight backpacking			Lakes			Historical features			Old-growth forest			Mountain peaks			Wilderness isolation			Geologic features		
		Easy	Moderate	Difficult	Easy	Moderate	Difficult	Easy	Moderate	Difficult	Easy	Moderate	Difficult	Easy	Moderate	Difficult	Easy	Moderate	Difficult	Easy	Moderate	Difficult	Easy	Moderate	Difficult	Easy	Moderate	Difficult	Easy	Moderate	Difficult
23	Lily Lake Trail 988													●																	
24	Root Lake															●															
25	Twin Sisters Trail 980, Deep Creek Campground to Deep Creek Horse Camp																			●											
26	Twin Sisters and Fryingpan Lakes Trails 980, 2000, and 43											●			●																
27	Tumac Mountain Trails 980, 1104, and 44														●									●			●				
28	Round Lake Trail 1105a													●																	
29	Pear Lake Loop Trails 1105 and 1148											●			●																
30	Pear Butte Trail 979						●																								
31	Copper City																●														
32	Richmond Lake via Richmond Mine Trail 973									●			●			●															
33	Mount Aix Trail 982									●			●												●			●			
34	Soda Springs Loop Trails 975 and 975a																													●	
35	Boulder Cave National Recreation Trail 962																												●		
36	Buck Lake via Mount Aix Trail 982		●												●																
37	Rattlesnake Trail 1114		●									●																			
38	MJB Trail 1101					●			●			●																		●	
39	Ironstone Mountain Trails 1141, 1111, and 1110											●																			
40	Indian Creek Trail 1105		●									●									●										
41	Little Buck Trail 1147																				●										
42	McCallister Trail 1109																				●										
43	Sand Ridge Trail 1104					●						●																			
44	Spiral Butte Trails 1106, 1142, and 1108														●										●			●			

Map Legend

Transportation

U.S. Highway	▬ ▭ ▬ ▭ ▬
State Highway	══════
Local Road	────────
Trail	─ ─ ─ ─ ─ ─ ─
Featured Trail	▬ ▬ ▬ ▬ ▬
Featured Shared Trail	▬ ▪ ▪ ▬ ▪ ▪ ▬
U.S. Highway	{12}
State Highway	(410)
Forest Road	1284

Boundaries

National Park	/////////
National Forest	············
Wilderness Area	⌐¬⌐¬⌐¬

Hydrology

Reservoir or Lake	Lake
River or Creek	Creek
Geyser/Spring	⌐°
Waterfall	≈

Grids

UTM Number and Ticks	51₉1₀₀₀	Lat / Long Number and Ticks	121°26'00"

Symbols

Campgound	⌂	Peak	▲
Bridge	⋊	Picnic Area	⊼
Ford	▪	Point of Interest	▪
Horse Camp	⌂	Trailhead	➊
Pass	)(	Trail Direction	◀1
Parking	🅿	Hike End	⬢18
		Viewpoint	👁

Southwest Region

This region is accessed from U.S. Highway 12 west of White Pass, with the exceptions of Hikes 1, 2, and 3, which begin just east of the summit. Most of the trails in this region lead to a plateau that was once covered by an ice cap. The smoothing and scouring of the ice created many depressions that now hold lakes and ponds. The plateau is mostly forested with subalpine timber, and between the stands of trees are many meadows and areas covered with mountain heather and huckleberry bushes. This is the home of the largest animal that inhabits the Cascade Mountains, the Roosevelt elk. Elk are common along all the trails in this region. Unfortunately mosquitoes are also very common because of the abundance of standing water.

Hike 1, Cramer Lake–Dumbbell Lake Trails, climbs gently through the forest to Cramer Lake, where fishing for trout can be excellent. Hike 2, Dark Meadow Trails, passes through old-growth midmountain forest for most of its length. Farther west Hike 5, Cortright Trail, is lightly used, making for a true wilderness experience. If you're interested in testing your route-finding skills, try Hike 7, Jug Lake–Chain Lakes Trails. All of the trails in this region except Hike 8, Soda Springs, interconnect, providing the hiker with a wide variety of options for one-way shuttle hikes.

Roosevelt elk bulls.

1 Cramer Lake–Dumbbell Lake Trails 1106 and 56

Hike through pristine old-growth forest to Cramer Lake. From there explore the lake-studded plateau that makes up much of the southern part of the William O. Douglas Wilderness.

Start: Dog Lake Trailhead.
Type of hike: Out-and-back day hike or backpack.
Total distance: 10.6 miles round-trip to the Pacific Crest National Scenic Trail.
Difficulty: Easy to moderate.
Maps: USDA Forest Service William O. Douglas and Norse Peak Wilderness or Spiral Butte and White Pass USGS quads.

Permits and fees: William O. Douglas Wilderness permit. A Northwest Forest Pass is required at Dog Lake Campground and Trailhead.
Best months: July–September.
Special considerations: Mosquitoes can be a problem, especially July–August.

Finding the trailhead: To reach Dog Lake Campground and Trailhead from the **Seattle-Tacoma** area, drive to Enumclaw. From Enumclaw take State Route 410 for 41 miles east and south to Cayuse Pass and the junction with State Route 123. Turn right (nearly straight ahead) on SR 123 and follow it for 16.5 miles south to the junction with U.S. Highway 12. Turn left (east) on US 12 and drive 15 miles east over White Pass to the Dog Lake Campground and Trailhead. From **Portland,** Oregon, drive north on Interstate 5 to exit 68 (68 miles north of the Interstate Bridge), then follow US 12 east for 87 miles to the Dog Lake Campground. Dog Lake Campground is 2.1 miles east of White Pass. Turn left into the campground and go to its western edge to reach the Dog Lake Trailhead, at 4,290 feet elevation.
Parking and trailhead facilities: Campsites, a boat launch, restrooms, and limited parking are available at the trailhead.

The Hike

As you leave the trailhead, the Cramer Lake Trail climbs gently to the northwest. The route here is through a mixed conifer forest of Douglas fir, Engelmann spruce, western red cedar, tamarack, hemlock, and western white pine. In 0.1 mile you have climbed to 4,330 feet elevation and reached the junction with the Dark Meadow Trail 1107. The Dark Meadow Trail turns to the left (west) to connect with the Pacific Crest Trail in 1.8 miles. Bear right (northwest and nearly straight ahead) at the junction. Another 0.2 mile of hiking brings you to the William O. Douglas Wilderness boundary. For the next 0.8 mile, the trail is nearly level, never gaining or losing more than a few feet of elevation. You will cross a small wooden bridge over a sluggish stream as you stroll through the old-growth forest.

Beargrass.

The route then turns west and climbs along the north fork of Clear Creek for 0.2 mile. Then you must cross the north fork without the benefit of the bridge that once spanned the stream. The crossing is generally easy but could be difficult during times of high water. When I hiked this trail, there were logs across the creek, both above and below the crossing, but the logs were wet and very slippery. This creek crossing is at 4,350 feet elevation and 1.3 miles from the trailhead.

Once across the creek the trail climbs gently to the northwest. In slightly less than 0.3 mile, you will make a sweeping turn to the right to head northeast. You now climb along a south-facing slope, with a couple of talus slopes below the trail. These open slopes allow views of Dog Lake, which is now well below to the southeast. The route climbs this slope until you have reached about 4,800 feet elevation, then turns north and continues to climb on gentler ground. The route levels out at 5,090 feet elevation 2.1 miles after crossing the north fork of Clear Creek. Here Cramer Lake can be spotted through the trees to the northeast. You then descend very slightly for the next 0.3 mile, crossing a tiny stream along the way to the junction with the path to Cramer Lake, at 5,030 feet elevation and 3.7 miles from the trailhead.

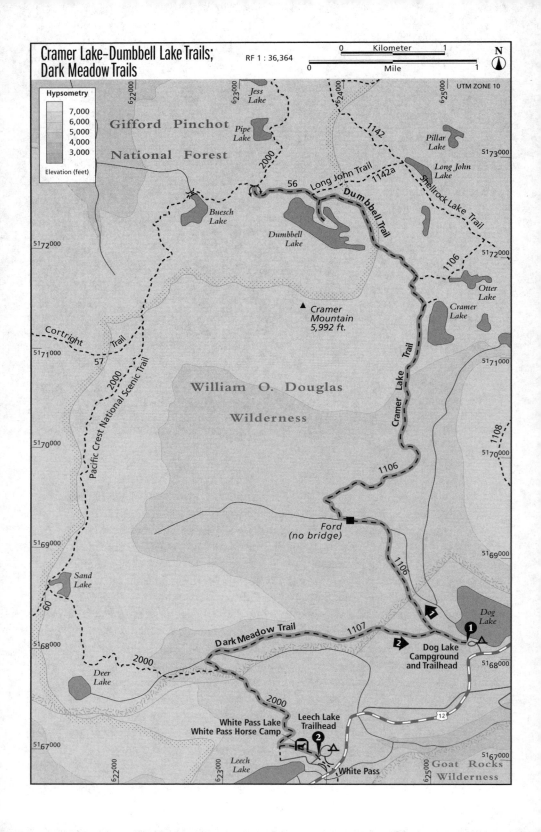

Cramer Lake-Dumbbell Lake Trails; Dark Meadow Trails

RF 1 : 36,364

Kilometer

Mile

N

UTM ZONE 10

Hypsometry

7,000
6,000
5,000
4,000
3,000

Elevation (feet)

Gifford Pinchot

National Forest

Jess Lake

Pipe Lake

Pillar Lake

Long John Lake

1142

Long John Trail

1142a

56

Shellrock Lake Trail

Dumbbell Trail

Buesch Lake

Dumbbell Lake

1106

Otter Lake

Cramer Lake

▲ Cramer Mountain 5,992 ft.

Cortright Trail

57

William O. Douglas

Wilderness

Cramer Lake Trail

2000

Pacific Crest National Scenic Trail

1106

1108

1106

Ford (no bridge)

Sand Lake

60

1

Dog Lake

Dark Meadow Trail

1107

2

Dog Lake Campground and Trailhead

2000

Deer Lake

2000

White Pass Lake
White Pass Horse Camp

Leech Lake Trailhead

2

12

Leech Lake

White Pass

Goat Rocks Wilderness

The path to Cramer Lake turns to the right just as the main trail enters a meadow. The lake is about 75 yards east along this path. Cramer Lake is surrounded with forest, which is mostly made up of hemlock, cedar, spruce, and true firs. Lily pads in the lake bloom in the summer, adding a splash of yellow color. There is a large campsite where the path reaches the lake. Be sure to camp at least 100 feet back from the lakeshore.

To continue on the main trail, turn left (northwest) at the junction with the path to Cramer Lake. The route skirts the meadow for about 0.1 mile, then turns right (north), crossing a couple of tiny streams in culverts to the junction with the Dumbbell Trail 56. This junction is 0.2 mile past the path to the shore of Cramer Lake (3.9 miles from Dog Lake Trailhead), at 5,040 feet elevation. To the right the Cramer Lake Trail heads east to Otter Lake and a junction with the Shellrock Lake Trail. See the options below to continue on the Cramer Lake Trail.

Turn left at the junction and head northwest on the Dumbbell Trail, through the old-growth forest of Douglas fir, hemlock, cedar, and true firs. The route climbs very gently for 0.3 mile to the first view of Dumbbell Lake. Then you continue to climb gently, well north of the lake, which is no longer visible. Soon you pass a broken-down wooden bridge. One-half mile from the junction with the Cramer Lake Trail, the course passes three small ponds. Then you pass between a tiny pond on your left and a larger one on your right. A little less than 0.2 mile after passing between the ponds, there is an unmarked path to your left leading to the shore of Dumbbell Lake.

In another 0.1 mile, at 5,140 feet elevation, there is another well-used but also unmarked path to your left (south). This path leads through an area of burned timber to several campsites on a peninsula in Dumbbell Lake. If you camp here, be sure to pitch your tent at least 100 feet from the lakeshore. The elevation of Dumbbell Lake is 5,091 feet.

The Dumbbell Trail continues west from the junction with the unmarked path to the peninsula, and in 0.3 mile you will reach the junction with the Long John Trail 1142a. This junction is near the northwest corner of Dumbbell Lake, in an area that was burned several years ago. The Long John Trail leads northeast for 0.7 mile to a junction with the Shellrock Lake Trail near Long John Lake. The Long John Trail is not shown on the White Pass and Spiral Butte USGS quad maps.

The Dumbbell Trail heads on to the west from the junction, quickly leaving the burn area. In 0.2 mile you will pass a small pond to the left of the trail. Another 0.1 mile brings you to a larger pond on your right and the junction with the Pacific Crest National Scenic Trail 2000 (PCT). From this junction it's only a short hike southwest on the PCT to Buesch Lake. Return the way you came to Dog Lake Trailhead.

Miles and Directions

0.0   Dog Lake Trailhead. GPS 46 39.278N 121 21.696W.

0.1   Junction with Dark Meadow Trail 1107. Bear right (nearly straight ahead).

1.3   Cross the north fork of Clear Creek.

3.7   Junction with path to Cramer Lake. GPS 46 41.135N 121 22.069W. Turn left.

3.9   Junction with Dumbbell Trail 56. GPS 46 41.261N 121 22.144W. Turn left.

4.7   Path to the peninsula of Dumbbell Lake. 46 41.723N 121 22.888W. Bear right.

5.0   Junction with the Long John Trail 1142a. GPS 46 41.731N 121 23.008W. Bear left.

5.3   Junction with the Pacific Crest National Scenic Trail 2000. GPS 46 41.781N 121 23.328W. Turnaround point.

10.6   Dog Lake Trailhead.

Options: To continue on the Cramer Lake Trail, bear right (east) at the junction with the Dumbbell Trail. The route soon climbs over a small, poorly defined ridge, reaching 5,090 feet elevation. After crossing the ridge, the tread makes a descending switchback and quickly crosses a small sluggish stream. There will be a pond to your right at the stream crossing. Just east of this pond is Otter Lake. About 0.1 mile farther along, you will pass a vague path to your right, which leads a short distance to the shore of Otter Lake. The course passes a couple more ponds as you hike through the now smaller and thinner subalpine timber. Between the groves of trees are small meadows, and the ground here is nearly covered with short huckleberry bushes. Elk often use these meadows. You may note that a few of the small trees have much of their bark torn off and their lower limbs shredded. This is caused by bull elk cleaning their antlers in preparation for the rut (breeding season). They really beat the heck out of these little trees at times. If you are here in late August or September, you may hear these huge animals bugling. The shrill call often sounds like it was made by some kind of a bird. Varied thrush are also often seen in these meadows.

The route crosses the small meadows and reaches the junction with the Shellrock Trail 1142, 0.7 mile from the junction with the Dumbbell Trail and 4.6 miles from the trailhead. This junction, at 5,060 feet elevation, is the end of the Cramer Lake Trail. The GPS coordinates at the junction are 46 41.461N 121 21.619W.

2 Dark Meadow
Trails 2000, 1107, and 1106

Dark Meadow Trail is an easy hike through old-growth forest just north of White Pass.

See map on page 24.
Start: Leech Lake Trailhead.
Type of hike: Shuttle day hike.
Total distance: 3 miles.
Difficulty: Easy.

Maps: USDA Forest Service Norse Peak and William O. Douglas Wilderness or White Pass USGS quad.
Permits and fees: Northwest Forest Pass and William O. Douglas Wilderness permit.
Best months: Late June through October.

Finding the trailhead: To reach Leech Lake Trailhead, near White Pass, from the **Seattle-Tacoma** area, drive to Enumclaw. From Enumclaw take State Route 410 for 41 miles east and south to Cayuse Pass and the junction with State Route 123. Turn right (nearly straight ahead) on SR 123 and follow it for 16.5 miles south to the junction with U.S. Highway 12. Turn left (east) on US 12 and drive 13 miles east to the junction with the entrance road for Leech Lake Campground. From **Portland,** Oregon, drive north on Interstate 5 to exit 68 (68 miles north of the Interstate Bridge), then follow US 12 east for 84 miles to the junction with the entrance road for Leech Lake Campground. This road is 0.5 mile northeast of the summit of White Pass. Turn left (northwest) at the junction and go 0.2 mile to the trailhead, which is on the right side of the road. The trailhead is near the northeast corner of Leech Lake, at 4,420 feet elevation.

To reach Dog Lake Trailhead, where this hike ends, go back to US 12 and turn left. Then drive 1.6 miles northeast to Dog Lake Campground. Turn left into the campground and go to its western edge to reach the Dog Lake Trailhead.

Parking and trailhead facilities: There is parking for several cars at Leech Lake Trailhead. Leech Lake Campground is located a few yards west of the trailhead, and a horse camp with stock facilities is 0.1 mile to the east. Parking is limited at the Dog Lake Trailhead, but there is room for two or three cars. Campsites and restrooms are also available.

The Hike

The first 1.1 miles of this hike follow the Pacific Crest National Scenic Trail 2000 (PCT). As you leave the trailhead, the route climbs gently for 30 yards to the wilderness registration box. Get your wilderness permit here, then enter the old-growth forest of mostly Douglas fir and western hemlock. In a little over 0.2 mile, the tread makes a switchback to the right. You soon make another switchback and, 0.4 mile from the trailhead, cross a roadbed at 4,630 feet elevation. This roadbed is part of the 18-kilometer White Pass Nordic Ski Trail System.

After crossing the roadbed, the course soon makes two more switchbacks. Above the switchbacks the trail flattens out. About 1 mile into the hike, you may notice another roadbed about 100 yards to the right of the trail. This roadbed is also part

Huckleberry bush in bloom.

of the nordic trail system. Soon you pass the William O. Douglas Wilderness boundary and reach the junction with the Dark Meadow Trail 1107, at 4,790 feet elevation, 1.1 miles from the trailhead.

Bear right at the junction and descend gently along the Dark Meadow Trail. The old-growth forest here consists of mostly western hemlock trees with a few true firs mixed in. On the ground beneath the dense canopy are lots of huckleberries, which ripen in August. A little over 0.1 mile from the junction, there is a small meadow to the left of the trail. Then the route crosses a small stream, which may be dry by late summer. A few western red cedars grow close to the stream, adding diversity to the old-growth woods, and vanilla leaf covers the ground in places.

You will pass another small meadow, located below and to the right of the trail, 0.5 mile after crossing the small stream. Beargrass sprouts from the forest floor here, between the huckleberry bushes, and many true fir trees have entered the old-growth forest mix. The trail becomes deeply eroded for a short distance, about 1 mile from the junction with the PCT. In another 0.2 mile you will pass the wilderness boundary sign and leave the William O. Douglas Wilderness. Close to the wilderness boundary, some large Douglas firs grow next to the trail. After leaving the wilderness, the route descends moderately to the junction with the Cramer Lake Trail 1106, at 4,330 feet elevation and 2.9 miles from the Leech Lake Trailhead. Turn right on the Cramer Lake Trail and descend the last 0.1 mile to the Dog Lake Trailhead, at 4,290 feet elevation.

Miles and Directions

0.0   Leech Lake Trailhead. GPS 46 38.702N 121 22.947W.

1.1   Junction with Dark Meadow Trail 1107. GPS 46 39.138N 121 23.623W. Turn right.

2.9   Junction with Cramer Lake Trail 1106. Turn right.

3.0   Dog Lake Trailhead. GPS 46 39.278N 121 21.696W.

Options: From the junction of the PCT and the Dark Meadows Trail, it is only another mile along the PCT to Deer Lake.

3 Pacific Crest National Scenic Trail 2000 Leech Lake Trailhead to Fish Lake

Hike along the Pacific Crest National Scenic Trail through the lake–studded southern part of the William O. Douglas Wilderness.

Start: Leech Lake Trailhead.
Type of hike: Out-and-back backpack.
Total distance: 27.4 miles out and back.
Difficulty: Moderate.
Maps: USDA Forest Service William O. Douglas and Norse Peak Wilderness or White Pass and Cougar Lake USGS quads.

Permits and fees: Northwest Forest Pass and William O. Douglas Wilderness permit.
Best months: Mid-July through September.
Special considerations: This is a fairly long hike so be sure all members of the party are up to it. Mosquitoes can be a problem, especially in July and early August.

Finding the trailhead: To reach Leech Lake Trailhead, near White Pass, from the **Seattle-Tacoma** area, drive to Enumclaw. From Enumclaw take State Route 410 for 41 miles east and south to Cayuse Pass and the junction with State Route 123. Turn right (nearly straight ahead) on SR 123 and follow it for 16.5 miles south to the junction with U.S. Highway 12. Turn left (east) on US 12 and drive 13 miles east to the junction with the entrance road for Leech Lake Campground. From **Portland,** Oregon, drive north on Interstate 5 to exit 68 (68 miles north of the Interstate Bridge), then follow US 12 east for 84 miles to the junction with the entrance road for Leech Lake Campground. This road is 0.5 mile northeast of the summit of White Pass. Turn left (northwest) at the junction and go 0.2 mile to the trailhead, which is on the right side of the road. The trailhead is near the northeast corner of Leech Lake, at 4,420 feet elevation.

Parking and trailhead facilities: There is parking for several cars at the trailhead. Leech Lake Campground is located a few yards west of the trailhead, and a horse camp with stock facilities is 0.1 mile to the east.

The Hike

The Pacific Crest National Scenic Trail (PCT) climbs gently for the first 30 yards to the wilderness registration box, where you can fill out your wilderness permit. Past the wilderness registration box, the route enters old-growth forest. The large timber consists mostly of western hemlock and Douglas fir. The course makes a couple of switchbacks as you climb and crosses a roadbed at 4,630 feet elevation 0.4 mile from the trailhead. This roadbed is part of the White Pass Nordic Ski Trail System. After crossing the roadbed the course soon makes two more switchbacks, then flattens out. About 1 mile into the hike, you'll pass the William O. Douglas Wilderness boundary and reach the junction with the Dark Meadow Trail 1107, at 4,790 feet elevation, 1.1 miles from the trailhead. The Dark Meadow Trail turns to the right to join the Cramer Lake Trail in 1.8 miles.

Bear left (straight ahead) at the junction and climb gently to the west. The route soon passes below a small, narrow talus slope. Pikas inhabit these rocks and may let out a whistle to announce your passing. A couple hundred yards after leaving the talus, the course crosses a small stream. Then you pass a meadow and climb a couple of switchbacks. Above the switchbacks there is another small meadow to your right. The tread climbs a little more, then comes alongside of a much larger meadow, where elk are often grazing. Along the southern side of this meadow, at 5,200 feet elevation and 2.1 miles from the trailhead, is the junction with the path to Deer Lake. There are no signs at the junction, but the path to the left, leading to the lake, is obvious.

The path to the lake leads south from the PCT, reaching the lakeshore in about 100 yards. Fir and hemlock forest surrounds the sparkling waters of Deer Lake, with a few cedars close to the shore. The campsite on the northern shore of the lake has been heavily used and is in need of restoration. If you camp here, be sure to set up at least 100 feet from the lakeshore.

The PCT heads west from the junction with the path to Deer Lake but soon turns north, skirting the meadow. Sand Lake comes into view to your right 0.4 mile past the junction; 0.1 mile farther along is the junction with the Sand Lake Trail 60. The junction is at 5,300 feet elevation, 2.6 miles from Leech Lake Trailhead. Sand Lake Trail leads southwest from the junction, climbing over the shoulder of Cortright Point before descending to a trailhead on Forest Road 1284 in 3.4 miles. A short distance from the PCT on the Sand Lake Trail is the three-sided Sand Lake Shelter. There are several possible campsites close to the shelter.

From the junction with the Sand Lake Trail, the PCT continues north, crossing a meadow and then climbing gently. In a little less than 0.3 mile, the route passes a pond to the right of the trail. The forest has now become semiopen, and patches of

Buesch Lake.

pink mountain heather dot the landscape. There is a path leaving the trail to the left 0.5 mile from the junction with the Sand Lake Trail. This short side path leads to a campsite next to another pond.

The PCT continues to climb, passing several more tiny ponds. A little less than 1.5 miles from the junction with the Sand Lake Trail, you'll reach 5,570 feet elevation. From here the course descends gently for 0.5 mile to the junction with the Cortright Trail 57. The lightly used Cortright Trail heads southwest from the junction, climbs over the ridgeline, and then descends to a trailhead on Forest Road 45, 4.8 miles to the west. The junction with the Cortright Trail is 4.6 miles from the Leech Lake Trailhead, at 5,480 feet elevation. Just past the junction the PCT passes two very pretty little ponds, and in another 0.1 mile it begins to descend steeply. As you lose elevation, the timber becomes larger. The trace passes another small pond, makes a couple of switchbacks, and then flattens out at about 5,100 feet elevation. Then you traverse wet meadows to the bridge over the outlet stream from Buesch Lake. As you approach the bridge, Buesch Lake is on your right. You are now 5.7 miles from the trailhead. Campsites can be had to the right of the trail as you near the bridge.

Across the bridge the PCT follows the shore of the lake for a short distance, then veers to the left through small meadows and passes a couple more ponds to the junction with the Dumbbell Trail 56. This junction, at 5,100 feet elevation, is 6.3 miles from the Leech Lake Trailhead. To the right on the Dumbbell Trail, it's only 0.5 mile to Dumbbell Lake. See the options below for an alternate return loop hike via Dumbbell and Cramer Lakes.

Bear left (northeast) at the junction to stay on the PCT. In a little more than 0.4 mile, the route begins to skirt the eastern shore of Pipe Lake. Then you pass a long, narrow lake that may have once been an arm of Pipe Lake. The PCT reaches the first junction with the Cowlitz Trail 44, 1.3 miles from the junction with the Dumbbell Trail.

To the right (east) the Cowlitz Trail climbs to the summit of Tumac Mountain. For the next 0.2 mile, the PCT and the Cowlitz Trail follow the same route, heading northwest. You pass another pond and soon come to the second junction with the Cowlitz Trail. From here the Cowlitz Trail heads west, passing Penoyer Lake, then descending to Soda Springs Campground and Trailhead.

The PCT heads north from the second junction with the Cowlitz Trail, through hemlocks and subalpine firs. In 0.25 mile the route crosses a streambed, which is usually dry by late summer. The route winds generally northwest, passing several ponds and undulating over the small bumps in the terrain. Snow Lake comes into view to your right a little less than 2 miles from the second junction with the Cowlitz Trail. Soon you will pass a path to the right, which leads to campsites near the lake. Then the route crosses Snow Lake's outlet stream on a one-log bridge. The route then follows the lake's shoreline for a short distance before bearing left away from the lake to continue its northerly course.

The PCT climbs slightly after leaving Snow Lake and passes several more ponds before descending to the junction with the Twin Sisters Trail 980, 0.6 mile after leaving Snow Lake. This junction, at 4,870 feet elevation, is 10.6 miles from the Leech Lake Trailhead. To the right the Twin Sisters Trail leads east and north for 3.7 miles to the Deep Creek Campground and Trailhead, passing Twin Sisters Lakes along the way.

Bear left at the junction and head west along the PCT. In 0.1 mile you will come to the junction with the Pothole Trail 45. Pothole Trail is a 2-mile-long connector that leads south from this junction to a junction with the Cowlitz Trail 44 near Penoyer Lake. The PCT continues west from the junction with the Pothole Trail but soon turns north, skirting a meadow. Soon the tread swings around to the northwest and reaches the junction with the Jug Lake Trail 43, 1 mile from the junction with the Pothole Trail. At the junction with the Jug Lake Trail, you have descended to 4,670 feet elevation. There is no trail sign at present at this junction. The Jug Lake Trail heads south from the junction, passing Fryingpan and Little Snow Lakes before reaching a short side trail to Jug Lake and descending to meet the Cowlitz Trail.

Turn right at the junction with the Jug Lake Trail, staying on the PCT, and descend gradually to the north. The tread passes along the sides of meadows, traverses

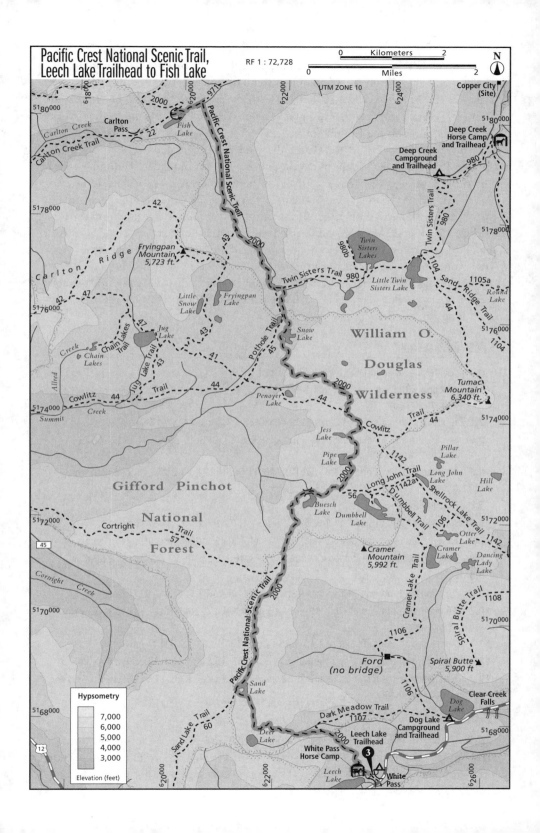

Pacific Crest National Scenic Trail,
Leech Lake Trailhead to Fish Lake

RF 1 : 72,728

Kilometers
0   2

Miles
0   2

N

UTM ZONE 10

Copper City
(Site)

Carlton Creek

Carlton
Pass

Fish Lake

22

Deep Creek
Horse Camp
and Trailhead

Deep Creek
Campground
and Trailhead

980

Carlton Creek Trail

Pacific Crest National Scenic Trail

2000

971

5180000

6180000

6120000

6124000

5180000

42

Carlton Ridge

Fryingpan
Mountain
5,723 ft.

43

2000

Twin Sisters Trail

980b

Twin
Sisters
Lakes

Twin Sisters Trail

1104

Sand Ridge Trail

1105a

Round
Lake

5178000

5178000

42

47

Little
Snow
Lake

Fryingpan
Lake

Jug Lake

Chain Lakes Trail

43

43

41

Pothole Trail

45

Snow
Lake

Twin Sisters Trail

980

Little Twin
Sisters Lake

William O.

Douglas

44

1104

1104

5176000

5176000

47

Creek

Chain
Lakes

Jug Lake Trail

Cowlitz

44

Trail

44

Penoyer
Lake

2000

Wilderness

Tumac
Mountain
6,340 ft.

Allred

Summit

Creek

Cowlitz

44

Trail

44

5174000

5174000

Jess
Lake

Pipe
Lake

2000

Cowlitz

1142

Pillar
Lake

Long John
Lake

Shellrock Lake Trail

Hill
Lake

Gifford Pinchot

National

Cortright

Trail

57

Forest

45

Buesch
Lake

Dumbbell
Lake

Long John Trail

1142a

56

Dumbbell Trail

1106

Otter
Lake

Cramer
Lake

1142

Dancing
Lady
Lake

5172000

5172000

Cortright

Cortright

Creek

2000

Cramer
Mountain
5,992 ft.

Cramer Lake Trail

Spiral Butte Trail

1108

5170000

5170000

Pacific Crest National Scenic Trail

1106

Ford
(no bridge)

Spiral Butte
5,900 ft

Clear Creek
Falls

Dog
Lake

5168000

5168000

Sand Lake Trail

60

Sand
Lake

Deer
Lake

Dark Meadow Trail

1107

1106

2000

Leech Lake
Trailhead

3

Dog Lake
Campground
and Trailhead

12

White Pass
Horse Camp

Leech
Lake

White
Pass

6120000

6122000

6124000

6126000

Hypsometry

Elevation (feet)

- 7,000
- 6,000
- 5,000
- 4,000
- 3,000

the mountain forest, crosses a stream, and reaches the junction with the Bumping Lake Trail 971 just after fording the Bumping River. The junction with the Bumping River Trail is at 4,120 feet elevation, 1.7 miles from the junction with the Jug Lake Trail. There are several campsites near this junction both on the PCT and the Bumping Lake Trail. To the right on the Bumping Lake Trail, it's 7.7 miles to the Fish Lake Way Trailhead. See the options below for exiting the wilderness by this route.

The PCT turns left at the junction and heads west along the Bumping River. The tread never gets really close to the river but rather traverses small meadows, fingers of timber, and brushy areas. In 0.2 mile you enter the large meadow that extends east from the shore of Fish Lake, and in another 0.1 mile is the junction with the Carlton Creek Trail. The Carlton Creek Trail skirts the northern shore of Fish Lake, then crosses Carlton Pass to descend to a trailhead on Forest Road 44. Carlton Creek Trail would make a good access route to and from the PCT if FR 44 was open to the trailhead; however, the road has been washed out and is presently not passable. Return the way you came or check the options below for an alternate return involving a long car shuttle.

Miles and Directions

0.0 Leech Lake Trailhead. GPS 46 38.702N 121 22.947W.

1.1 Junction with Dark Meadow Trail 1107. GPS 46 39.138N 121 23.623W. Bear left (nearly straight ahead).

2.1 Junction with path to Deer Lake. GPS 46 39.186N 121 24.602W. Bear right.

2.6 Sand Lake and junction with the Sand Lake Trail 60. GPS 46 39.577N 121 24.822 W. Proceed straight ahead.

4.6 Junction with the Cortright Trail 57. GPS 46 41.008N 121 24.239W. Proceed straight ahead.

5.7 Buesch Lake.

6.3 Junction with the Dumbbell Trail 56. GPS 46 41.781N 121 23.328W. Bear left.

7.6 First junction with the Cowlitz Trail 44. Bear left (nearly straight ahead).

7.8 Second Junction with the Cowlitz Trail 44. GPS 46 42.579N 121 23.232W. Bear right.

9.9 Snow Lake.

10.6 Junction with the Twin Sisters Trail 980. GPS 46 43.940N 121 24.192W. Bear left.

10.7 Junction with the Pothole Trail 45. GPS 46 43.939N 121 24.312W. Bear right (nearly straight ahead).

11.7 Junction with the Jug Lake Trail 43. GPS 46 44.604N 121 24.918W. Turn right.

13.4 Junction with the Bumping Lake Trail 971. GPS 46 45.843N 121 25.559W. Turn left.

13.7 Junction with the Carlton Creek Trail 22 near Fish Lake. GPS 46 45.815N 121 25.731W. Turnaround point.

27.4 Leech Lake Trailhead.

Options: If you would like to shorten your hike and make it a loop, you can turn right on the Dumbbell Trail 56, 6.3 miles from Leech Lake Trailhead. Follow the

Dumbbell Trail for 1.4 miles southeast to the junction with the Cramer Lake Trail 1106. Then turn right on the Cramer Lake Trail and head south for 3.8 miles to the junction with the Dark Meadow Trail 1107. Turn right again on the Dark Meadow Trail and hike 1.8 miles west to the junction with the PCT. Turn left on the PCT and retrace your steps 1.1 miles to the Leech Lake Trailhead, completing the 14.4-mile lollipop loop.

To make this a 21.1-mile one-way hike, you can turn right (northeast) on the Bumping Lake Trail 971. Then descend along the Bumping River for 5.9 miles, to the junction with Fish Lake Way 971a. Turn right on Fish Lake Way and hike 1.8 miles northeast to the Fish Lake Way Trailhead. Hiking Fish Lake Way requires fording the Bumping River, so it is best to take this route in August or later when the water is low.

The car shuttle from Leech Lake Trailhead to Fish Lake Way Trailhead is a long one at 68.5 miles. To reach Fish Lake Way Trailhead from the Leech Lake Trailhead, go back to US 12 and turn right. Follow US 12 west for 13 miles to the junction with SR 123. Turn right on SR 123 and go north for 16.5 miles to Cayuse Pass and the junction with SR 410. Turn right on SR 410 and head east for 22.9 miles, over Chinook Pass and down to the junction with the Bumping Lake Road (Forest Road 1800). Turn right (southwest) on Bumping Lake Road. Drive 11 miles to Bumping Lake Dam. Continue another 2.5 miles on FR 1800, leaving the pavement, to the junction with FR 1808. Turn right, staying on FR 1800, and head west for 2.6 miles to Fish Lake Way Trailhead.

4 Sand Lake Trail 60

Hike from an out-of-the-way trailhead west of White Pass over a shoulder of Cortright Point. Then descend to Sand Lake and the Pacific Crest National Scenic Trail.

Start: Sand Lake Trailhead.
Type of hike: Out-and-back day hike or backpack or access route to the Pacific Crest Trail.
Total distance: 6.8 miles.
Difficulty: Moderate with a few steep and sometimes muddy spots.
Maps: USDA Forest Service Norse Peak and

William O. Douglas Wilderness or White Pass USGS quad.
Permits and fees: William O. Douglas Wilderness permit.
Best months: Mid-July through September.
Special considerations: Mosquitoes can be a problem, especially in July.

Finding the trailhead: To reach the Sand Lake Trailhead from the **Seattle-Tacoma** area, drive to Enumclaw. From Enumclaw take State Route 410 for 41 miles east and south to Cayuse Pass and the junction with State Route 123. Turn right (nearly straight ahead) on SR 123 and follow it for 16.5 miles south to the junction with U.S. Highway 12. Turn left (east) on US 12 and drive 12 miles east to the junction with Forest Road 1284. From **Portland,** Oregon, drive north on Interstate 5 to exit 68 (68 miles north of the Interstate Bridge), then follow US 12 east for 83 miles to the junction with FR 1284. This junction is 0.7 mile west of (before reaching) White Pass.

Turn left (northwest) off US 12 on the paved road, which leads to the White Pass Highway Maintenance Station. In 0.1 mile turn right (north-northwest), continuing on FR 1284, and follow it for 2.8 miles to the Sand Lake Trailhead. The poorly marked trailhead is on the right (northeast) side of the road, at 4,640 feet elevation. The Sand Lake Trailhead is a couple hundred yards before the end of FR 1284, so if you reach the end of FR 1284, turn around and backtrack.
Parking and trailhead facilities: There is parking for a couple of vehicles at the trailhead but no other facilities.

The Hike

The trail climbs a road-cut bank as you begin the hike. In a few yards, at the first switchback, there will be a wilderness registration box, where you should get your wilderness permit. The course then climbs through the thick forest of Douglas fir, noble fir, and hemlock. The route makes three more switchbacks and gains 560 feet of elevation in the next 0.8 mile to the point where you enter the William O. Douglas Wilderness. Just before reaching the wilderness boundary, you cross below a small talus slope.

Slightly less than 0.2 mile past the wilderness boundary, the tread enters an area that was burned some years ago. Shortly after entering the burn area, the route flattens out at 5,410 feet elevation and passes a tiny pond. As you hike through the burned area, the trail may be a little vague in a couple of spots as it heads north.

Sand Lake shelter.

Above the huckleberry bushes and between the standing silvered snags, Mount Rainier looms above the surrounding country to the northwest.

After hiking through the burn area for 0.6 mile, you leave the burnt timber and quickly pass another tiny pond. If this pond is full, the trail will be hard to see as you pass this pond. Go around it on the left side (west and north) and pick up the route again at the northeast corner of the pond. There is a blaze on a tree where the trail leaves the pond.

Soon after passing the second pond, the tread begins to climb. After ascending a little less than 200 feet, the way flattens again. Look to the right here for a view of Goat Rocks to the south-southeast. Keep your eyes open for elk in this area; when I hiked this trail, I encountered one of the best specimens of Roosevelt elk bull that I have ever seen.

Soon the trace descends a little as you pass beneath a talus slope, where pikas often screech their annoyance at your presence. Past the talus the trail climbs again, reaching its highest point as you cross a ridgeline at 5,590 feet above sea level, 2.4 miles from the trailhead. After crossing the ridgeline, the route descends steeply for

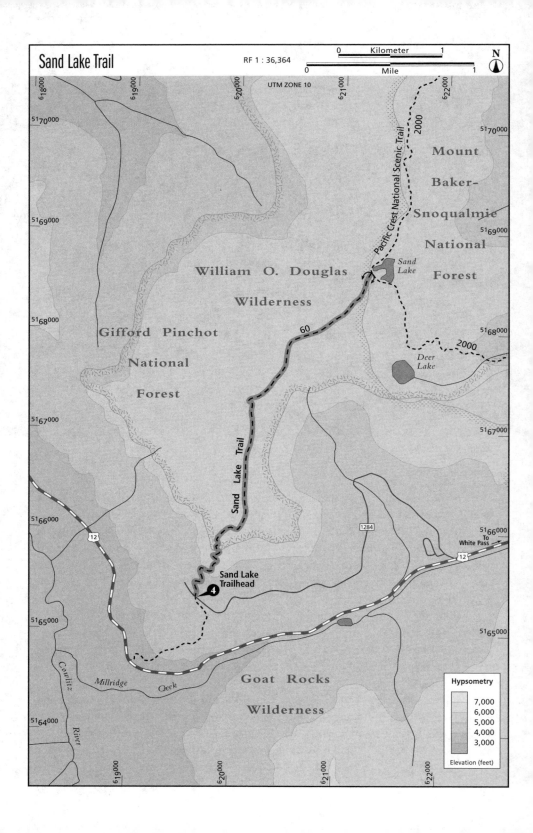

about 0.25 mile, then flattens to pass between two more small ponds. You will quickly pass yet another tiny pond, then descend slightly as you hike through the small wet meadows between the timber for about a mile. Watch for blacktail deer, as well as elk, as you stroll along.

The three-sided Sand Lake shelter will be a few feet to your right as you approach the junction with the Pacific Crest National Scenic Trail 2000 (PCT). The junction with the PCT is 3.4 miles from the trailhead, at 5,300 feet elevation. Aptly named Sand Lake is a few yards to your east at the junction.

Groves of hemlocks and true firs surround the lake between the grassy meadows. Huckleberry bushes, lupine, and beargrass complete the ground cover. If the bear grass has already bloomed, you may notice that nearly all the flowers have been bitten off: These flowers are a favorite food for both deer and elk. Gray jays, also called camp robbers, are usually around near the lake and at the shelter, waiting for a handout from hikers. Return by retracing your route to Sand Lake Trailhead or see the options below for an alternate return hike.

Miles and Directions

0.0   Sand Lake Trailhead. GPS 46 37.934N 121 26.282W.

0.8   Cross the wilderness boundary.

2.4   Attain the ridgeline.

3.4   Junction with the PCT at Sand Lake. GPS 46 39.577N 121 24.822 W. Turnaround point.

6.8   Sand Lake Trailhead.

Options: A one-way shuttle hike can be made by turning right on the PCT at the junction with the Sand Lake Trail next to Sand Lake. From the junction follow the PCT southeast for 2.6 miles to Leech Lake Trailhead near White Pass, passing Deer Lake along the way. This would, of course, require a short car shuttle to and from Leech Lake Trailhead.

To reach Leech Lake Trailhead by car from the Sand Lake Trailhead, drive back to US 12 and turn left. Head east on US 12 for 1.2 miles to the junction with the access road to the Leech Lake Trailhead. Turn left and follow the access road for 0.2 mile to the trailhead.

5 Cortright Trail 57

Hike a lightly used trail from an out-of-the-way trailhead, over the crest of the Cascade Range to a junction with the Pacific Crest National Scenic Trail. Roosevelt elk are common along this trail; in fact, they seem to use it more than people do. If you are backpacking, this route provides places for true wilderness camping.

Start: Cortright Trailhead.
Type of hike: Out-and-back day hike or backpack.
Total distance: 9.6 miles round-trip to the Pacific Crest National Scenic Trail.
Difficulty: Moderate.
Maps: USDA Forest Service William O. Douglas and Norse Peak Wilderness or White Pass USGS quad.

Permits and fees: William O. Douglas Wilderness permit.
Best months: July–September.
Special considerations: Good route-finding and map-reading skills are required to complete this hike safely.

Finding the trailhead: To reach the Cortright Trailhead from the **Seattle-Tacoma** area, drive to Enumclaw. From Enumclaw take State Route 410 for 41 miles east and south to Cayuse Pass and the junction with State Route 123. Turn right (nearly straight ahead) on SR 123 and follow it for 16.5 miles south to the junction with U.S. Highway 12. Turn left (east) on US 12 and drive about 1 mile to the junction with Forest Road 45. From **Portland,** Oregon, drive north on Interstate 5 to exit 68 (68 miles north of the Interstate Bridge), then follow US 12 east for 72 miles to the junction with FR 45. The junction with FR 45 is next to milepost 140 and 10.9 miles west of (before reaching) White Pass.

Turn left (north) off US 12 on FR 45. Be sure to make the hard right turn, staying on FR 45, 0.3 mile after leaving the highway. Follow FR 45 for 8.8 miles to the Cortright Trailhead, which will be on the right (northeast) side of the road.

Parking and trailhead facilities: There is parking for several cars close to the trailhead but no other facilities.

The Hike

There is a sign marking the trailhead; however, the trail starts about 100 feet northwest of the sign, at 4,240 feet elevation. Walk a few steps down the trail to the wilderness registration box and pick up your wilderness permit. A short distance past the wilderness registration box, the route enters the William O. Douglas Wilderness. From the trailhead, at 4,240 feet elevation, the trail first descends about 30 feet through the mature forest of fir and hemlock. Beargrass, bunchberry, vanilla leaf, and huckleberry bushes cover the ground beneath the stately trees. Soon the route begins to climb. After gaining about 100 feet of elevation, the course flattens for a few yards before resuming its ascent. You will need to negotiate a short but rough and rocky stretch of trail 0.6 mile into the hike. Hike quietly along the route and

Pond near the Cortright Trail.

you may see elk. When I hiked this trail in mid-July, I saw a magnificent six-point Roosevelt bull elk along this part of the trail.

Slightly over 1 mile from the trailhead, the tread flattens to traverse the north-facing hillside, then passes below a brushy talus slope. Past the talus the trail climbs again before flattening out at 4,920 feet elevation, 1.7 miles from the trailhead. Here the trail enters a small meadow, where it may disappear completely. On this as well as several other lightly used trails in the William O. Douglas Wilderness, the meadows can cause problems in route finding. Unless at least a few parties with stock have crossed the meadow fairly recently, it may have grown up to grass, making the trail nearly invisible. Head south-southeast across the meadow, watching slightly to the left for the trail. Soon the route shows up again as it reenters the woods.

The trail soon climbs again, flattening out at about 5,150 feet elevation, 2.2 miles from the trailhead. There is a pond on the right side of the trail 0.1 mile farther along. The grade is gentle for the next 0.9 mile as the route travels through the now smaller and more alpine forest. The track then passes a series of small ponds. Beargrass, lupine, and pink mountain heather cover the landscape between the trees and ponds.

Cortright Trail; Cowlitz Trail; Jug Lake–Chain Lakes Trails

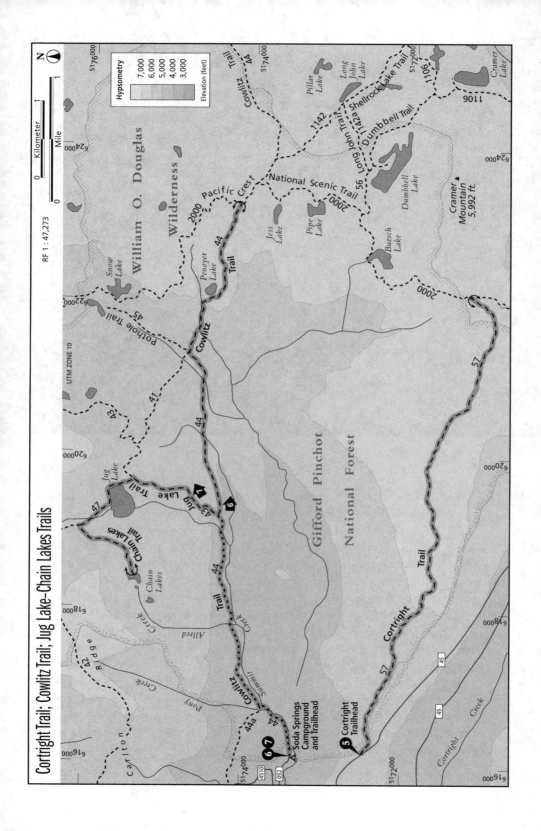

RF 1 : 47,273

N

Hypsometry
7,000
6,000
5,000
4,000
3,000
Elevation (feet)

Kilometer
Mile

UTM ZONE 10

William O. Douglas

Wilderness

Snow Lake

Pothole Trail 45

Penoyer Lake

Pacific Crest

National Scenic Trail

2000

Cowlitz Trail

Cowlitz Trail 44

5176000
5174000
5172000

Pillar Lake

Long John Lake

Shellrock Lake Trail

1142

Long John Trail 1142a

56

Dumbbell Trail

1106

Cramer Lake

Jess Lake

Pipe Lake

Dumbbell Lake

2000

Buesch Lake

Cramer Mountain 5,992 ft.

57

Jug Lake

Jug Lake Trail

47

Chain Lakes Trail

Chain Lakes

Allred Creek

Cowlitz Trail 44

Summit Creek

Pony Creek

Carlton Ridge

Soda Springs Campground and Trailhead

4510
052
44a
44

Cortright Trailhead

Cortright Trail

57

45

Cortright Creek

Gifford Pinchot

National Forest

43

41

44

44

43

7

6

6 7

5

624000
622000
620000
618000
616000

There is a small stream to the right of the trail 3.5 miles from the trailhead. A few more yards bring you to another pond at the northwest end of a long meadow. The trail soon enters the meadow and promptly disappears as it did 1.8 miles back. This is, however, a much larger meadow, making the point where the trail leaves it more difficult to spot. Head south-southeast, staying close to the left side of the meadow. In about 200 yards the trail will leave the meadow to the left (east). If you reach another pond before turning east, you have gone about 20 yards too far. To complicate things, there are two elk trails that continue past this pond that are visible before you can see the correct trail where it heads east. See the options below for wilderness campsites a short distance south of here at an unnamed lake.

The route leaves the meadow at 5,320 feet elevation. The GPS coordinates where the trail leaves the meadow are 46 41.028N 121 25.355W. The route is marked with old, partially scarred-over blazes as you quickly begin to climb to the east. The tread is steep, rough, and rocky in places as you head for the crest of the Cascade Range. You will cross a tiny stream, which may be dry by late summer, at 5,550 feet elevation, 0.4 mile after leaving the meadow. Shortly after crossing the stream, the trail intersects a well-used elk trail at nearly right angles. Another 0.2 mile of hiking brings you to the summit of the Cascade Range, at 5,700 feet elevation.

As you cross the crest, the trail gradually turns to the northeast and descends. You then hike downhill, through the alpine timber for 0.3 mile to the junction with the Pacific Crest National Scenic Trail 2000 (PCT). This junction, at 5,480 feet elevation, is 4.8 miles from the Cortright Trailhead where this hike began. A short distance to the left (north) on the PCT is a pretty little pond. To make the return trip, retrace your steps back to the Cortright Trailhead.

Miles and Directions

0.0 Cortright Trailhead. GPS 46 41.734N 121 28.896W.

3.9 Trail reappears on edge of meadow. GPS 46 41.028N 121 25.355W. Head east.

4.5 Summit.

4.8 Junction with the Pacific Crest National Scenic Trail 2000. GPS 46 41.008N 121 24.239W. Turnaround point.

9.6 Cortright Trailhead.

Options: If you continue south on the elk trails, from the meadow 3.9 miles from the trailhead, and hike around the pond, soon you will come to an unnamed lake. The timbered islands in the meadows near this lake make great campsites. Unless you are here during the fall hunting seasons, you will probably be completely alone except for the elk. The Cortright Trail can also be used as an access route for a longer backpack on the PCT.

6 Cowlitz Trail 44

Hike into the lush southwestern portion of the William O. Douglas Wilderness, climbing to the plateau and passing Penoyer Lake before reaching the Pacific Crest National Scenic Trail.

See map on page 42.
Start: Soda Springs Campground and Trailhead.
Type of hike: Out-and-back day hike or backpack.
Total distance: 11 miles round-trip to the Pacific Crest National Scenic Trail 2000 (PCT).
Difficulty: Moderate.

Maps: USDA Forest Service Norse Peak and William O. Douglas Wilderness or White Pass USGS quad.
Permits and fees: William O. Douglas Wilderness permit.
Best months: July–September.
Special considerations: Mosquito presence can be very thick on the plateau, especially in July and early August.

Finding the trailhead: To reach the Soda Springs Trailhead from the **Seattle-Tacoma** area, drive to Enumclaw. From Enumclaw take State Route 410 for 41 miles east and south to Cayuse Pass and the junction with State Route 123. Turn right (nearly straight ahead) on SR 123 and follow it for 16.5 miles south to the junction with U.S. Highway 12. Turn left (east) on US 12 and drive about 1 mile to the junction with Forest Road 45. From **Portland,** Oregon, drive north on Interstate 5 to exit 68 (68 miles north of the Interstate Bridge), then follow US 12 east for 72 miles to the junction with FR 45. The junction with FR 45 is next to milepost 140 and 10.9 miles west of (before reaching) White Pass.

Turn left (north) off US 12 on FR 45 and drive 0.3 mile, then bear left (northeast) on Forest Road 4510. Follow FR 4510 for 4.1 miles to the junction with Forest Road 052, signed to Soda Springs Campground. Turn right (east) on FR 052 and go 0.6 mile to Soda Springs Trailhead, which is at the northeastern corner of the campground.

Parking and trailhead facilities: Campsites and restrooms are available at Soda Springs Campground and Trailhead.

The Hike

The Cowlitz Trail leaves the trailhead at 3,170 feet elevation, heading east. Soon the route appears to fork—bear left, the trail to the right is now abandoned. You will quickly enter the William O. Douglas Wilderness. Soon the trail climbs for a short distance, then levels to traverse a forested hillside. Slightly over 0.2 mile into the hike, you will cross a small stream at 3,290 feet elevation. Another 0.3 mile of hiking brings you to the crossing of Pony Creek. Just after crossing Pony Creek is the junction with Trail 44a. This junction is 0.5 mile from Soda Springs Trailhead, at 3,420 feet elevation. Trail 44a, which is normally used by parties with stock, turns to the left and leads northwest for 1 mile to the Cowlitz Trailhead on FR 4510. Stock is not permitted in the Soda Springs Campground.

Penoyer Lake.

Just past the junction the Cowlitz Trail crosses a tiny stream on a wooden bridge, as you continue to hike to the northeast. Skunk cabbage grows from the wet areas along this stream. The track crosses Allred Creek 0.3 mile past the junction. You will cross two more streams, which may be dry by midsummer, before reaching the outlet stream from Jug Lake, 2.2 miles from the trailhead, at 3,880 feet elevation.

Once you have forded the stream, the route climbs, passing a possible campsite on the left in a short distance. One-tenth mile after crossing the stream, you will reach the junction with the Jug Lake Trail 43, at 3,930 feet elevation. At the junction the Jug Lake Trail appears more used than the continuation of the Cowlitz Trail. See the options below for the route to Jug Lake.

Bear right at the junction to continue on the Cowlitz Trail. The course continues to climb through mixed-age forest, including some large Douglas firs and western hemlocks. Bracken fern, vanilla leaf, and an occasional columbine grow on the forest floor, often beneath an understory of vine maple. The tread climbs moderately for 0.6 mile, crossing a couple of tiny streams as it ascends to 4,250 feet elevation. The route reaches a streambed 0.1 mile farther along. This streambed may or may not have water in it depending on the season. The trail follows the streambed down-stream (straight ahead) for 50 yards and then climbs out steeply. At the point where the route climbs out, there is another streambed, which generally has at least some water, entering the streambed you have been walking in.

The route then climbs moderately again, crossing several tiny streams in the 0.8 mile to a creek crossing. Along the way beargrass and white-flowered rhododendron crowd the sides of the trail. Another 0.1 mile brings you to the junction with the Pothole Trail 45 and Trail 41. This junction, at 4,740 feet elevation, is 4 miles from the Soda Spring Campground and Trailhead. Trail 41 leads northwest to join the Jug Lake Trail in about 1 mile. The Pothole Trail heads north for a couple of miles to a junction with the PCT. By the time you reach the junction, you are on the plateau, and the forest has become subalpine in nature. The trees are mostly subalpine fir and spruce, and in the openings huckleberry bushes and an occasional mountain heather cover the ground.

Bear right (east-southeast) at the junction and you'll soon cross a couple of tiny streams. In slightly over 0.3 mile, after climbing to 4,860 feet elevation, the route reaches the rim of a small canyon. Here the trail turns to head east, climbing along the rim, with the canyon to your right. You climb along the rim for a little less than 0.2 mile, then turn to the right at the head of the canyon to cross a streambed, which is made of nearly solid rock. By mid-August this stream is usually dry, but if you are here when it has water, there is a waterfall a few feet below (to the right of) the trail crossing. After crossing the streambed the tread heads southeast for 0.1 mile to Penoyer Lake.

Penoyer Lake, at 4,940 feet elevation, is relatively small. It is a shallow lake with grasses growing over a large part of its area. Mountain heather and huckleberries, backed by subalpine timber, surround the shoreline.

The Cowlitz Trail skirts Penoyer Lake on the south then climbs gently to the east, through timber and openings. In about 0.4 mile you will pass a small pond on the left side of the trail. Then the route crosses a streambed and continues its gentle climb to the junction with the Pacific Crest Trail 2000. The junction with the PCT is 5.5 miles from Soda Springs Trailhead, at 5,140 feet above sea level.

This is not the end of the Cowlitz Trail 44, but if you wish to hike the eastern part of it, over Tumac Mountain, it is much easier to begin your hike at Deep Creek Trailhead south of Bumping Lake. The Cowlitz Trail turns right at the junction with the PCT and follows the same route as the PCT for 0.2 mile before heading on to the east.

Miles and Directions

0.0   Soda Springs Campground and Trailhead. GPS 46 42.258N 121 28.858W.
0.5   Junction with Trail 44a. GPS 46 42.534N 121 28.260W. Bear right.
2.3   Junction with Jug Lake Trail 43. GPS 46 42.775N 121 26.430W. Bear right.

4.0 Junction with Pothole Trail 45 and Trail 41. GPS 46 42.964N 121 24.758W. Bear right.

4.6 Penoyer Lake.

5.5 Junction with PCT 2000. GPS 46 42.579N 121 23.232W. Turnaround point.

11.0 Soda Springs Campground and Trailhead.

Options: Make the side trip to Jug Lake by turning left on Jug Lake Trail 43, 2.3 miles from the trailhead, and hiking 1.3 miles to the junction with the Judkin Trail 47. Turn left on the Judkin Trail, and it's only 0.1 mile to Jug Lake.

7 Jug Lake–Chain Lakes Trails 44, 43, and 47

Hike the moderate trail to Jug Lake to camp and fish, or if your route-finding skills are up to it, go on to Chain Lakes for an isolated campsite.

See map on page 42.

Start: Soda Springs Campground and Trailhead.

Type of hike: Out-and-back day hike or backpack.

Total distance: 10 miles round-trip to Chain Lakes.

Difficulty: Moderate to Jug Lake, strenuous with excellent route-finding skills required from there to Chain Lakes.

Maps: USDA Forest Service William O. Douglas and Norse Peak Wilderness and White Pass USGS quad.

Permits and fees: William O. Douglas Wilderness permit.

Best months: July–September.

Special considerations: If you are not sure of your ability to follow a very faint trail, it is best not to attempt the hike from Jug Lake to Chain Lakes.

Finding the trailhead: To reach the Soda Springs Trailhead from **Portland,** Oregon, drive north on Interstate 5 to exit 68 (68 miles north of the Interstate Bridge), then follow U.S. Highway 12 east for 72 miles to the junction with Forest Road 45. From the **Seattle-Tacoma** area, drive to Enumclaw. Then take State Route 410 east and south for 41 miles to Cayuse Pass and the junction with State Route 123. Bear right on SR 123 and go 16.5 miles south to the junction with US 12. Turn left (east) on US 12 and drive 1 mile to the junction with FR 45. The junction with FR 45 is next to milepost 140 and 10.9 miles west of (before reaching) White Pass.

Turn left (north) off US 12 on FR 45 and drive 0.3 mile, then bear left (northeast) on Forest Road 4510. Follow FR 4510 for 4.1 miles to the junction with Forest Road 052, signed to Soda Springs Campground. Turn right (east) on FR 052 and go 0.6 mile to Soda Springs Trailhead, which is at the northeastern corner of the campground, at 3,170 feet elevation.

Parking and trailhead facilities: Campsites and restrooms are available at Soda Springs Campground and Trailhead.

Chain Lakes.

The Hike

This hike begins on the Cowlitz Trail 44. Get your wilderness permit at the trail-head and then head east on the Cowlitz Trail. Soon the route appears to fork, at which point you should bear left—the trail to the right is now abandoned. In a short distance the route enters the William O. Douglas Wilderness. The trail climbs fairly steeply for a short distance after entering the wilderness. Then the grade moderates as you traverse a forested hillside. The course crosses a small stream a little over 0.2 mile from the trailhead. Pony Creek is crossed 0.3 mile farther along. Shortly after crossing Pony Creek, you will reach the junction with Trail 44a, at 3,420 feet elevation. Trail 44a turns to the left and leads northwest for 1 mile to Cowlitz Trailhead on FR 4510. As horses and other stock are prohibited in Soda Springs Campground, parties with stock normally use Trail 44a.

The Cowlitz Trail crosses a wooden bridge over a tiny stream just past the junction. Three-tenths mile past the junction, the route crosses Allred Creek. You will cross two more streams, which may be dry by midsummer, before reaching the outlet stream from Jug Lake, 2.2 miles from the trailhead, at 3,880 feet elevation. There is a possible campsite on the left side of the trail a short distance after crossing the stream.

One-tenth mile after crossing the stream, the junction with the Jug Lake Trail 43 is reached at 3,930 feet elevation. The Jug Lake Trail receives more use than the continuation of the Cowlitz Trail and appears to be the main route at the junction.

Bear left (northeast) at the junction and begin your climb toward Jug Lake. The wide but somewhat rocky course climbs fairly steeply through the forest of mostly Douglas and true fir timber. Vine maple forms an understory in places, while bracken fern, bunchberry, and vanilla leaf cover the ground. In a short distance you make the first of seven switchbacks that ease the grade as you climb to about 4,350 feet elevation. The grade moderates 0.7 mile from the junction but continues to climb gently, reaching 4,470 feet elevation as you cross an indistinct, rounded ridgeline. Then the route descends very gently to the junction with the Judkin Trail 47. Before reaching the junction, there is a pond to the right of the trail. The junction with the Judkin Trail is at 4,440 feet elevation, 3.6 miles from the Soda Springs Campground and Trailhead. See the options below to continue on the Jug Lake Trail.

You would think that the Jug Lake Trail would go to Jug Lake, but it bypasses the lake completely. To reach Jug Lake, turn left (northwest) on the Judkin Trail. In 0.1 mile the lake will come into view to your left. Jug Lake, at 4,416 feet above sea level, has some campsites along its north shore and to the right of the trail at its northeast corner. Be sure to camp at least 100 feet from the lake and keep stock, if you have them, at least 200 feet from the shoreline.

Unless you are sure of your route-finding abilities, Jug Lake should be your stopping point. The trail from here to Chain Lakes can be very difficult to follow. If you decide to head for Chain Lakes, continue west-northwest on the Judkin Trail. Shortly you will cross a stream that empties into Jug Lake near the campsites along the northern shoreline. After crossing the stream the tread bears right to head northwest. Just after turning to the northwest, the trail crosses a small meadow, where it becomes very vague. Follow along the right side of the meadow and pick up the trail again at its northern end. Once back in the timber, the trail is obvious again for a short distance. Then you cross a streambed, which is often dry by midsummer, and enter a much larger meadow, where the trail may disappear completely. The GPS coordinates where the trail enters this meadow are 46 43.619N 121 26.517W. Elk often use this meadow—watch for them early in the morning and in the evening. To continue on the trail to Chain Lakes, cross the meadow, heading west-southwest. The trail shows up again on the far side of the meadow at GPS coordinates 46 43.571N 121 26.647W.

The meadow is not the end of your route-finding task, because much of the rest of the trail to Chain Lakes is also hard to follow. Leaving the meadow the trail climbs to the southwest. Watch for cut logs indicating that the route here was once maintained. There are also very old blazes marking the route, but these have mostly healed over and the scars are difficult to spot. To complicate matters, there are several game trails on this slope that are at least as well used as is the route to Chain Lakes.

The route climbs generally southwest for about 0.3 mile, reaching a poorly defined pass at about 4,750 elevation. Then you begin to descend to the west. The portion of the trail descending west from the pass is a bit easier to follow than the route climbing up from the meadow. After descending to the west for 0.2 mile, the route reaches a meadow with two ponds in it. The meadow and ponds will be to your left. Enter the meadow and skirt the ponds, keeping them on your left, and in about 200 yards you will reach the northern shore of the largest of the Chain Lakes. The second pond that you skirt is really a cove of this lake. If you want to get away from it all and camp by yourself, Chain Lakes is a great place to do it. The GPS coordinates where you reach the shore of the largest of the Chain Lakes are 46 43.251N 12127.116W and the elevation is 4,660 feet.

The Chain Lakes Trail used to continue on past the lakes and eventually reach FR 4510 at its end just north of the Cowlitz Trailhead. This section of trail is still shown on the USGS White Pass quad map, but it hasn't been maintained for many years and is even more difficult to follow than is the route to Chain Lakes. Make the return hike by retracing your steps back to the Soda Springs Campground and Trailhead.

Miles and Directions

0.0 Soda Springs Campground and Trailhead. GPS 46 42.258N 121 28.858W.

0.5 Junction with Trail 44a. GPS 46 42.534N 121 28.260W. Bear right.

2.3 Junction with Jug Lake Trail 43. GPS 46 42.775N 121 26.430W. Turn left.

3.6 Junction with Judkin Trail 47. GPS 46 43.282N 121 26.054W. Turn left.

3.7 Jug Lake.

4.3 Junction with Chain Lakes Trail. Turn left.

5.0 Chain Lakes. GPS 46 43.251N 12127.116W Turnaround point.

10.0 Soda Springs Campground and Trailhead.

Options: If you continue northeast from the junction with the Judkin Trail on Jug Lake Trail, you'll reach Little Snow Lake in about a mile, and a little farther along is Fryingpan Lake. There is a campsite next to Little Snow Lake and there are several around Fryingpan Lake. Either of these lakes makes a good alternate destination. The meadows around Fryingpan Lake often have elk grazing or bedding in them.

8 Soda Springs

Hike the steep but only 60–yard–long trail to colorful, bubbling Soda Springs.

Start: Poorly marked trailhead 130 yards west of Soda Springs Campground and Trailhead on Forest Road 4510-052.
Type of hike: Out-and-back 10-minute hike.
Total distance: 0.06 mile.
Difficulty: Moderate but very short.
Maps: USDA Forest Service Gifford Pinchot National Forest map may be helpful for finding the trailhead. White Pass USGS quad covers the area but does not show this short trail.

Permits and fees: None.
Best months: June–October.
Special considerations: Although this trail is very short, it may not be suitable for people whose balance isn't quite good. A watchful eye should be kept on children because of the drop-off just past the spring into Summit Creek.

Soda Springs.

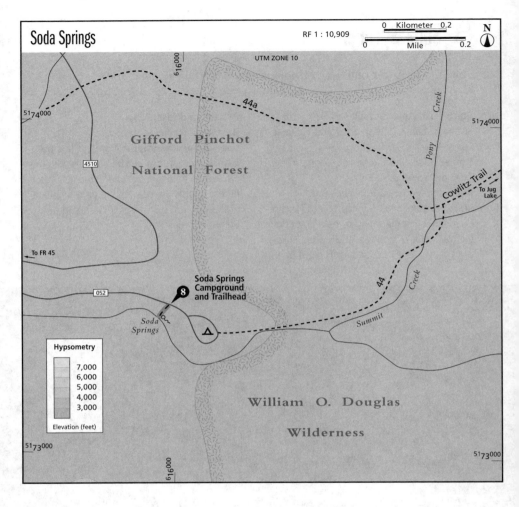

Soda Springs

RF 1 : 10,909

0   Kilometer   0.2

0   Mile   0.2

N

UTM ZONE 10

51⁷⁴000

Gifford   Pinchot

National   Forest

4510

51⁷⁴000

Pony   Creek

Cowlitz Trail

To Jug Lake

To FR 45

052

Soda Springs
Campground
and Trailhead

8

Soda
Springs

44

44a

Creek

Summit

Hypsometry

	7,000
	6,000
	5,000
	4,000
	3,000

Elevation (feet)

William O. Douglas

Wilderness

51⁷³000

51⁷³000

Finding the trailhead: To reach Soda Springs Campground and Trailhead from the **Seattle-Tacoma** area, drive to Enumclaw. From Enumclaw take State Route 410 for 41 miles east and south to Cayuse Pass and the junction with State Route 123. Turn right (nearly straight ahead) on SR 123 and follow it for 16.5 miles to the junction with U.S. Highway 12. Turn left (east) on US 12 and go slightly over 1 mile to the junction with Forest Road 45. From **Portland,** Oregon, drive north on Interstate 5 to exit 68 (68 miles north of the Interstate Bridge), then follow US 12 east for 72 miles to the junction with FR 45. The junction with FR 45 is next to milepost 140 and 10.9 miles west of (before reaching) White Pass.

Turn left (north) off US 12 on FR 45 and drive 0.3 mile, then bear left (northeast) on FR 4510. Follow FR 4510 for 4.1 miles to the junction with FR 052, signed to Soda Springs Campground. Turn right (east) on FR 052 and go 0.6 mile to Soda Springs Campground. From the western end of the campground, backtrack west 130 yards along FR 052 to the unmarked trailhead. **Parking and trailhead facilities:** There is parking for a couple of cars at the trailhead. Adequate parking, campsites, and restrooms are available at Soda Springs Campground.

The Hike

From the unmarked trailhead the trail heads south for a few feet before turning west-southwest and beginning its steep descent. Maidenhair ferns, huckleberry bushes, and bunchberries line the route as you descend. The huckleberries are generally ripe here in mid-August. About halfway down, the trail makes a steep switchback to the left. This area is often muddy and slick, making this hike unsuitable for people with poor balance. A few more steps bring you to the spring, which is encased with rocks. The mineral water draining from the spring makes an orange course as it splashes down the slope into Summit Creek.

Miles and Directions

0.00 Trailhead on FR 052.

0.03 Soda Springs. Turnaround point.

0.06 Trailhead on FR 052.

Options: Soda Springs Campground is also the trailhead for the Cowlitz Trail 44, from where you can reach Jug and Penoyer Lakes, as well as much of the central William O. Douglas Wilderness.

Northwest Region

The northwestern portion of the William O. Douglas Wilderness includes the rugged backbone of the Cascades along the eastern boundary of Mount Rainier National Park, as well as the northern slope of 15-mile-long American Ridge. Hikes 9, 10, 11, 14, and 16 all access high subalpine and alpine ridges that provide spectacular views in all directions, including the ice-shrouded eastern face of Mount Rainier. Hikes 13 and 15 offer easy hiking in the river bottom along

American Lake at the head of the American River.

the American River. Elk are especially common along Hike 14, which follows the American River for over 7 miles. High on American Ridge and on Naches Peak Loop (Hike 9), mountain goats are sometimes encountered. In July the subalpine meadows of the high country bring forth some of the best flower displays to be found anywhere.

All of the hikes in this region are accessed directly from or very close to State Route 410, making them easily accessible for regular cars. With the exception of Hike 13, Pleasant Valley Nature Loop, these trails all interconnect, providing a wealth of hiking opportunities. Hike 13 is a barrier-free paved route. This short loop is an excellent place to take small children hiking. The reader boards along Hike 13 provide much insight as to what goes on in this forest.

9 Naches Peak Loop
National Park Trail and Trail 2000

Early in the summer (July), the flower gardens along this loop rival those to be found anywhere. The first 1.6 miles of this hike are within Mount Rainier National Park.

Start: Trailhead across State Route 410 from Tipsoo Lake.
Type of hike: Shuttle day hike with the option of continuing and making a loop.
Total distance: 3.2 miles.
Difficulty: Easy to moderate.
Maps: USDA Forest Service Norse Peak and William O. Douglas Wilderness, Chinook Pass and Cougar Lake USGS quads, or U.S. Department of the Interior National Park Service Mount Rainier National Park.

Permits and fees: None for this loop trail, even though it does enter the William O. Douglas Wilderness.
Best months: July–September.
Special considerations: The timing of the snowmelt is variable at Chinook Pass. Some years portions of this trail may be snow-covered well into July. The best flowers can be seen about 2 weeks after the snow melts.

Finding the trailhead: To reach the trailhead where this hike begins, drive north from **Portland,** Oregon, on Interstate 5 for 68 miles to the junction with U.S. Highway 12. Then head east on US 12 for 71 miles (7 miles east of Packwood) to the junction with State Route 123. Turn left off US 12 on SR 123 and drive north for 16.5 miles to Cayuse Pass and the junction with SR 410. From the **Seattle-Tacoma** area, drive to Enumclaw. From Enumclaw follow SR 410 for 41 miles east and south to Cayuse Pass.

Turn left (right if coming from Portland) on SR 410 and head east for 3.2 miles to the trailhead, which is across the highway from Tipsoo Lake. Park on the left side of the road (5,330 feet elevation).

To reach the Chinook Pass Trailhead, where this hike ends, continue east and north on SR 410 for 0.6 mile, crossing Chinook Pass to the parking area, which is on the left side of the highway. The Chinook Pass Trailhead is 0.1 mile past (north of) Chinook Pass.
Parking and trailhead facilities: There is adequate parking at both trailheads. Restrooms are available at the Chinook Pass Trailhead, where this hike ends.

The Hike

Cross the highway from the parking area and pass the trail sign that marks the trailhead. This trail is open to hikers only, as are most of the trails in Mount Rainier National Park. The meadows here are covered with western pasqueflowers and buttercups in early summer (July). In about 50 yards you will reach the junction with the East Side Trail. The East Side Trail is to the right at the junction, and to the left is a path that leads east to a small, unnamed lake. Hike straight ahead (south) at the junction, climbing through the mountain hemlocks and subalpine firs.

Naches Peak.

In about 0.2 mile the trail crosses a tiny stream where there is a great view of ice-covered Mount Rainier to the west. Mount Rainier, at 14,408 feet above sea level, is Washington's highest peak and the fifth highest in the contiguous forty-eight states. The trail continues to climb south, through the subalpine timber and glacier lilies for 0.2 mile more, then turns to the southeast. By now you have reached 5,600 feet altitude. To the south the bulky form of Mount Adams cuts the skyline in the distance. Mount Adams, at 12,276 feet elevation, is the second-highest peak in Washington.

Soon the trail turns east, crossing a semiopen slope, where Nelson Ridge comes into view ahead. The route crosses another tiny stream that may be dry by midsummer, then comes to a trail junction. The path to the right goes a few yards to a viewpoint. Bear left at the junction and soon cross another tiny stream, which may also be dry. There will be a pond on your left just after crossing the stream. Past the pond the trail climbs slightly to another path to the right. This path leads 30 yards to a viewpoint overlooking Dewey Lake. Just past the path to the viewpoint, the trail reaches its highest elevation at 5,850 feet and passes a sign that says you are entering the William O. Douglas Wilderness. According to the USGS quad maps, this sign

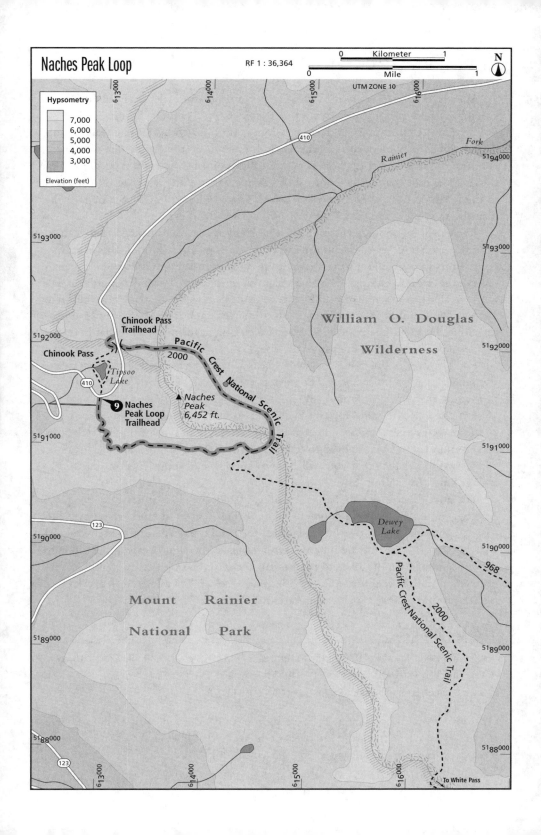

Naches Peak Loop

RF 1 : 36,364

Hypsometry

7,000
6,000
5,000
4,000
3,000

Elevation (feet)

UTM ZONE 10

N

410

Rainier *Fork*

5¹94000

5¹93000

5¹93000

Chinook Pass Trailhead

William O. Douglas

Wilderness

5¹92000

5¹92000

Chinook Pass

Pacific Crest National Scenic Trail

2000

410

Tipsoo Lake

9 Naches Peak Loop Trailhead

▲ *Naches Peak 6,452 ft.*

5¹91000

5¹91000

123

5¹90000

Dewey Lake

5¹90000

968

Mount Rainier

Pacific Crest National Scenic Trail

2000

5¹89000

National Park

5¹89000

5¹88000

5¹88000

123

6¹3000

6¹4000

6¹5000

6¹6000

To White Pass

may be slightly misplaced as the wilderness boundary is shown to be a short distance east of here.

After passing the wilderness boundary sign, the route descends slightly to a switchback and the junction with the Pacific Crest National Scenic Trail 2000 (PCT). This junction, at 5,800 feet elevation, is 1.5 miles from the trailhead next to Tipsoo Lake. Turn left at the switchback and junction on the Pacific Crest Trail and climb to the top of a rise. There is another viewpoint to the right near the top of the rise. The route flattens here for a short distance, after which you begin to descend to the north, into the Rainier Fork drainage. This is where the USGS Cougar Lake map shows you entering the William O. Douglas Wilderness.

There will be another viewpoint to the right as the route makes a left turn to head northwest. As you descend the mostly open slope, the Chinook Pass Highway comes into view to the north. If you are here early in the summer, you will cross several tiny streams and pass beneath a small waterfall as you descend along this slope, but by August they will likely all be dry. Snowdrifts covering parts of the trail here are possible well into July. There is a path to the right 0.6 mile after you begin hiking along the PCT. The path, at 5,620 feet elevation, leads to the lake that has been in view since you crossed the top of the rise. This is a beautiful spot to stop and take a break. The precipitous slopes of Naches Peak, where mountain goats are occasionally seen, rise above to the west. The flowers are fantastic here early in the season, as they are in many places along this loop.

Past the lake the trail crosses a creek and soon enters subalpine timber as you continue to traverse the slope, heading northwest. Early in the season you will cross several more tiny streams along this slope, and the route may be muddy in spots. There is also a chance that you will have to cross several snowdrifts on this north-facing slope early in the season.

The route leaves the William O. Douglas Wilderness 2.9 miles into the hike. Another 0.2 mile of slightly downhill hiking brings you to the footbridge over SR 410 at Chinook Pass. Cross the bridge and turn right, paralleling the highway, and walk another 0.1 mile to the junction with a trail to the right. Leave the PCT here and descend a few more yards to the parking area at Chinook Pass Trailhead. By the time you reach the trailhead, you have descended to 5,390 feet elevation and are 3.2 miles from the trailhead where you started this hike.

Miles and Directions

0.0 Trailhead across SR 410 from Tipsoo Lake. GPS 46 52.018N 121 31.074N. Cross highway.

1.5 Junction with Pacific Crest Trail. GPS 46 51.732N 121 29.782W. Turn left.

3.2 Chinook Pass Trailhead. GPS 46 52.502N 121 31.070W.

Options: If you didn't arrange for a car shuttle to the Chinook Pass Trailhead, there is a trail from near the footbridge over the highway that goes about 0.6 mile southwest, back to the trailhead where you started this hike.

10 Cougar Lake
Trails 2000, 958, and 958a

Hike from Chinook Pass along the backbone of the Cascade Range to gorgeous Cougar Lake, passing Dewey and American Lakes as you go.

Start: Chinook Pass Trailhead.
Type of hike: Out-and-back backpack.
Total distance: 19.2 miles round-trip to Cougar Lake.
Difficulty: Moderate.
Maps: USDA Forest Service Norse Peak and William O. Douglas Wilderness or Cougar Lake USGS quad.

Permits and fees: William O. Douglas Wilderness permit.
Best months: Mid-July through September.
Special considerations: Some route-finding skills are necessary because of trail rerouting on the Cougar Lake Trail. Much of the Cougar Lake Trail is very rough and rocky. Mosquitoes can be terrible in July.

Finding the trailhead: To reach Chinook Pass, where this hike begins, drive north from **Portland,** Oregon, on Interstate 5 for 68 miles to the junction with U.S. Highway 12. Then head east on US 12 for 71 miles (7 miles east of Packwood) to the junction with State Route 123. Turn left off US 12 on SR 123 and drive north for 16.5 miles to Cayuse Pass and the junction with State Route 410. From the **Seattle-Tacoma** area, drive to Enumclaw. From Enumclaw follow SR 410 for 41 miles east and south to Cayuse Pass

Turn left (right if coming from Portland) on SR 410 and head east for 3.7 miles to Chinook Pass. The parking area is about 0.1 mile past the pass on the left side of SR 410.
Parking and trailhead facilities: You'll find adequate parking and restrooms at the trailhead.

The Hike

The first 6.6 miles of this route follow the Pacific Crest National Scenic Trail 2000 (PCT). The trail leaves from the west side of the parking area, at 5,390 feet elevation, quickly climbing a few yards west to meet the PCT. Early in the season western pasqueflowers *(Anemone occidentalis)* bloom in profusion here. By August their blooms are gone, replaced by the hairy seedpods that give them their other common name, "mouse on a stick." Turn left on the PCT and hike along the wide trail that parallels SR 410 for 0.1 mile to the footbridge over SR 410 at Chinook Pass.

Cross the bridge over the highway and begin the ascending traverse along the northern slope of Naches Peak. In another 0.2 mile you enter the William O. Douglas Wilderness. No permit is required for this section of the trail, so just keep hiking. Behind you to the west, Mount Rainier lifts its huge ice-covered dome high above the lesser surrounding peaks and timbered canyons. Early in the season the route crosses several tiny streams as you traverse this slope through the

subalpine timber, but by mid-August they are mostly dry. Mountain goats are occasionally seen on the slopes of Naches Peak—look above to your right, through the thinning timber, for a possible glimpse of one of these white crag monarchs.

There will be a path to your left, at 5,620 feet elevation, 1.1 miles from the trailhead. The side trail leads a few yards to a small but very pretty lake. This lake is a popular destination and may be crowded on summer weekends. Past the path to the lake, the route continues to climb, crossing a small creek beneath a waterfall in another 0.2 mile. Like the other small streams in the area, this one may be dry by mid-August. The route then climbs across a rocky slope for another 0.3 mile to a switchback. To the left at the switchback, a short path leads to a viewpoint overlooking the Rainier Fork Canyon. Above the switchback the tread soon flattens out, crossing the top of a rise at 5,880 feet elevation. As you cross the nearly flat open area, the peaks and ridges of the eastern part of the William O. Douglas Wilderness come into view. There is another short side path to the left, to another viewpoint near the top of the rise. Once across the rise the tread descends for a little over 0.1 mile to the junction with the Naches Peak Loop Trail at 5,800 feet elevation, 1.7 miles from the Chinook Pass Trailhead.

Bear left at the junction with the Naches Peak Loop Trail, staying on the PCT, and continue your descent. In a short distance you will reach the wilderness registration box. Stop here and fill out your wilderness permit, then traverse southwest along a semiopen slope, with a view of the Tatoosh Range ahead. The tread is a little rocky in places here and has a few water bars. These water bars create steps that you descend. A quarter mile from the junction, the course makes a switchback to the left and heads east-southeast. Mount Rainier comes into view to the northwest as you make the switchback. The wide array of flowers beside the trail include phlox, lupine, and avalanche and glacier lilies, as well as many other varieties of flowers. Alpine spiraea and huckleberry bushes also cover part of the slope. The huckleberries are ready for picking in late August.

The course makes a couple more switchbacks 0.3 mile farther along and crosses a couple of tiny streams as you enter larger timber. The trees here are mostly hemlocks. The tread crosses a small wooden bridge 0.8 mile from the junction with the Naches Peak Loop. After the bridge two short boardwalks ease the passage across a muddy area. Slightly over 0.1 mile past the boardwalks, the route passes a couple of signs on a tree that state NO FIRES WITHIN ½ MILE OF DEWEY LAKES and that you must camp at least 100 feet from the lakes and keep stock back 200 feet.

A short distance past the signs, there is a path to the left that leads to campsites along the northern shore of the larger of the Dewey Lakes. The route passes between the two Dewey Lakes. Shortly you'll cross another wooden bridge, this one over the stream that connects the lakes. This bridge is 2.8 miles from the Chi-

◀ *Little Cougar Lake*

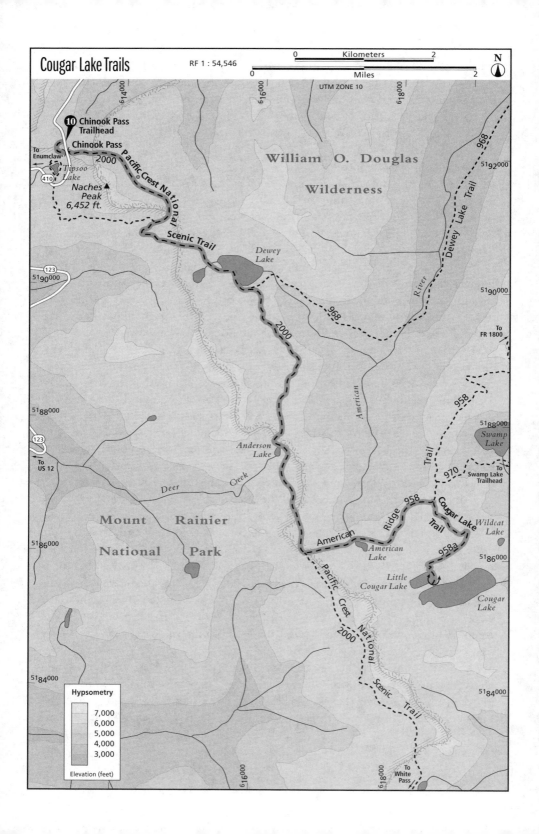

Cougar Lake Trails

RF 1 : 54,546

Kilometers
0   2

Miles
0   2

UTM ZONE 10

N

6¹4°°°

6¹6°°°

6¹8°°°

10 Chinook Pass
Trailhead

Chinook Pass

To
Enumclaw

410

2000

Tipsoo
Lake

Pacific Crest National

Naches
Peak
6,452 ft.

Scenic Trail

Dewey
Lake

William O. Douglas

Wilderness

968

Dewey Lake Trail

51⁹²°°°

123

51⁹⁰°°°

2000

968

American

River

51⁹⁰°°°

To
FR 1800

958

51⁸⁸°°°

Swamp
Lake

51⁸⁸°°°

123

To
US 12

Anderson
Lake

Deer   Creek

970

To
Swamp Lake
Trailhead

Ridge

958

Trail

Cougar Lake

Trail

Wildcat
Lake

Mount   Rainier

American

American
Lake

958a

51⁸⁶°°°

National   Park

51⁸⁶°°°

Little
Cougar Lake

Cougar
Lake

Pacific Crest National

2000

51⁸⁴°°°

Scenic   Trail

51⁸⁴°°°

Hypsometry

	Elevation (feet)
	7,000
	6,000
	5,000
	4,000
	3,000

6¹6°°°

6¹8°°°

To
White
Pass

nook Pass Trailhead, at 5,140 feet elevation. Just past the bridge, a path to the right leads to campsites at upper Dewey Lake. Upper Dewey Lake is much smaller than the lower lake. After crossing the bridge the route heads southeast, skirting the shore of the larger lake. Several side paths lead to campsites. If Dewey Lake is your destination, find a spot 100 or more feet back from the shoreline, and set up camp. Dewey Lake has a good population of trout to keep the anglers in your party busy.

The tread continues along the southern shore of the lake to a junction with the Dewey Lake Trail 968. This junction is at 5,150 feet elevation and is 3.4 miles from the Chinook Pass Trailhead. Dewey Lake Trail descends to Mesatchee Creek Trail, which in turn continues to Mesatchee Creek Trailhead near SR 410, 8.9 miles from here. Large firs and hemlocks stand guard over the trail near the junction. Bear right (straight ahead to the southeast) at the junction and stay on the PCT.

The PCT enters a meadow 0.2 mile from the junction with the Dewey Lake Trail. In the meadow are a pond and a stream, which the route crosses. At the southern end of the meadow, the course crosses a couple of small wooden bridges over wet areas, then begins to climb. Both pink and white mountain heather grow beside the tread as you climb. The track soon makes a switchback to the left and crosses another bridge over a small stream. You pass beneath a talus slope 0.3 mile farther along. Watch and listen for pikas in the rocks. Soon there will be talus below the trail, allowing for a great view of the American River Canyon and Fife's Peak, to the east and northeast. Mount Aix and Bismarck Peak are also in view here to the southeast.

The route flattens out at 5,420 feet elevation a little less than 1 mile from the junction with the Dewey Lake Trail. From here you descend very gently, crossing a wooden bridge over a tiny stream, then crossing a larger creek without benefit of a bridge. The route reaches Anderson Lake 1.8 miles from the Dewey Lake Trail junction. Small Anderson Lake lies at a little over 5,300 feet elevation, to the right of the trail.

At Anderson Lake the PCT makes a hard left turn and begins to climb, soon passing a metal sign pointing left to CAMP. As you climb there are views of Mount Rainier. The route makes a switchback, then tops out at 5,610 feet above sea level, 0.6 mile after passing Anderson Lake. Before long you begin to descend toward the junction with the American Ridge Trail. As the trace begins to head down, you pass through meadowland that blooms profusely with wildflowers in late July. Just before reaching the junction, the trail crosses another small wooden bridge over a marshy spot. The junction with the American Ridge Trail 958 is reached 6.6 miles from the Chinook Pass Trailhead, at 5,300 feet elevation. To continue south on the PCT, see the options below.

At the junction turn left, leaving the PCT, and continue to descend on the American Ridge Trail, heading to the east. The route drops gently through the subalpine forest of mountain hemlock and subalpine fir. Between the stands of trees are small flower-covered meadows. In about 0.1 mile the track crosses a tiny stream upon whose banks grow white mountain heather.

There will be a path to your right 0.5 mile from the junction with the PCT. The short path leads to small but picturesque American Lake. American Lake, at 5,250 feet elevation and 7.1 miles from Chinook Pass Trailhead, makes a great destination for your hike. There are several campsites here. Remember that you must camp at least 100 feet back from the shoreline and observe the areas that are closed for restoration.

The trail crosses the American River, which is only a creek here, close to where it flows from American Lake. The route follows the north shore of the lake for a short way, then descends very gently, crossing several tiny streams, to the junction with the Cougar Lake Trail 958a, 8.1 miles from Chinook Pass Trailhead. The junction with the Cougar Lake Trail is in a small meadow next to a creek, at 5,050 feet elevation.

Turn right at the junction on the Cougar Lake Trail and climb south-southwest, soon leaving the meadow. As you climb through the subalpine fir, Alaska cedar, and hemlock timber, the trailside is covered with pink mountain heather, white-flowered rhododendron, and huckleberry bushes. The path is fairly steep in places as you climb toward the rounded ridgeline.

After gaining 350 feet of elevation in 0.6 mile, the tread flattens on the ridge. For the next 0.7 mile, the trail has been rerouted to follow a different route than is shown on the Cougar Lake USGS quad map. First you turn to the northeast to descend a semiopen slope. Then the course turns right (southeast), descends more gently, and crosses a tiny stream that may be dry by midsummer. Soon the route swings around to the southwest, heading directly toward Little Cougar Lake. Alpine spiraea graces the sides of the rough trail as you gradually descend. Little Cougar Lake soon comes into view. The tread makes the first of four switchbacks 1.1 miles from the junction with the American Ridge Trail. The switchbacks allow for an easier descent to the northeast corner of Little Cougar Lake. When you reach the lakeshore, you have lost all the elevation you gained climbing to the top of the rounded ridgeline, plus a few feet more.

There are campsites to your right as you pass Little Cougar Lake heading south-southeast toward Cougar Lake. In a couple hundred more yards, you'll reach the shore of Cougar Lake, where there are more campsites. Remember to camp at least 100 feet away from the lakes, as is stated in the wilderness regulations. If you have stock, they must be kept at least 200 feet back from the lakes.

The route soon heads southwest, passing between Cougar Lake and Little Cougar Lake. From here an unmaintained path climbs steeply over the ridgeline to the southwest to the PCT. Use this path only if you are good at route finding and accustomed to cross-country travel. Return the way you came.

Miles and Directions

0.0   Chinook Pass Trailhead. GPS 46 52.502N 121 31.070W.

1.7   Junction with Naches Peak Loop Trail. GPS 46 51.732N 121 29.782W. Turn left.

3.4   Junction with Dewey Lake Trail 968 near Dewey Lakes. GPS 46 51.156N 121 28.756W. Proceed straight ahead.

6.6   Junction with American Ridge Trail 958. GPS 46 49.029N 121 28.117W. Turn left.

7.1   American Lake.

8.1   Junction with Cougar Lake Trail 958a. GPS 46 49.591N 121 26.667W. Turn right.

8.7   Trail crosses rounded ridgeline

9.6   Cougar Lake. Turnaround point.

19.2   Chinook Pass Trailhead.

Options: From the junction with the American Ridge Trail, the PCT climbs to the southeast. The route stays west of the crest and within Mount Rainier National Park for about 2.5 miles. Then you cross the crest to the east side and traverse above Two Lakes and One Lake. A side trail leads down to Two Lakes. You reach the junction with the Laughingwater Trail 4.2 miles from the junction with the American Ridge Trail. Laughingwater Trail descends to the west to a trailhead on SR 123. Past the junction with the Laughingwater Trail, the PCT soon begins to descend toward Fish Lake, passing Crag and Buck Lakes along the way. You reach the junction with the Carlton Creek Trail 22, next to Fish Lake, 8.1 miles from the junction with the American Ridge Trail. Three-tenths mile farther is the junction with the Bumping Lake Trail, which descends northeast to Bumping Lake. From this junction you can continue on along the PCT for another 13.7 miles to Leech Lake Trailhead near White Pass or descend the Bumping River Trail and Fish Lake Way to Fish Lake Way Trailhead south of Bumping Lake.

11 Mesatchee Creek Trail 969

Hike from a trailhead along the American River to lovely Mesatchee Falls, then on to the top of American Ridge.

Start: Mesatchee Creek Trailhead.
Type of hike: Out-and-back day hike or backpack.
Total distance: 11.4 miles to American Ridge.
Difficulty: Moderate.
Maps: Norse Peak and Cougar Lake USGS quads or USDA Forest Service William O. Douglas and Norse Peak Wilderness.

Permits and fees: Northwest Forest Pass and William O Douglas Wilderness permit.
Best months: July through mid-October.
Special considerations: The American River must be forded, so take sandals or other water shoes along. Early in the season when the river is high, the crossing could be difficult.

Finding the trailhead: From the **Seattle-Tacoma** area, drive to Enumclaw. From Enumclaw follow State Route 410 for 41 miles east and south to Cayuse Pass. From **Portland,** Oregon, drive north on Interstate 5 for 68 miles to the junction with U.S. Highway 12. Then head east on US 12 for 71 miles (7 miles east of Packwood) to the junction with State Route 123. Turn north (left) off US 12 on SR 123 and drive 16.5 miles to Cayuse Pass and the junction with SR 410.

Turn right (left if coming from Seattle) on SR 410 and head east for 10.4 miles to the Mesatchee Creek Forest Road 460. This junction is 6.7 miles east of Chinook Pass. Turn right at the junction and follow FR 460 for about 0.3 mile to its end at Mesatchee Creek Trailhead, at 3,640 feet elevation.

Parking and trailhead facilities: Adequate parking, restrooms, and some stock facilities are available at the trailhead.

The Hike

A few yards west of the trailhead, you'll reach the wilderness registration box. Stop and fill out your wilderness permit, then continue west, passing some large Douglas firs. Vanilla leaf and bunchberries cover the ground beneath the stately conifers. Watch for elk all along this hike—when I hiked this route, I saw far more elk than people. The route soon bears to the southwest and crosses a small stream; 0.25 mile farther along, you will cross another small stream. The trail intersects a roadbed 0.5 mile from the trailhead. Follow the roadbed, heading southwest, and shortly you will cross another creek.

Just after crossing this creek, another roadbed crosses the one you are hiking on; continue straight ahead to the southwest and pass between the boulders, which block the road to vehicles. It is possible to reach this point with a high–clearance vehicle via an unsigned road that leaves SR 410 about 0.75 mile west of the junction with FR 460. If you are going to start your hike here rather than at the

Mesatchee Falls.

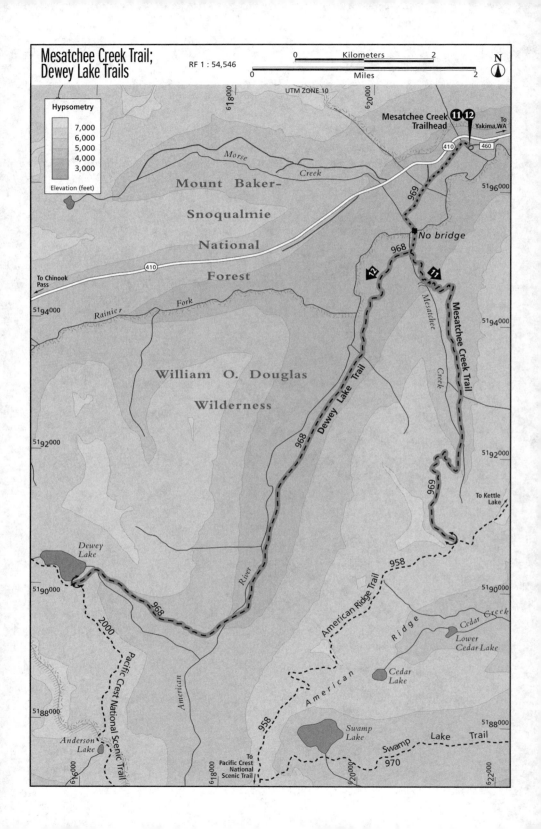

Mesatchee Creek Trail;
Dewey Lake Trails

RF 1 : 54,546

Kilometers
0   2
0   2
Miles

N

UTM ZONE 10

Hypsometry

7,000
6,000
5,000
4,000
3,000

Elevation (feet)

Mesatchee Creek
Trailhead

11 12

To
Yakima, WA

410

460

969

No bridge

968

12

11

Morse

Creek

Mount Baker-

Snoqualmie

National

Mesatchee

To Chinook
Pass

410

Forest

Rainier   Fork

Creek

Mesatchee Creek Trail

William O. Douglas

Wilderness

968

Dewey Lake Trail

996

To Kettle
Lake

958

American Ridge Trail

Dewey
Lake

968

Cedar   Creek

R i d g e

Lower
Cedar Lake

2000

River

Cedar
Lake

Pacific Crest National Scenic Trail

A m e r i c a n

958

American

Swamp
Lake

Swamp   Lake   Trail

Anderson
Lake

To
Pacific Crest
National
Scenic Trail

970

5196000

5194000

5192000

5190000

5188000

618000

620000

622000

Mesatchee Creek Trailhead, it will be necessary to drive to the trailhead first and get your wilderness permit.

The tread leaves the roadbed 0.3 mile farther along. Shortly you will cross a footbridge over Morse Creek. The trail quickly turns left after crossing the bridge. Now you are heading south-southeast toward the American River, and soon you are on the abandoned roadbed again. Another 0.2 mile of hiking brings you to the American River.

There is no bridge over the American River here. The USGS Norse Peak quad map shows a footbridge but it washed out some time ago, so to continue your hike, you must ford the river. During the low water of late summer and fall, this slow section of river is an easy crossing. If you head straight across the river, the water may be 2 or more feet deep, but a few yards downstream it is much shallower. About 100 yards downriver there is a logjam that may offer a dry-footed crossing, but be careful because the logs can be very slippery, especially when they are wet. Don't, under any circumstances, try to cross just above the logjam: The current can easily pull you beneath the logs. During times of high water, this could be a difficult and possibly dangerous crossing.

You enter the William O. Douglas Wilderness as you cross the river. After crossing the American River, the trail climbs very gently, heading south. In another 0.2 mile you reach the junction with the Dewey Lake Trail 968. This junction is 1.4 miles from the Mesatchee Creek Trailhead, at 3,640 feet elevation. Dewey Lake Trail turns to the right (west-southwest), climbing to lower Dewey Lake in 7.4 miles and reaching the Pacific Crest National Scenic Trail 0.2 mile farther along.

Hike straight ahead (south) from the junction with the Dewey Lake Trail, through the hemlock, fir, and tamarack forest. Shortly after leaving the junction, the route turns to the left and begins to climb more steeply. Then you make a switchback to the right and cross a small stream. The course makes a couple more switchbacks before reaching a viewpoint at 3,920 feet elevation, 0.5 mile from the junction with the Dewey Lake Trail. The viewpoint is just to the right of the trail at a switchback. From here Mesatchee Falls is in full view to the south and Mount Rainier juts skyward, to the west over Chinook Pass. There are two more smaller falls in Mesatchee Creek above the main falls, but they cannot be seen from the trail.

The course makes nine switchbacks and climbs fairly steeply for the next 0.5 mile. Above the switchbacks you follow a poorly defined ridge with Mesatchee Creek in a small canyon below and to your right. The trace quickly moves away from the canyon to make a gently ascending traverse, along the west-facing slope, for the next 1.2 miles. Then you cross a streambed and in a few more yards you cross Mesatchee Creek, at 4,850 feet elevation. Just after crossing Mesatchee Creek, there is a good campsite on the right side of the trail. As you cross the creek, you enter an area that was burned many years ago. This slope is now densely covered with small subalpine firs, Alaska cedars, and hemlocks, 10 to 30 feet tall. A little less than 0.25 mile from the crossing, the tread makes a switchback to the right. Here you leave the canyon bottom and begin to climb along an east-facing slope. The view quickly improves as you climb. Across Mesatchee Creek Canyon to your left, the hillside is mostly open, with just a scattering of small trees, making it prime elk range.

Soon the route turns to the left to head south again, continuing to climb along the slope. The course twists and turns a couple of times but generally heads south for slightly over 0.3 mile to a possible campsite, at 5,430 feet elevation, close to a tiny but dependable stream. After crossing the tiny stream, the track continues its ascending traverse, crossing a couple of small sloping meadows and getting into larger timber. White-flowered rhododendrons grow in the openings between the trees. In July these bushes are covered with beautiful white blooms, but if you are here in early October, their bright yellow leaves are almost as pretty. About 0.8 mile after crossing the tiny stream, you reach the junction with the American Ridge Trail 958. The unsigned junction is in a timbered saddle, on the top of American Ridge, at 5,870 feet elevation, 5.7 miles from the Mesatchee Creek Trailhead.

At the junction there is a possible dry campsite. There isn't much of a view from the junction, but if you turn left and walk a couple hundred yards to the east-southeast along the American Ridge Trail, the timber opens up and the views improve immensely. From the junction you can retrace your steps back to Mesatchee Creek Trailhead or see the options below for more information about the American Ridge Trail.

Miles and Directions

0.0 Mesatchee Creek Trailhead. GPS 46 54.766N 121 24.360W.

1.2 Trail fords American River.

1.4 Junction with Dewey Lake Trail 968. GPS 46 53.912N 121 24.963W. Proceed straight ahead.

1.9 Mesatchee Falls viewpoint.

3.9 Cross Mesatchee Creek.

5.7 Junction with American Ridge Trail 958. GPS 46 51.562N 121 24.462W. Turnaround point.

11.4 Mesatchee Creek Trailhead.

Options: Mesatchee Creek Trail is a good way to access this remote section of the American Ridge Trail. If you turn right at the junction of the American Ridge and Mesatchee Creek Trails, the American Ridge Trail descends to the southwest, reaching the junction with the Swamp Lake Trail in about 4.5 miles. From there it's only about a mile east to Swamp Lake, or 1.6 miles south to Cougar Lake.

To make a fairly strenuous alternate return hike, which requires a short car shuttle, turn left (northeast) on the American Ridge Trail at its junction with Mesatchee Creek Trail. You will soon be hiking along the semiopen ridgeline of American Ridge, where you stand a good chance of spotting elk. Follow the American Ridge Trail northeast for 6 miles along spectacular American Ridge to the junction with the

Kettle Creek Trail 957, near Kettle Lake. From the junction with the American Ridge Trail, descend the Kettle Creek Trail, heading north for 6 miles to a junction with the Pleasant Valley Loop Trail 999. This junction is just across the American River from the Pleasant Valley Campground. There is no bridge over the American River here, so you must ford the stream or turn left and hike southwest along the Pleasant Valley Loop Trail for 3.2 miles to an unmarked trailhead on SR 410. This strenuous, 20-mile hike can be made in one day by an athletic and determined hiker, but it's much more pleasant and rewarding to allow three days, with camps near the junction of the Mesatchee and American Ridge Trails and close to Kettle Lake.

To reach the unmarked trailhead from the Mesatchee Creek Trailhead by car, go back to SR 410. Turn right and drive 1.8 miles northeast to the trailhead, which is next to a bridge over the American River at milepost 78. Pleasant Valley Campground is another 2.7 miles northeast along SR 410.

12 Dewey Lake
Trails 969 and 968

Hike the somewhat challenging trails, mostly through old-growth forest, from deep in the American River Canyon to picturesque Dewey Lakes.

See map on page 70.
Start: Mesatchee Creek Trailhead.
Type of hike: Out-and-back backpack or long day hike.
Total distance: 17.8 miles.
Difficulty: Moderate to strenuous.
Maps: USDA Forest Service Norse Peak and William O. Douglas Wilderness or Norse Peak and Cougar Lake USGS quads.

Permits and fees: William O. Douglas Wilderness permit.
Best months: July–September.
Special considerations: There are two river crossings on this route. Sandals or other extra river-crossing shoes will make the rest of the trip much more comfortable.

Finding the trailhead: From the **Seattle-Tacoma** area, drive to Enumclaw. From Enumclaw follow State Route 410 for 41 miles east and south to Cayuse Pass. From **Portland,** Oregon, drive north on Interstate 5 for 68 miles to the junction with U.S. Highway 12. Then head east on US 12 for 71 miles (7 miles east of Packwood) to the junction with State Route 123. Turn north (left) off US 12 on SR 123 and drive 16.5 miles to Cayuse Pass and the junction with SR 410.

Turn right (left if coming from Seattle) on SR 410 and head east for 10.4 miles to the Mesatchee Creek Forest Road 460. This junction is 6.7 miles east of Chinook Pass. Turn right at the junction and follow FR 460 for about 0.3 mile to its end at Mesatchee Creek Trailhead.
Parking and trailhead facilities: Adequate parking, restrooms, and some stock facilities are available at the trailhead.

The Hike

The first 1.4 miles of this hike follow the Mesatchee Creek Trail 969. Large Douglas firs guard the route as you leave the trailhead at 3,640 feet elevation. The route first heads west to the wilderness registration box, where you can stop and get your wilderness permit. Bunchberries and vanilla leaf line this part of the trail, as do several ant piles. Soon the course bears to the southwest and crosses a small stream. You cross another small stream 0.25 mile farther along and intersect a roadbed 0.5 mile from the trailhead.

The route follows the roadbed, heading southwest, quickly crossing another creek. Just after crossing the creek, another roadbed crosses the one you are hiking on; continue straight ahead to the southwest and pass between the boulders, which block the road to vehicles. The route veers off the roadbed 0.3 mile farther along to cross a bridge over frothing Morse Creek. Just after crossing the bridge, the tread turns left to head south-southeast. Soon you are following a long-abandoned roadbed again. Another 0.2 mile of hiking brings you to the American River.

The USGS map shows a footbridge over the American River here, but there is none, so to continue your hike you must ford the river. The river is slow here, and during the low water of late summer and fall, this is an easy crossing, although it may still be 2 or more feet deep. During times of high water, this could be a difficult and possibly dangerous crossing. As you cross the river, you also enter the William O. Douglas Wilderness. Once across the river the route climbs gently to the south for another 0.2 mile to the junction with the Dewey Lake Trail 968. This junction, at 3,640 feet elevation, is 1.4 miles from the Mesatchee Creek Trailhead.

Turn right at the junction and hike southwest on the Dewey Lake Trail. In 0.1 mile the trail crosses Mesatchee Creek without the benefit of a bridge. There will be a pond below the trail to the right 0.4 mile farther along. Another 0.1 mile of hiking brings you to an area of dead snags. Since there is no forest canopy here and the sunlight can reach the ground, white-flowered rhododendrons crowd the trailsides. For the next 3.5 miles, from here to the next crossing of the American River, the trail climbs gently up the canyon bottom, mostly through beautiful old-growth forest. The course undulates a few feet in places and crosses many small streams, a couple of them on wooden bridges, as you hike south-southwest along the river bottom. The only place where the route gets close to the American River is at about 0.3 mile before you reach the next crossing. Just before you reach the crossing, there is a good campsite next to the river. At the crossing you are at 3,980 feet elevation and 5.6 miles from the Mesatchee Creek Trailhead.

Like the first crossing of the American River, this one also has no bridge, but the river is considerably smaller here and this ford is quite easy during low water.

◀ *Falls in Dewey Creek.*

It could, however, be difficult and dangerous during spring runoff. Put on your water shoes and cross the cold knee-deep water.

The trail from the river crossing to Dewey Lake is shown somewhat incorrectly on the USGS Cougar Lake quad map and on all other maps that I have checked. The trail has been rerouted and makes many switchbacks, which ease the grade but lengthen the distance. The switchbacks start right after you cross the river. The route makes seven switchbacks in the next 1.2 miles, then crosses a small creek before reaching a great viewpoint at the eighth switchback. This viewpoint, at 4,500 feet elevation, is a good place to stop for a break and look at the colorful canyon, with a waterfall to the southwest.

The route continues to climb, making eleven more switchbacks in the next 0.5 mile. Then you will cross several tiny streams. These streams may be dry by late summer, but earlier in the year this area can be quite muddy. The last of the tiny streams has a broken-down wooden bridge over it. Soon after crossing the broken-down bridge, there is a wet meadow on your right. The trail continues to wind its way on up through the Alaska cedars and firs to another drier meadow, which is on your left, at 4,900 feet elevation. Lupine, phlox, and hellebore dominate this meadow. Above the meadow the sometimes muddy route soon crosses a small stream. Just after crossing the stream, there will be a short path to your left. This path leads to a viewpoint with a view of a pretty, little waterfall. There are actually several waterfalls in this creek, which is the outlet stream of Dewey Lake.

Above the path to the viewpoint, the now steeper route makes six more switchbacks in the next 0.2 mile. Then the trail flattens out a little and leads west for a short distance to a sign that warns that no fires are allowed within 0.5 mile of Dewey Lakes. Just past the sign the trail turns left to cross the outlet stream, and quickly reaches the junction with Dewey Lake Way. There are usually logs on which to make a dry-footed crossing a few yards upstream from the point where the trail crosses the creek. Dewey Lake Way turns to the right and leads to the shore of Dewey Lake. From the creek crossing and junction, the Dewey Lake Way route heads south for slightly more than 0.2 mile to the junction with the Pacific Crest National Scenic Trail 2000 (PCT). This junction, at 5,180 feet elevation, is 8.9 miles from the Mesatchee Creek Trailhead.

There are two Dewey Lakes: The one you are next to is the larger and lower of them. The PCT to your right follows the shore of the larger of the lakes. There are several good campsites around the lakes, but remember to camp back at least 100 feet from the shore, and if you have stock, keep them at least 200 feet back. Also remember that campfires are prohibited within 0.5 mile of either lake. Trout fishing can be good in Dewey Lakes. Return the way you came, or see the options below for an alternate one-way hike.

Miles and Directions

0.0 Mesatchee Creek Trailhead. GPS 46 54.766N 121 24.360W.

1.2 Trail fords American River.

1.4 Junction with Dewey Lake Trail 968. GPS 46 53.912N 121 24.963W. Turn right.

5.6 Trail fords American River.

8.9 Junction with the PCT near Dewey Lakes. GPS 46 51.156N 121 28.756W. Turnaround point.

17.8 Mesatchee Creek Trailhead.

Options: Dewey Lake Trail is not the easiest way to reach Dewey Lakes. They can be reached via a 3.4-mile hike along the Pacific Crest National Scenic Trail from Chinook Pass. Making a shuttle hike and reaching Dewey Lakes via the PCT, then hiking down the Dewey Lake and Mesatchee Creek Trails to Mesatchee Creek Trailhead makes a great two- or three-day, mostly downhill backpack.

To reach Chinook Pass Trailhead from Mesatchee Creek Trailhead, go back to SR 410 and turn left (west). Drive 6.6 miles to the large paved parking area on the right side of the highway, 0.1 mile before reaching Chinook Pass.

From the parking area a short path leads west and quickly connects with the PCT. Turn left on the PCT and you'll soon cross the footbridge over the highway at Chinook Pass. Then continue for 3.3 miles southeast on the PCT to Dewey Lakes. If you are going to make this hike, it is a good idea to check the water level in the American River where you must ford it, 1.2 miles from the Mesatchee Creek Trailhead, before you make the hike down from Dewey Lakes.

13 Pleasant Valley Nature Loop

Pleasant Valley Nature Loop is indeed a pleasant and very informative stroll through the wonders of a mature east-slope Cascades forest. The route is paved all the way.

Start: Pleasant Valley Nature Loop Trailhead.
Type of hike: 1-hour loop.
Total distance: 0.8 mile.
Difficulty: Very easy and wheelchair accessible.

Maps: The Goose Prairie USGS quad map covers the area but doesn't show this trail. The map in this book should be all you need.
Permits and fees: None.
Best months: June–November.

Finding the trailhead: From the **Seattle-Tacoma** area, drive to Enumclaw. From Enumclaw follow State Route 410 for 41 miles east and south to Cayuse Pass. From **Portland,** Oregon, drive north on Interstate 5 for 68 miles to the junction with U.S. Highway 12. Then head east on US 12 for 71 miles (7 miles east of Packwood) to the junction with State Route 123. Turn left onto SR 123 and head north for 16.5 miles to Cayuse Pass and the junction with SR 410.

Turn right (left if coming from Seattle) and drive 14.9 miles on SR 410 to the access road for Pleasant Valley Campground. Turn right (south) on the access road, then take another quick right. In a short distance you will reach the trailhead, at 3,370 feet elevation.
Parking and trailhead facilities: There is parking for several vehicles at the trailhead, and there are also some informative reader boards.

The Hike

The paved trail heads southwest from the parking area, through the forest of Douglas fir and tamarack. Much of the forest floor is covered with vanilla leaf *(Achlys triphylla),* also known as deer foot. In about 100 yards you reach a reader board that describes some of the flowers of the old-growth forest. A bit farther on you'll cross a small wooden bridge over a tiny stream and come to a reader board that discusses red ants *(Formica rufa).* These ants create huge anthills, locally called ant piles, and are very common in this forest.

Shortly the trail forks; turn right and soon cross another small wooden bridge, then pass a bench. About 60 yards past the bench is another signboard with information about the lichen that grows in this forest. In the next 0.2 mile, the tread makes a turn to the left and you reach another bench. These benches may seem unnecessary on this short and very easy trail, but stopping and sitting quietly on one of them allows the walker to look and listen carefully to the forest that surrounds them.

There are some fairly large Douglas fir *(Pseudotsuga menziesii)* trees in this area; many of them have fire scars attesting to a long ago forest fire. As you can tell, Douglas fir is a very fire-resistant species when it is mature. Red firs, or just Dougs, as Douglas firs are often called, are the largest trees in the Northwest and can live

Anthill (aka ant pile) next to the Pleasant Valley Nature Loop.

to be 1,000 years old. There are also a few large tamaracks (western larch, *Larix occidentalis*) here. Tamaracks are unusual trees; they are conifers (needle leaf) but are also deciduous. In the autumn the needles of the tamarack turn a bright yellow and then fall off, leaving the tree looking dead. Tamarack wood is some of the best firewood to be had.

Shortly after leaving the bench, there is a reader board explaining how fire shapes nature's landscape. Soon there is another bench; a short distance past this bench is a path to the right leading to a viewpoint overlooking the river. Next to the viewpoint is a reader board reviewing the spawning cycle of Chinook salmon (*Oncorhynchus tshawytscha*). To reach the spawning beds (reeds), these marvelous fish have had to make a 400-mile upstream swim from the Pacific Ocean.

Another 0.2 mile of gentle walking, crossing another small wooden bridge and passing a reader board discussing forest meadows, brings you back to the fork in the trail. Turn right at the fork and retrace your steps back to the trailhead.

Pleasant Valley Nature Loop; Pleasant Valley Lake Trail; Pleasant Valley Loop Trail; Goat Peak Trails

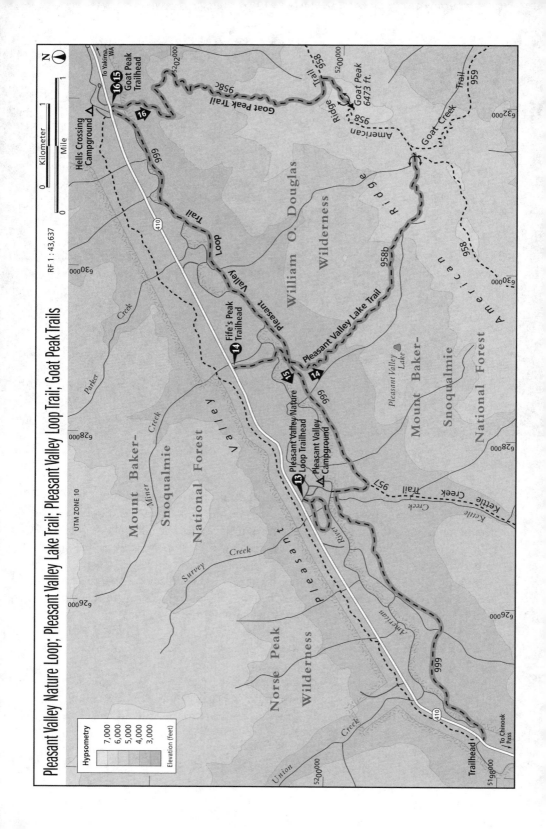

RF 1 : 43,637

UTM ZONE 10

Hypsometry

7,000
6,000
5,000
4,000
3,000

Elevation (feet)

Miles and Directions

0.0 Pleasant Valley Nature Loop Trailhead. GPS 46 56.631N 121 19.677W.
0.1 Trail forks. Turn right.
0.5 Viewpoint overlooking the American River.
0.7 Fork in trail. Bear right.
0.8 Pleasant Valley Nature Loop Trailhead.

14 Pleasant Valley Lake Trail 958b

Ford the clear, cold waters of the American River, then climb the challenging route, taking in the ever-increasing views, to the top of American Ridge and a junction with the American Ridge Trail.

See map on page 80.
Start: Fife's Peak Viewpoint and Trailhead.
Type of hike: Out-and-back day hike or backpack.
Total distance: 7.4 miles round-trip to American Ridge Trail.
Difficulty: Moderate to strenuous following the trail to the top of American Ridge. Strenuous with excellent route-finding skills required to reach Pleasant Valley Lake via the optional cross-country route.

Maps: USDA Forest Service William O. Douglas and Norse Peak Wilderness or Goose Prairie USGS quad.
Permits and fees: William O. Douglas Wilderness permit and Northwest Forest Pass.
Best months: June–October to Pleasant Valley Lake, July–September to American Ridge Trail.
Special considerations: The American River must be forded near the beginning of this hike. This river crossing can be difficult and dangerous at times. See the options below for an alternate access route.

Finding the trailhead: To reach Fife's Peak Viewpoint and Trailhead, drive north from **Portland,** Oregon, on Interstate 5 for 68 miles to the junction with U.S. Highway 12. Then head east on US 12 for 71 miles (7 miles east of Packwood) to the junction with State Route 123. Turn left off US 12 on SR 123 and go north for 16.5 miles to Cayuse Pass and the junction with State Route 410. From the **Seattle-Tacoma** area, drive to Enumclaw. From Enumclaw follow SR 410 for 41 miles east and south to Cayuse Pass.

Turn left (right if coming from Portland) on SR 410 and head east for 16.2 miles over beautiful Chinook Pass and down to Fife's Peak Viewpoint and Trailhead, which is on the left (north) side of the highway. The viewpoint is between mileposts 81 and 82. Drive into the viewpoint, passing the main parking area. Just past the main parking area, there are two more smaller parking areas with room for only three or four cars each. Park in one of these smaller parking areas. The Pleasant Valley Lake Trail heads south from between the two small parking areas. There is no sign here, and the path may be very faint or not even visible on the ground. The USGS Goose Prairie quad map shows this trailhead correctly. The elevation at the parking area is 3,390 feet.

Pleasant Valley Lake.

Parking and trailhead facilities: There are restrooms and some stock facilities at the trailhead. Campsites can be had for a fee at Pleasant Valley Campground 1.3 miles west on SR 410.

The Hike

Hike south-southeast from the parking areas and cross SR 410 in about 25 yards. After crossing the highway the trail becomes obvious. There is also a sign marking the trail here. Once across the highway, continue south through the medium-age forest of Douglas and true firs, Engelmann spruce, and western red cedar. Beneath the trees on the forest floor, vanilla leaf grows in profusion between scattered Oregon grape and trilliums. A few fairy slipper orchids are also present. About 0.2 mile from the parking area, the Pleasant Valley Lake Trail crosses a sometimes very well-used elk trail.

You will reach the American River 0.4 mile from the trailhead. There is no bridge here, so to continue, the river must be forded. This ford can be very difficult and dangerous during periods of high water. Don't make this ford if you are not sure of your party's ability to do it safely. See the options below for an alternate route to reach the south side of the American River. Notice the willow bushes close to the river: Many of their branches have been chewed off by something with broad teeth. There are beavers that work the banks of the river.

After crossing the American River, the trail quickly crosses another small stream, then makes a wide switchback to the right and climbs steeply for the last few yards to the junction with the Pleasant Valley Loop Trail 999. This junction, at 3,380 feet elevation, is 0.6 mile from the Fife's Peak Viewpoint and Trailhead. Turn right on the Pleasant Valley Loop Trail and walk 10 yards to another junction, both trails follow the same route between the junctions. There are signs at the second junction pointing out the routes.

To continue on the Pleasant Valley Lake Trail, turn left (south-southwest) at the second junction. The tread is fairly steep leaving the junction as you ascend through an open, mixed forest of tamarack, hemlock, grand fir, Engelmann spruce, and lodgepole and western white pine. A little less than 0.5 mile from the junction, the route reaches the first of seven switchbacks, which take you up to 3,880 feet elevation. Three hundred yards after passing the last switchback, there is an unmarked side path to the right. This path is slightly less than 1 mile from the junction with the Pleasant Valley Loop Trail, at 3,990 feet elevation. This is just a use path; it's not maintained and it's easy to miss.

The side path descends about 50 feet in elevation in the 150 yards to the shore of an unnamed lake. The small, sometimes slightly murky lake is nearly surrounded with small willows and mountain alders. Western red cedar, spruce, and tamarack complete the forest cover. There is a possible campsite near the eastern shore of the lake, and there are fish to be caught here. The elevation of the unnamed lake is 3,930 feet, and the GPS coordinates on its east shore are 46 56.360N 121 18.240W.

Past the junction with the side path to the unnamed lake, the Pleasant Valley Lake Trail continues its climb to the southeast. After climbing moderately for about 0.4 mile and reaching 4,180 feet in elevation, a cross-country route to Pleasant Valley Lake leaves the trail. There is no sign here and the route to the lake is not visible on the ground. It is very hard to find Pleasant Valley Lake without using an altimeter and/or GPS unit. For a description of the route to Pleasant Valley Lake, see the options below.

To continue on the Pleasant Valley Lake Trail (not to the lake), hike on to the southeast. The trail climbs along a small rounded ridge for a short distance. A little over 0.1 mile past the cross-country route to Pleasant Valley Lake and 2 miles from the trailhead, there is a tiny spring on the left side of the trail. This spring may be dry by midsummer, so don't count on it for water. Another 300 yards of fairly steep climbing and the tread enters a semiopen area. The course makes a couple of switchbacks as you climb through the thinning timber. The views are spectacular through the openings in the trees. Majestic Mount Rainier looms to the west over Chinook Pass, and to the north are the spires of Fife's Peak. In these openings you are at about 4,500 feet elevation and 2.4 miles from the trailhead.

Above the openings the trail bends around to a more easterly direction. You climb through the timber and pass a couple more open areas. Then you make some switchbacks to attain a ridgeline at 5,600 feet elevation. The route then traverses a north-facing slope and climbs the last 100 feet to the junction with the American Ridge Trail 958, at 5,710 feet elevation, 3.7 miles from the trailhead. Return by the same route or see the alternate return option over Goat Peak, below.

Miles and Directions

0.0 Fife's Peak Viewpoint parking area. GPS 46 57.119N 121 18.424W.

0.4 Ford the American River.

0.6 Junction with Pleasant Valley Loop Trail 999. GPS 46 56.763N 121 18.233W. Turn right then turn left.

1.5 Junction with path to unnamed lake. GPS 46 56.404N 121 18.215W. Proceed straight ahead.

1.9 Cross-country route to Pleasant Valley Lake leaves trail. GPS 46 56.275N 121 17.935W. Proceed straight ahead.

3.7 Junction with American Ridge Trail 958. GPS 46 55.938N 121 16.382W. Turnaround point.

7.4 Fife's Peak Viewpoint and Trailhead.

Options: If you don't want to try fording the American River, you can reach the Pleasant Valley Lake Trail via the Pleasant Valley Loop Trail 999. To reach the trailhead from Fife's Peak Viewpoint and Trailhead, drive 2 miles east on SR 410 to a bridge over the American River. The trailhead is on the right (south) side of the highway just after crossing the bridge, across the road from the Hells Crossing Campground entrance. This trailhead, at 3,270 feet elevation, is also the trailhead for the Goat Peak Trail 958c. From the parking area, head south a few yards to a trail junction with a signboard and wilderness registration box. Stop here and fill out your William O. Douglas Wilderness permit. Turn right at the junction and hike southwest along the banks of the American River. As cross-country skiers also use this trail, it is marked with plastic blue diamond markers. In a short distance you will enter the William O. Douglas Wilderness. After hiking 2.8 miles, you will cross a wooden bridge and quickly come to the junction with the Pleasant Valley Lake Trail 958b. Turn left at the signed junction and begin your hike up the Pleasant Valley Lake Trail. At this junction you are only 0.6 mile from the Fife's Peak Viewpoint and Trailhead. You have avoided the river crossing but have added 4.4 miles in distance to your round-trip hike.

An optional side trip off the Pleasant Valley Lake Trail can be made to reach Pleasant Valley Lake. The side trip to the lake requires excellent route-finding and map-reading skills for safe completion. It is also very difficult to find the lake without the use of an altimeter. A GPS unit can also be a big help. But if the altimeter on your GPS unit works off satellites rather than air pressure, it may not be accurate enough to follow a map contour line. Be sure that your altimeter is properly set when you begin this hike and check it at the junction with the path to the unnamed lake (which is at 3,990 feet elevation) 0.4 mile before you reach the spot where the cross-country route to Pleasant Valley Lake leaves the trail. Most altimeters have at least a little lag time. Stop for 2 or 3 minutes both at the side path and at the point where the cross-country route leaves the trail to make sure that your altimeter reading has stabilized. If you are not sure of your route-finding skills and your ability to use your compass, altimeter, and GPS unit, don't take this route.

When you have reached an elevation of 4,180 feet on the Pleasant Valley Lake Trail and the GPS coordinates of 46 56.275N 121 17.935W, bear to the right off the trail. There is no side trail here, so you are just walking through the forest and stepping over the downed trees. Watch your altimeter, staying as close as possible to 4,180 feet elevation, as you hike to the southwest along the slope. In approximately 0.25 mile you will cross a small creek. Just after crossing the creek, there will be a couple more tiny streams and some small springs. Cross this approximately 100-yard-wide wet area heading generally southwest and staying at the 4,180-foot contour. After crossing the wet area, there will be a small rise in the ground ahead of you. Contour westerly along this slope and climb slightly to cross the top of the rise at 4,220 feet elevation. From the top of the rise the lake should be in view to the south-southwest. Descend to the lake, which is at 4,170 feet elevation. The total distance to the lake from the trail is slightly less than 0.4 mile.

Pleasant Valley Lake is quite small and has no outlet. There is, however, a small inlet stream flowing into it from the southeast. There is a campsite available close to the inlet stream, and there are fish in the lake. The GPS coordinates at the point where the inlet stream enters the lake are 46 56.078N 121 18.191W.

Another option is to return from the junction of the Pleasant Valley Lake and American Ridge Trails via American Ridge Trail 958 and the Goat Peak Trail 958c. To make this hike, turn left on the American Ridge Trail and follow it for about 1.7 miles northeast, then over Goat Peak and down to the junction with the Goat Peak Trail. Then turn left again and descend the steep Goat Peak Trail for 3.4 miles to Goat Peak Trailhead.

Fife's Peak Viewpoint and Trailhead is about 2 miles west along SR 410 from the Goat Creek Trailhead. If you haven't arranged a car shuttle, the Pleasant Valley Loop Trail 999, which also starts at the Goat Creek Trailhead, connects with the Pleasant Valley Lake Trail in 2.8 miles.

15 Pleasant Valley Loop
Trail 999

Hike along the south side of the sparkling American River through mostly virgin forest. This trail offers an excellent opportunity to observe elk if you move quietly early in the morning or in the evening. Marked for cross-country skiing, this trail provides recreational opportunities in both winter and summer.

See map on page 80.
Start: Goat Peak Trailhead.
Type of hike: Shuttle day hike or backpack.
Total distance: 7.4 miles.
Difficulty: Easy.
Maps: USDA Forest Service William O. Douglas and Norse Peak Wilderness or Goose Prairie USGS quad.
Permits and fees: William O. Douglas Wilderness permit. Snopark permit during ski season.

Best months: Mid-May through October.
Special considerations: This description doesn't cover the entire Pleasant Valley Loop, which is generally used as a cross-country ski trail. Only the portion of the loop that follows the south side of the American River, providing access to the trails along the northern boundary of the William O. Douglas Wilderness, is described here.

Finding the trailhead: To reach Goat Peak Trailhead, drive north from **Portland,** Oregon, on Interstate 5 for 68 miles to the junction with U.S. Highway 12. Then head east on US 12 for 71 miles (7 miles east of Packwood) to the junction with State Route 123. Turn left onto SR 123 and head north for 16.5 miles to Cayuse Pass and the junction with State Route 410. From the **Seattle-Tacoma** area, drive to Enumclaw. From Enumclaw follow SR 410 for 41 miles east and south to Cayuse Pass.

Turn left (right if coming from Portland) and drive 17.9 miles east on SR 410, over Chinook Pass and down to a bridge over the American River. The trailhead is on the right (south) side of the highway just after crossing the bridge, across the road from the Hells Crossing Campground entrance. This trailhead, at 3,270 feet elevation, is also the trailhead for the Goat Peak Trail 958c.

To reach the trailhead (western) where this hike ends, drive 5.7 miles west on SR 410 (8.5 miles east of Chinook Pass) to another bridge over the American River. The unsigned trailhead is close to the west end of this bridge next to milepost 78, at 3,440 feet elevation. If this is to be a shuttle hike, which is the best way to do this trail, you may want to leave a car at this trailhead on your way to the Goat Peak Trailhead, where the hike begins.

Parking and trailhead facilities: There is parking for several cars at the Goat Peak Trailhead but no other facilities. Campsites are available across the highway at Hells Crossing Campground. There is parking for only a couple of cars and no other facilities at the trailhead where the hike ends.

The Hike

From the parking area head south a few yards to a trail junction with a signboard and wilderness registration box. Stop here and fill out your William O. Douglas

American River ford on the Pleasant Valley Lake Trail.

Wilderness permit. With your permit attached securely to the outside of your pack and the copy left in the slot, turn right to begin your hike along the American River. The Goat Peak Trail 958c, which is to the left at the registration box, climbs steeply to join the American Ridge Trail in 3.4 miles.

The route follows the banks of the sparkling American River through the dense forest of Douglas and true firs with scattered western red cedars and a few black cottonwoods. As cross-country skiers also use this trail, it is marked with plastic blue diamond markers. In a short distance you will enter the William O. Douglas Wilderness. Just before entering the wilderness, there is an information sign about spring chinook salmon on the right side of the trail. These marvelous fish, which may be as large as 40 inches or more in length, have had to swim 400 miles upstream, against sometimes swift currents, to reach this point.

About a quarter mile into the hike, the tread passes beneath a talus slope that is studded with a few large, old tamarack (western larch) trees. The course climbs gently past the talus, then descends and flattens out. Trilliums and Oregon grape nearly cover the forest floor in places as you continue upriver. A campground can be seen across the river 0.6 mile from the trailhead, and through the trees, ahead and to the right, Fife's Peak juts skyward. There are a few small meadows along the river. If you are here in the early morning or evening, there is a good chance of seeing elk grazing here.

About 1 mile from the trailhead, the trail leaves the riverbank for the first time. On these slightly drier slopes, lodgepole pines make their appearance between the tamaracks, firs, and spruce trees. There are also scattered western white pines in the mix of trees. After being away from the riverbank for a couple tenths of a mile, the track gets close to the water again for a short distance. Another 0.2 mile brings you to the first creek crossing. There is no bridge here but logs span the stream, which is easy to cross in any case.

The route gets close to the American River again 0.3 mile farther along. You soon pass a spring that is on the left side of the trail. This spring may be dry by early summer, so don't depend on it for water. The trail leaves the river again 0.3 mile past the spring. A little less than 0.2 mile after leaving the riverbank, you will cross a wooden bridge over a creek and shortly come to the junction with the Pleasant Valley Lake Trail 958b. This junction is 2.8 miles from the trailhead and at 3,380 feet elevation.

There are actually two junctions a few yards apart here. If you were to turn right (north) at the first one, the Pleasant Valley Lake Trail would take you to a ford of the American River in a little less than 0.2 mile. After crossing the river the route continues north, crosses SR 410, and reaches the Fife's Peak Viewpoint parking area in about another 0.4 mile. The ford of the American River can be difficult or even dangerous especially during times of high water, so don't take this route unless you are sure of your party's river-crossing ability. A few yards farther along the Pleasant Valley Loop Trail, there will be another junction, with signs. From here the Pleasant Valley Lake Trail climbs southeast, gaining 2,300 feet of elevation in 3.7 miles, to join the American Ridge Trail atop American Ridge. Unfortunately, the Pleasant Valley Lake Trail bypasses Pleasant Valley Lake.

Hike southwest from the junctions, staying on the Pleasant Valley Loop Trail. The route climbs and descends a few feet in several places but never strays far from the 3,400-foot contour line. One and one-tenth miles from the junction, the course crosses another creek. There are several logs laid together here to ease the crossing. Another 0.3 mile brings you to the junction with the Kettle Creek Trail 957. At the junction you are at 3,450 feet elevation and 4.2 miles from the Goat Peak Trailhead. Kettle Creek Trail turns left and climbs south to join the American Ridge Trail near Kettle Lake.

The Pleasant Valley Loop Trail makes a hard right turn at the junction and descends gently to the north. After heading north for 0.3 mile, the route makes a hard left turn. There is a rock cairn and a sign at this turn. In the past there was a trail continuing north from here to the Pleasant Valley Campground, but the bridge over the American River is no longer there and this trail has been abandoned.

Turn to the left (southwest) and continue along the Pleasant Valley Loop Trail. In about 100 yards the tread crosses a wooden bridge over the rushing waters of Kettle Creek. Watch for large anthills (locally called ant piles) as you hike. You will notice that most of these ant piles are very active, with thousands of red-headed ants on them. About 0.7 mile after crossing the bridge over Kettle Creek, the route gets relatively close to the American River again. Another 0.7 mile brings you to another wooden bridge over a small but swift creek. The tread crosses another small stream without the benefit of a bridge, 1.1 miles farther along. From this crossing, if you look upstream along the American River, you can see a highway bridge spanning it. This bridge is at the end of your hike. Continue southwest along the trail for 0.3 mile to the trailhead along the side of SR 410. Just before reaching the trailhead, the trail turns right and heads north for a few yards. At the turn another trail continues southwest for a short distance before fading out. This trailhead is 7.4 miles from your starting point, at 3,440 feet elevation.

Miles and Directions

0.0   Goat Peak Trailhead. GPS 46 57.860N 121 15.984W. Hike right.

2.8   Junction with Pleasant Valley Lake Trail 958b. GPS 46 56.761N 121 18.231W. Bear left then bear right.

4.2   Junction with Kettle Creek Trail 957. GPS 46 56.234N 121 19.536W. Bear right.

7.4   Trailhead (western). GPS 46 55.521N 121 21.944W.

Options: Either Goat Peak or Pleasant Valley Lake Trails make great side trips to a hike along the Pleasant Valley Loop. However, both of these trails are more strenuous.

16 Goat Peak
Trails 958c and 958

Climb a challenging trail to the summit of 6,473-foot-high Goat Peak, on top of American Ridge, where you can sit at the site of a long-abandoned lookout and take in the view, which includes most of the William O. Douglas Wilderness.

See map on page 80.
Start: Goat Peak Trailhead.
Type of hike: Out-and-back day hike.
Total distance: 8.2 miles.
Difficulty: Strenuous.
Maps: USDA Forest Service William O. Douglas and Norse Peak Wilderness or Goose Prairie USGS quad.
Permits and fees: William O. Douglas Wilderness permit.

Best months: Mid-June through October.
Special considerations: There is no water along the trail above the creek crossing, at 3,840 feet elevation and 0.6 mile into the hike. Early in the season an ice axe or ski poles can be helpful when crossing the steep side-sloping patches of snow that often persist about 3.3 miles from the trailhead, just before the route reaches the junction with the American Ridge Trail.

Finding the trailhead: To reach Goat Peak Trailhead, drive north from **Portland,** Oregon, on Interstate 5 for 68 miles to the junction with U.S. Highway 12. Then head east on US 12 for 71 miles (7 miles east of Packwood) to the junction with State Route 123. Turn left onto SR 123 and drive north for 16.5 miles to Cayuse Pass and the junction with State Route 410. From the **Seattle-Tacoma** area, drive to Enumclaw. From Enumclaw follow SR 410 for 41 miles east and south to Cayuse Pass.

Turn left (right if coming from Portland) and drive 17.9 miles east on SR 410, over Chinook Pass and down to a bridge over the American River. The trailhead is on the right (south) side of the highway just after crossing the bridge, across the road from the Hells Crossing Campground entrance. This trailhead, at 3,270 feet elevation, is also the trailhead for the Pleasant Valley Loop Trail 999.

Parking and trailhead facilities: There is parking for several cars at the trailhead but no other facilities.

The Hike

Walk a few yards south from the parking area to the signboard at the junction of the Pleasant Valley Loop and Goat Peak Trails. Get your wilderness permit here, then turn left at the junction to begin your climb toward American Ridge and the summit of Goat Peak. You'll quickly pass the William O. Douglas Wilderness boundary, and the grade moderates a bit. The tread continues its climb through the mixed conifer forest of Douglas fir, tamarack, western white pine, and lodgepole pine. Huckleberry bushes grow beneath the medium-size timber. About 0.2 mile from the trailhead, the route follows a small rounded ridge for a short distance. Then you

Mount Stuart from the Goat Peak Trail.

pass a small talus slope, above and to the left of the trail. Oregon grape sprouts between the rocks, and in shadier places trilliums bloom in May.

For the next 0.5 mile, the USGS Goose Prairie quad map shows the trail slightly incorrectly. The course comes alongside of a creek slightly over 0.5 mile into the hike and soon crosses the stream. Just after crossing the creek, the tread turns steeply upward, to the south-southwest. The next 250 yards of trail are very steep and rocky. The route follows the side of the streambed over and around the boulders. The trace then recrosses the intermittent stream, at 3,840 feet elevation, and traverses onto a north-facing slope. About 300 yards after making the second stream crossing, the trail makes a climbing switchback to the right, then one to the left. Another 0.1 mile brings you to a steep open slope, which the route traverses heading northeast. Fife's Peak comes into view to the northwest along this open slope. A few gnarled Alaska cedars and Douglas firs grow from the rocky slope, while stonecrop and penstemon cling to existence between the rocks.

Soon the trail crosses a ridgeline at 4,060 feet elevation, then continues to climb southeasterly on the now timbered slope. In about 0.2 mile the route makes a switchback to the right on a semiopen rocky slope. Shortly after making the switchback, there is a viewpoint a few feet to the left of the trail. The view from here is to the north and east and includes the valley of the American River. This spot, at nearly 4,300 feet elevation, makes a great place for a break.

Above the viewpoint the trail climbs along the right (west) side of the ridgeline for 150 yards, then crosses back to the more open left (east) side for a short distance. For the next 0.9 mile, you will climb close to the ridgeline, never getting very far below it on either the east or west side. There are a couple of places in this section where the trail has sloughed away and the footing is not very good. The route makes several switchbacks as you climb to the point where the ridgeline broadens and rounds out some, at 5,150 feet elevation, 2.9 miles from the trailhead. The route continues to climb the now less well-defined ridgeline for a couple hundred yards, then you bear slightly left and traverse the ridge's eastern slope. The course crosses a small opening in the timber, at 5,500 feet elevation, 0.2 mile after leaving the ridgeline. By now the timber is getting smaller and more alpine. The mix of trees includes hemlock, subalpine fir, lodgepole pine, and a scattering of western white pine. Kinnikinnick and huckleberry bushes cover the ground in places.

Soon the trail swings around to the southeast, and the timber changes to mostly hemlock. As you continue to climb along this northeast-facing slope, the route crosses a short section of talus. This talus slope is often snow-covered early in the season and could be dangerous to cross at times. An ice axe or at least ski poles can be helpful here if there is snow. A few yards after crossing the talus, the tread reaches the top of American Ridge, at 5,990 feet elevation. If you turn to the left as the Goat Peak Trail crosses American Ridge, there is a rocky outcrop a few yards to the northeast. From this outcrop there is a great view of the Stuart Range to the northeast in the distance.

The Goat Peak Trail turns right as you cross the ridge. From the ridgeline it's about 20 yards southwest to the signed junction with the American Ridge Trail 958. At the junction you are at 6,000 feet above sea level and 3.4 miles from the Goat Peak Trailhead. The American Ridge Trail below (left, east) this junction is only lightly used and vague in places, but to the right toward Goat Peak it is obvious.

Turn right at the junction and follow the American Ridge Trail, climbing to the southwest. The route makes many switchbacks as you ascend through the increasingly alpine forest and openings. White-bark pines are now included in the forest mix and flowers sometimes cover the openings. The steep trail climbs over 400 feet in the 0.6 mile to the junction with the path to the very summit of Goat Peak, at 6,420 feet elevation.

Turn right up the path and hike the short distance to the 6,473-foot-high summit of Goat Peak. From the peak, Bumping Lake and Nelson Ridge are in view to the south. To the northwest the jagged columns and spires of Fife's Peak rise above the American River Canyon, and to the west is the huge, ice-crowned, 14,408-foot-high summit of Mount Rainier. Stunted, wind-whipped subalpine fir, Alaska cedar, and white-bark pine grow scattered around the rocky outcrop that is the summit of Goat Peak. Between the rocks sprout buckwheat, penstemon, lupine, and Indian paintbrush. Chipmunks are often begging for food around the summit. Little is left today of the abandoned and dismantled American Ridge Lookout that once was atop Goat Peak. Make your return hike by retracing your steps to the Goat Peak Trailhead or see the options below for an alternate return route.

Miles and Directions

0.0   Goat Peak Trailhead. GPS 46 57.860N 121 15.984W. Take left trail.

3.4   Junction with American Ridge Trail 958. GPS 46 56.474N 121 15.718W. Turn right.

4.0   Path to Goat Peak summit. GPS 46 56.356N 121 15.899W. Turn right.

4.1   Summit of Goat Peak. Turnaround point.

8.2   Goat Peak Trailhead.

Options: An alternate return hike can easily be made from Goat Peak via the Pleasant Valley Lake Trail. To make this hike, go back to the American Ridge Trail and turn right. Follow the American Ridge Trail for 1.7 miles southwest to the junction with the Pleasant Valley Lake Trail 958b. Turn right on the Pleasant Valley Lake Trail and descend for 3.7 miles to the junction with the Pleasant Valley Loop Trail 999. Turn right on the Pleasant Valley Loop Trail and hike 2.8 miles northeast to the Goat Peak Trailhead.

Bumping River Region

The Bumping River Region reaches into the very heart of the William O. Douglas Wilderness. Bumping Lake Road (Forest Road 1800) is an access corridor, leading southwest from State Route 410 to Bumping Lake and beyond. There are numerous campsites all along the Bumping River and at Bumping Lake, making the area very popular for a few weeks in the summer. If you forgot something when you left home, there is a store and restaurant at Goose Prairie and

On the trail high above Bumping Lake.

another store at the marina on the northwest side of Bumping Lake. All of the hikes in this region are accessed by FR 1800, except Hike 24, Root Lake, which leaves from the end of Forest Road 1809.

Hiking in this region takes on two different flavors: bottomlands and high ridges. Hikes 19 and 23 are easy trails with negligible elevation gain, close to Bumping Lake. Both are suitable for very young hikers. While following a river bottom nearly its entire length, Hike 22, Fish Lake, is far more strenuous and requires crossing the Bumping River without the benefit of a bridge. Hikes 17, 18, and 19 climb the slopes of American Ridge all the way to its subalpine ridgeline, where you'll have a tremendous view of the surrounding terrain. Although it's fairly short, Hike 24, Root Lake, should not be taken lightly: It's steep and fairly easy to lose the route. Elk are common along all the trails in this region.

17 American Ridge Trail 958
Goat Creek Trail to American Ridge Trailhead

From an internal start, hike the eastern end of American Ridge from its junction with Goat Creek Trail, over Goat Peak and down to the American Ridge Trailhead on Forest Road 1800. This is a great early-season hike, when the trails along the Cascade crest are still snow-covered.

Start: Junction of Goat Creek Trail and American Ridge Trail (internal start).
Type of hike: Shuttle backpack or very long day hike.
Total distance: 10 miles.
Difficulty: Moderate, with some route-finding skills required.
Maps: USDA Forest Service William O. Douglas and Norse Peak Wilderness or Goose Prairie and Old Scab Mountain USGS quads.

Permits and fees: William O. Douglas Wilderness permit and Northwest Forest Pass.
Best months: Mid-June through September.
Special considerations: Water can be very scarce along the ridgeline after the snow has melted, so take along as much as you will need or be sure you fill up along Goat Creek Trail before reaching the junction where this hike description begins.

Finding the trailhead: To reach Goat Creek Trailhead, drive north from **Portland,** Oregon, on Interstate 5 for 68 miles to the junction with U.S. Highway 12. Then head east on US 12 for 71 miles (7 miles east of Packwood) to the junction with State Route 123. Turn left off US 12 on SR 123 and go north for 16.5 miles to Cayuse Pass and the junction with State Route 410. From the **Seattle-Tacoma** area, drive to Enumclaw. From Enumclaw follow SR 410 for 41 miles east and south to Cayuse Pass.

Turn left (right if coming from Portland) on SR 410 and head east for 22.9 miles over Chinook Pass and down to the junction with Bumping Lake Road (FR 1800). Turn right and follow FR 1800 for 5.9 miles southwest to the Goat Creek Trailhead, which will be on the right side of the road, at 3,090 feet elevation. Then hike northwest along Goat Creek Trail 959 for 4.9 miles to the junction with the American Ridge Trail, at 5,660 feet elevation. Turn right on the American Ridge Trail to begin your hike along American Ridge. See the options below for information about the American Ridge Trail in the other direction (southwest).

To reach the American Ridge Trailhead, where this hike ends, drive back (northeast) from the Goat Creek Trailhead along FR 1800 for 5.3 miles and turn left into the trailhead parking area. There is a sign marking this trailhead.

Parking and trailhead facilities: There is parking for several cars at the Goat Creek Trailhead but no other facilities. The American Ridge Trailhead, where this hike ends, also has parking for several cars but no other facilities.

The Hike

From the junction with Goat Creek Trail 959, the American Ridge Trail leads northeast, crossing small sloping meadows that bloom with lupine and yellow buckwheat.

Lower American Ridge.

At first the tread is slightly to the right of the ridge, but in about 0.2 mile it crosses the ridgeline to the left side. As you climb along the left (northwest) side of the ridge, Mount Rainier and Fife's Peak come into view. The course shortly makes the first of a series of eight switchbacks. The route gains 400 feet of elevation in slightly less than 0.8 mile as you climb the switchbacks. As you ascend, the country opens up. Between the groves of subalpine fir, Alaska cedar, and white-bark pine are sloping meadows covered with buckwheat, lupine, and paintbrush.

Just after making the eighth switchback, there will be a path to your left. A very short and well-worthwhile side trip up the path takes you to the 6,473-foot-high summit of Goat Peak. From the peak, Bumping Lake and Nelson Ridge are in view to the south. Chipmunks are often around, begging for food on the summit. Goat Peak was once the site of the American Ridge Lookout, although little is left of the abandoned and dismantled lookout today.

After passing the path to Goat Peak summit, the trail begins to descend through patches of subalpine timber and openings. You will make several switchbacks in the next 0.6 mile to the junction with the Goat Peak Trail 958c. The junction, at 6,000

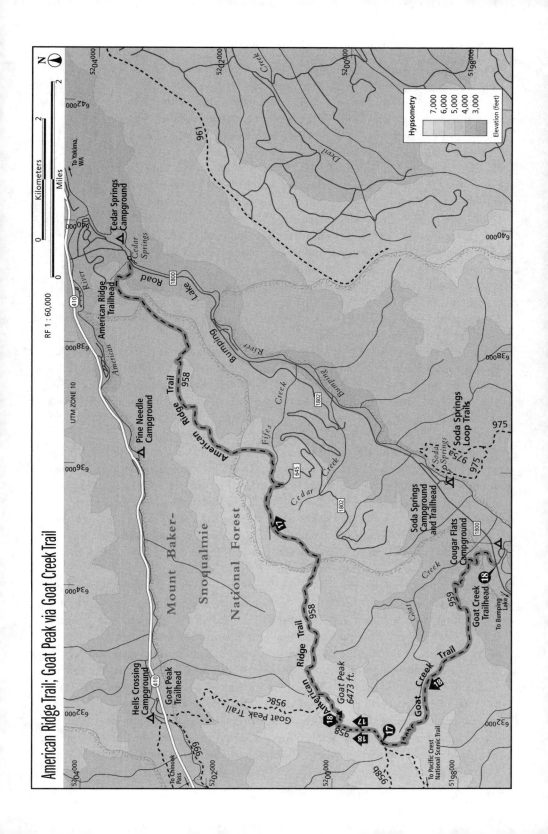

American Ridge Trail; Goat Peak via Goat Creek Trail

RF 1 : 60,000

Hypsometry

7,000
6,000
5,000
4,000
3,000

Elevation (feet)

feet elevation, is marked with a sign, but you may not notice the American Ridge Trail bearing slightly to the right. The American Ridge Trail below here is only lightly used for the next couple of miles and can be hard to follow in places. On the other hand, the Goat Peak Trail receives quite a bit of traffic and appears here to be the main trail. Goat Peak Trail descends steeply for 3.4 miles to a trailhead on SR 410.

To continue along the American Ridge Trail, bear right (east-northeast) and keep descending the switchbacks along the semiopen ridge. Before long the timber thickens, and at about 5,200 feet elevation you end the series of switchbacks. Below 5,200 feet elevation, the route flattens out, then about 1 mile from the junction with the Goat Peak Trail, it climbs slightly, reaching 5,240 feet elevation in another 0.4 mile before beginning to gently descend again. The trail makes two switchbacks 0.5 mile after you started the descent, and the downgrade steepens for a short distance. Watch for a spring on the left side of the trail, a short distance past the second switchback, as you hike through the mixed forest of western white pine, lodgepole pine, tamarack, grand fir, and Douglas fir.

Six-tenths mile below the switchbacks, you'll pass a tiny meadow where paintbrush and columbines bloom in late spring (June). The route makes two more descending switchbacks 0.4 mile farther along, then descends a short distance to cross the closed and abandoned Forest Road 645, at 4,440 feet elevation, 5.4 miles from the junction with Goat Creek Trail. To the southwest along abandoned FR 645, it is only 1 mile to Forest Road 1802, which is an open and well-maintained gravel road. If a car shuttle can be made and you can find the obscure spot where FR 645 meets FR 1802, you can exit your hike here if you like.

If not, turn right on the old roadbed of FR 645 and walk a few yards south, then turn left to continue on the American Ridge Trail. The trail heads east from FR 645 through timber and small meadows. In 0.3 mile the course turns north and begins a descending traverse along the slopes of American Ridge. The tread soon turns east again, as you descend to 4,100 feet elevation. Then the course turns north to cross a flat area before resuming the sidehill traverse. About 1.5 miles from the junction with FR 645, you begin to climb a series of switchbacks that take you back to the crest of American Ridge, at 4,500 feet elevation.

The route then descends along the ridgeline, reaching a small saddle at about 4,250 feet elevation in 0.3 mile. A few yards to the right of the saddle is a viewpoint overlooking the Bumping River Canyon. Past the saddle the trail climbs very slightly, passing some large ponderosa pines, then continues its descent. Three hundred yards from the saddle, the course starts a series of eight steep switchbacks, which descend 270 feet in the next 0.5 mile. As you head down the ridgeline, the timber gradually thickens and the views become more limited. The route leaves the William O. Douglas Wilderness in another mile, at 3,350 feet elevation.

Soon after crossing the wilderness boundary, the tread bears slightly to the left to descend along a north-facing slope. Shortly you return to the ridgeline in another small saddle, at 3,140 feet elevation. A couple hundred yards past the saddle, a road and building can be seen below and to the left. The track makes a switchback to the left a little farther along and soon reaches an unsigned trail junction. Hike straight ahead at the junction; the trail to the left descends to the road and building. The route soon makes four more switchbacks, then bears left to follow an abandoned roadbed. Another 150 yards of hiking along the roadbed brings you to the American Ridge Trailhead. The trailhead is at 2,760 feet elevation, next to FR 1800, 10 miles from the junction with the Goat Creek Trail.

Miles and Directions

0.0 Junction of Goat Creek Trail 959 and American Ridge Trail 958. GPS 46 55.967N 121 16.337W. Turn right.

1.7 Path to Goat Peak summit. GPS 46 56.356N 121 15.899W. Proceed straight ahead.

2.3 Junction with Goat Peak Trail 958c. GPS 46 56.474N 121 15.718W. Bear right.

5.4 Cross FR 645. Turn right, then turn left.

10.0 American Ridge Trailhead on FR 1800. GPS 46 58.161N 121 10.104W.

Options: If you turn left (southwest) on the American Ridge Trail at the junction with the Goat Creek Trail, it's only 0.1 mile to the junction with the Pleasant Valley Lake Trail 958b. Pleasant Valley Lake Trail descends 3.7 miles northwest to a junction with the Pleasant Valley Loop Trail along the American River. From the junction with the Pleasant Valley Lake Trail, it's about another 5 miles southwest along the American Ridge Trail to the junction with the Goose Prairie Trail 972. Goose Prairie Trail descends 5.2 miles east to Goose Prairie Trailhead on FR 1800. Another mile of hiking along the American Ridge Trail brings you to the junction with the Kettle Creek Trail near Kettle Lake. Kettle Creek Trail 957 descends for 6 miles north, to another junction with the Pleasant Valley Loop Trail. Any of these trails can be used as alternate return routes from your hike along American Ridge, provided the appropriate car shuttle can be made.

18 Goat Peak via Goat Creek
Trails 959 and 958

Hike from the bottom of the Bumping River Canyon to the alpine summit of Goat Peak, where you get a panoramic view of Mount Rainier and much of the Norse Peak and William O. Douglas Wilderness Areas. While Goat Creek Trail is not the shortest route to the summit of Goat Peak, it is probably the easiest.

See map on page 99.
Start: Goat Creek Trailhead.
Type of hike: Out-and-back day hike or backpack.
Total distance: 13.4 miles.
Difficulty: Moderate.
Maps: USDA Forest Service Norse Peak and William O. Douglas Wilderness or Old Scab Mountain and Goose Prairie USGS quads.

Permits and fees: William O. Douglas Wilderness permit.
Best months: Mid-June through September.
Special considerations: Water is very limited along this trail, especially in late summer and fall. Take along all that you will need.

Finding the trailhead: To reach Goat Creek Trailhead, drive north from **Portland,** Oregon, on Interstate 5 for 68 miles to the junction with U.S. Highway 12. Then head east on US 12 for 71 miles (7 miles east of Packwood) to the junction with State Route 123. Turn left off US 12 on SR 123 and go north for 16.5 miles to Cayuse Pass and the junction with State Route 410. From the **Seattle-Tacoma** area drive to Enumclaw. From Enumclaw follow SR 410 for 41 miles east and south to Cayuse Pass.

Turn left (right if coming from Portland) on SR 410 and drive 22.9 miles east to the junction with Bumping Lake Road (Forest Road 1800). Turn right and follow FR 1800 for 5.9 miles southwest to the Goat Creek Trailhead, which will be on the right, at 3,090 feet elevation.
Parking and trailhead facilities: There is only limited parking and no other facilities at the trailhead. Cougar Flats Campground is across FR 1800 from the trailhead.

The Hike

The William O. Douglas Wilderness Map shows the trailhead slightly incorrectly. Leaving the trailhead the trail leads northeast following FR 1800 for about 200 yards, through the mixed forest of ponderosa pine, Douglas fir, and true firs. Then the route turns to the northwest, passing the William O. Douglas Wilderness boundary 0.3 mile from the trailhead. Past the wilderness boundary, the course begins its climb toward American Ridge.

Shortly the tread makes the first of seven switchbacks as it winds its way up to a tiny spring at 3,930 feet elevation, 1.6 miles from the trailhead. Soon after passing the spring, the timber thins out a little, allowing views of Nelson Ridge to the south. The route continues to climb along a slope in and out of the timber for another 0.9

Path to Goat Peak summit.

mile before reaching a rounded ridgeline at about 4,400 feet elevation. On the ridge Goat Peak comes into view through the trees to the right (northwest). The timber now mostly consists of tamarack, hemlock, and Douglas fir, with beargrass covering the ground in places.

The trail crosses a tiny stream at 4,730 feet elevation, 3.2 miles from the trailhead. This stream may be dry by midsummer. After crossing the tiny stream, the tread continues to wind uphill, making ten switchbacks and gaining slightly over 800 feet of elevation in the next 1.5 miles. As you climb, cardinal flowers and kinnikinnick line the trail in the openings. After the last switchback the route soon leaves the timber and crosses an open slope to the poorly marked junction with the American Ridge Trail 958. This junction is 4.9 miles from the trailhead, at 5,660 feet elevation. Cell phone service is marginal but can usually be had at the junction.

Turn right at the junction on the American Ridge Trail and soon cross small sloping meadows on the right side of the ridgeline. These meadows bloom with lupine and yellow buckwheat in midsummer. In about 0.2 mile the route crosses the ridgeline to the left side. Look to your left as you climb along this slope.

Mount Rainier and Fife's Peak soon are in view, to the west and northwest. The trail soon makes the first of eight switchbacks, in which you gain 400 feet of elevation. The country opens up as you climb. Between the groves of subalpine fir, Alaska cedar, and white-bark pine are sloping meadows covered with buckwheat, lupine, and paintbrush.

There will be a path to your left just after you make the eighth switchback, 1.7 miles from the junction with the Goat Creek Trail. Turn on the path and hike to the 6,473-foot-high summit of Goat Peak. Looking south from the summit, Bumping Lake and Nelson Ridge are in view, and majestic Mount Rainier dominates the scene to the west. Chipmunks are often begging for food at the summit. Goat Peak was once the site of the American Ridge Lookout, but little is left of the abandoned and dismantled lookout today. Return the way you came or see the options below for an alternate return route.

Miles and Directions

0.0 Goat Creek Trailhead. GPS 46 55.031N 121 13.984W.

4.9 Junction with American Ridge Trail 958. GPS 46 55.967N 121 16.337W. Turn right.

6.6 Path to the summit of Goat Peak. GPS 46 56.356N 121 15.899W. Turn left.

6.7 Summit of Goat Peak. Turnaround point.

13.4 Goat Creek Trailhead.

Options: A shorter but steeper return trip, requiring a car shuttle, can be made via Goat Peak Trail 958c. To hike down by way of Goat Peak Trail, go back the short distance to the American Ridge Trail and turn left. Follow the American Ridge Trail east for 0.6 mile to the junction with the Goat Peak Trail. Turn left on the Goat Peak Trail and descend steeply for 3.4 miles to Goat Peak Trailhead on SR 410.

To reach Goat Peak Trailhead by car, drive back the way you came on FR 1800 to the junction with SR 410. Turn left on SR 410 and go 5 miles west to the Goat Peak Trailhead. The trailhead is nearly straight across the highway from the Hells Crossing Campground entrance.

19 Goose Prairie Trail 972

Hike from the trailhead next to the Bumping River to the top of American Ridge.

Start: Goose Prairie Trailhead.
Type of hike: Out-and-back day hike or access route to American Ridge Trail.
Total distance: 10.4 miles.
Difficulty: Moderate.

Maps: USDA Forest Service William O. Douglas and Norse Peak Wilderness or Goose Prairie USGS quad.
Permits and fees: William O. Douglas Wilderness permit.
Best months: Mid-June through October.

Finding the trailhead: To reach Goose Prairie Trailhead from the **Seattle-Tacoma** area, drive to Enumclaw. From Enumclaw follow State Route 410 for 41 miles east and south to Cayuse Pass. From **Portland,** Oregon, drive north on Interstate 5 for 68 miles to the junction with U.S. Highway 12. Then head east on US 12 for 71 miles (7 miles east of Packwood) to the junction with State Route 123. Turn left off US 12 on SR 123 and go north for 16.5 miles to Cayuse Pass and the junction with SR 410.

Turn right (left if coming from Seattle) on SR 410 and drive 22.9 miles east to the junction with Bumping Lake Road (Forest Road 1800). Follow FR 1800 for 9.4 miles to Goose Prairie Trailhead. The trailhead is on the right (northwest) side of FR 1800 at 3,350 feet elevation.
Parking and trailhead facilities: There is parking for several cars across FR 1800, from the trailhead and several unimproved campsites but no other facilities.

The Hike

Fill out your wilderness permit and start your hike by paralleling FR 1800 for a few yards to the northeast. The route then makes a left turn to begin its climb up American Ridge, through the tall pine, fir, tamarack, and hemlock forest. After climbing moderately for 0.4 mile and gaining about 200 feet of elevation, an opening in the timber allows for views to your left. In another 0.4 mile you will reach the William O. Douglas Wilderness boundary, at 3,710 feet elevation. A sign marks the wilderness boundary.

After entering the wilderness the tread winds its way up through the woods for 0.4 mile to a creek crossing. There is no bridge so you must ford the shallow, clear water. Beyond the creek crossing the path crosses several tiny streams, some with wooden bridges over them. You start to climb a series of nine switchbacks 1.6 miles into the hike. This 0.5-mile-long set of switchbacks takes you up to 4,310 feet elevation. A quarter mile past the last switchback, the course crosses another small stream. After crossing the small stream, the trail continues to climb, making a couple more switchbacks and reaching another creek crossing at 4,990 feet elevation.

After crossing the creek the timber starts to thin, allowing more views of the surrounding mountains. White-bark pine and subalpine fir are now included in the

Kinnikinnick beside the Goose Prairie Trail.

forest mix of trees, and kinnikinnick covers the ground in places. You will cross a couple more tiny streams about 0.6 mile farther along. These streams will probably be dry by midsummer. In June you are likely to encounter patches of snow here, and this could be your turnaround point since the trail is difficult to follow when it's snow-covered. The route makes several more switchbacks as you climb up to 5,890 feet elevation. Above the switchbacks you climb the last 0.2 mile to the junction with the American Ridge Trail on the top of American Ridge.

This junction, just a few feet before you reach the ridgeline of American Ridge, 5.2 miles from the trailhead, at 5,970 feet elevation, is easy to miss. It is a Y junction, and the part of the American Ridge Trail coming in from your left is very vague. There are a couple of old weathered signs on a tree to the left of the junction, but they can be a bit hard to see. If you continue straight ahead (north) at the junction, you will be on American Ridge Trail heading for Goat Peak. Return the way you came or see the options below for an alternate return hike.

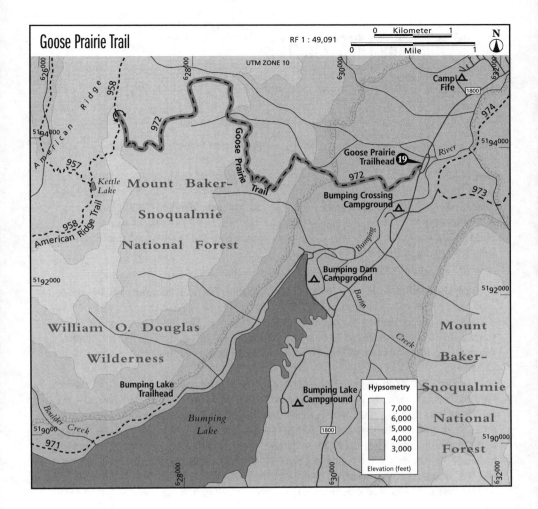

Goose Prairie Trail

RF 1 : 49,091

0   Kilometer   1

0   Mile   1

N

UTM ZONE 10

Camp Fife 1800

974

Goose Prairie Trailhead 19 River

972

973

Bumping Crossing Campground

American Ridge

958

972

Goose Prairie Trail

Kettle Lake

957

Mount Baker-

958

American Ridge Trail

Snoqualmie

National Forest

Bumping

Bumping Dam Campground

Baren

William O. Douglas

Mount

Wilderness

Creek

Baker-

Bumping Lake Trailhead

Bumping Lake Campground

Hypsometry

Snoqualmie

National

Boulder Creek

Bumping Lake

1800

7,000
6,000
5,000
4,000
3,000

Forest

971

Elevation (feet)

Miles and Directions

0.0   Goose Prairie Trailhead. GPS 46 53.026N 121 16.851W.

0.8   William O. Douglas Wilderness boundary.

5.2   Junction with American Ridge Trail. GPS 56 53.572N 121 19.887W. Turnaround point.

10.4 Goose Prairie Trailhead.

Options: You can make an alternate return requiring a car shuttle by heading north-east on the American Ridge Trail for a little less than 5 miles to the junction with the Goat Creek Trail 959. Turn right on the Goat Creek Trail and descend for 4.9 miles to the Goat Creek Trailhead on FR 1800.

    To reach Goat Creek Trailhead by car, drive back the way you came (northeast) on FR 1800 for 3.5 miles to Goat Creek Trailhead.

20 Bumping Lake Trail 971

Hike along the shore of Bumping Lake, watching for elk and possibly stopping to fish as you go.

Start: Bumping Lake Trailhead on the northwest side of Bumping Lake.
Type of hike: Out-and-back day hike or short backpack with shuttle options.
Total distance: 9 miles out and back.
Difficulty: Easy to the head of Bumping Lake.
Maps: USDA Forest Service William O. Douglas and Norse Peak Wilderness or Bumping Lake and Cougar Lake USGS quads.

Permits and fees: William O. Douglas Wilderness permit.
Best months: Mid-May through October out and back, mid-July through October shuttle.
Special considerations: If you camp along this trail, be sure you are at least some distance from any of the many large anthills.

Finding the trailhead: To reach Bumping Lake Trailhead, drive north from **Portland,** Oregon, on Interstate 5 for 68 miles to the junction with U.S. Highway 12. Then head east on US 12 for 71 miles (7 miles east of Packwood) to the junction with State Route 123. Turn left off US 12 on SR 123 and go north for 16.5 miles to Cayuse Pass and the junction with State Route 410. From the **Seattle-Tacoma** area, drive to Enumclaw. From Enumclaw follow SR 410 for 41 miles east and south to Cayuse Pass.

Turn left (right if coming from Portland) on SR 410 and head east for 22.9 miles over Chinook Pass and down to the junction with Bumping Lake Road (Forest Road 1800). Turn right on FR 1800 and follow it for 11 miles, then turn right on the road across the top of Bumping Lake Dam. Once across the dam the road first turns right, then swings around to the left to follow the northwest shore of Bumping Lake. Continue along the shoreline road for 1.5 miles to its end at the trailhead. The elevation at the trailhead is 3,460 feet. A sign at the trailhead reads SWAMP LAKE TRAIL 970 and BUMPING LAKE TRAIL 971.
Parking and trailhead facilities: There is parking for several cars at the trailhead but no other facilities.

The Hike

The trail first descends a short distance, then turns right to head southwest along the lakeshore. The forest along the lake consists of mixed-age conifers, and much of the ground is covered with vanilla leaf. Vanilla leaf blooms in June here. Scattered around between the trees and above the vanilla leaf are a few shrubby Rocky Mountain maples and mountain ash bushes.

After a short distance along the lake, the shoreline steepens, forming talus slopes, which in places reach nearly to the water's edge. Penstemon sprouts from between the rocks, blooming by mid-June, and Oregon grape and hazel brush dot the slopes. About 1.1 miles from the trailhead, you'll leave the talus, and the steep sidehill backs away from the lake. In another couple tenths of a mile, the route fords Boulder

Elk in meadows close to the Bumping Lake Trail.

Creek. When I hiked this trail in 2004, there was a good, if a bit high off the water, log to cross, just upstream from the ford. The area around Boulder Creek seems to have a good population of cross deer (blacktail–mule deer cross). I spotted small groups here both heading out and hiking back along this section of trail. The trail is eroded and washed out for about 100 yards 0.8 mile past Boulder Creek. Rock cairns mark the route through the washout area, making it easy to follow.

In several places along the trail, you may notice large mounds of twigs and other forest duff. These piles, which are up to and sometimes over 3 feet high and 6 or more feet in diameter, are anthills. Red ants, *Formica rufa,* build these huge anthills, and when most of them are at home, there may be thousands of them covering the tops of the piles. Red ants do bite so it's best if you don't take a rest break on or next to the piles.

There is a campsite to the left of the trail next to the lake, 2.5 miles from the trailhead. If this is to be a short backpack, this makes a good place to camp. Another 0.5 mile of hiking brings you to Cedar Creek. Cedar Creek also has no bridge crossing it and must be forded. Watch for elk as you approach Cedar Creek; this seems to

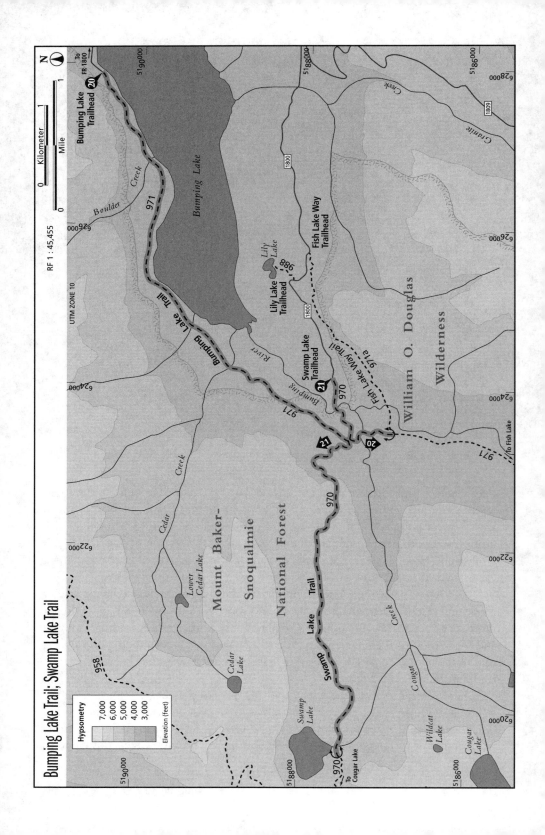

Bumping Lake Trail; Swamp Lake Trail

RF 1 : 45,455

N

Kilometer

Mile

Bumping Lake Trailhead 20
To FR 1800

5190000

UTM ZONE 10

5188000

5186000

6288000

Boulder Creek

971

Bumping Lake

Lily Lake

988

Lily Lake Trailhead

Fish Lake Way Trailhead

1800

1809

Granite Creek

6286000

6288000

Bumping Lake Trail

Bumping River

971

Swamp Lake Trailhead 21

970

Fish Lake Way Trail 971a

1800

William O. Douglas Wilderness

6284000

6284000

17

20

971

To Fish Lake

Cedar Creek

970

Mount Baker-

Lower Cedar Lake

Snoqualmie

Cedar Lake

National Forest

958

Swamp Lake Trail

970

Swamp Lake

Cougar Creek

Wildcat Lake

Cougar Lake

970

To Cougar Lake

6282000

6280000

5188000

5186000

Hypsometry

| Elevation (feet) |
7,000
6,000
5,000
4,000
3,000

be a favorite bedding area for these huge animals. Just across the creek the trail has been obliterated for a short distance by a flood. The route across the debris is marked with cairns and is easy to follow.

The route climbs gently after crossing Cedar Creek, reaching the William O. Douglas Wilderness boundary in 0.6 mile. Another 0.4 mile brings you to the junction with the Swamp Lake Trail 970, at 3,700 feet elevation. See the options below for ending this hike at Swamp Lake Trailhead. If you turn right on the Swamp Lake Trail, it's a 3.4-mile climb to Swamp Lake.

The Bumping Lake Trail goes straight ahead (southwest) from the junction. In 0.25 mile the route fords Cougar Creek. Cougar Creek is swift and knee-deep in mid-July and could be a difficult crossing early in the season. After crossing Cougar Creek it's another 0.25 mile to the junction with Fish Lake Way 971a and the end of this hike. To exit via Fish Lake Way rather than returning the way you came, see the options below. Along the Bumping Lake Trail, it's another 5.9 miles to Fish Lake. If Fish Lake is your destination, it is better to reach the Bumping Lake Trail here via Fish Creek Way.

Miles and Directions

- **0.0** Bumping Lake Trailhead. GPS 46 51.455N 121 19.142W.
- **1.2** Cross Boulder Creek.
- **3.0** Cross Cedar Creek.
- **4.0** Junction with Swamp Lake Trail 970. GPS 46 49.773N 121 22.843W. Proceed straight ahead or turn left for shuttle return.
- **4.5** Junction with Fish Lake Way 971a. GPS 46 49.433N 121 22.852W. Turn around or turn left for shuttle return.
- **9.0** Bumping Lake Trailhead.

Options: To the left on the Swamp Lake Trail, it's 0.9 mile to Swamp Lake Trailhead. If you turn left on Fish Lake Way, it's 1.8 miles to Fish Lake Way Trailhead. Both Fish Creek Way and Swamp Lake Trails ford the Bumping River between the Bumping River Trail and their trailheads on FR 1800. If the water is high, both of these fords can be difficult and dangerous.

To reach either Fish Creek Way or Swamp Lake Trailhead by car, first head back the way you came from the Bumping Lake Trailhead and cross the Bumping Lake Dam. After you cross the dam, turn right on FR 1800. Drive south for 2.5 miles on FR 1800 to the junction with FR 1808. Turn right, staying on FR 1800, and head west for 2.6 miles to Fish Lake Way Trailhead. The trailhead is on the left side of FR 1800, at 3,850 feet elevation. To continue to Swamp Lake Trailhead, drive another 0.9 mile west to the road's end at 3,630 feet elevation. Forest Road 1800 is rough for the 0.9 mile between the trailheads and may require a high-clearance vehicle.

21 Swamp Lake Trail 970

Hike through the pristine forest from Swamp Lake Trailhead to the Bumping River. Then ford the clear, cold stream and climb to Swamp Lake high on the slopes of American Ridge.

See map on page 110.
Start: Swamp Lake Trailhead.
Type of hike: Out-and-back backpack or day hike.
Total distance: 8.6 miles.
Difficulty: Moderate.
Maps: Bumping Lake and Cougar Lake USGS quads or USDA Forest Service Norse Peak and William O. Douglas Wilderness.

Permits and fees: Northwest Forest Pass and William O. Douglas Wilderness permit.
Best months: July–September.
Special considerations: Fording the Bumping River 0.6 mile into the hike could be dangerous during times of high water. Take sandals or other water shoes for the crossing.

Finding the trailhead: To reach the Swamp Lake Trailhead, drive north from **Portland,** Oregon, on Interstate 5 for 68 miles to the junction with U.S. Highway 12. Then head east on US 12 for 71 miles (7 miles east of Packwood) to the junction with State Route 123. Turn left off US 12 on SR 123 and go north for 16.5 miles to Cayuse Pass and the junction with State Route 410. From the **Seattle-Tacoma** area drive to Enumclaw. From Enumclaw follow SR 410 for 41 miles east and south to Cayuse Pass

Turn left (right if coming from Portland) on SR 410 and head east for 3.7 miles to Chinook Pass. Then continue on SR 410 for 19.2 miles down to the junction with Bumping Lake Road (Forest Road 1800). Turn southwest on Bumping Lake Road (FR 1800) off SR 410. Drive 11 miles to the Bumping Lake Dam. Continue another 2.5 miles on FR 1800, leaving the pavement, to the junction with FR 1808. Turn right, staying on FR 1800, and head west for 3.5 miles to its end at Swamp Lake Trailhead.

Parking and trailhead facilities: The trailhead has restrooms and a few unimproved campsites.

The Hike

Leaving the trailhead at 3,630 feet elevation, the Swamp Lake Trail quickly crosses a small wooden bridge. The route heads southwest through the mixed-age conifer forest. A little over 0.1 mile from the trailhead, you will pass a swampy pond to the left of the trail. A little farther along there will be a short path to your right. This path leads to a viewpoint overlooking a falls in the Bumping River. There are cliffs below and some exposure at the viewpoint so be careful, especially if the ground and rocks are wet. Past the viewpoint the tread crosses a semiopen slope where pink mountain heather blooms in June. Soon the course makes a descending switchback to the right. Then you wind down gently, passing a campsite, to the shore of the Bumping River, at 3,550 feet elevation. There is no bridge here so you must ford the cold, clear waters. This ford could be dangerous during spring and early sum-

Bumping River ford.

mer. See the options below for an alternate access route if the Bumping River is too high and the ford is dangerous.

After crossing the river the trail climbs the riverbank, then heads south for a short distance, entering the William O. Douglas Wilderness. The route then turns west and reaches the junction with the Bumping Lake Trail, at 3,710 feet elevation, 0.3 mile after crossing the river. To the left at the junction, the Bumping Lake Trail heads southwest for a little more than 6 miles to a junction with the Pacific Crest National Scenic Trail near Fish Lake. If you turn right on the Bumping Lake Trail, it's 4 miles to the trailhead on the northwest shore of Bumping Lake.

To continue on toward Swamp Lake, hike straight ahead (west), crossing the Bumping Lake Trail. The tread quickly begins to climb. Soon you make a couple of switchbacks as the route ascends through the western red cedar and western hemlock forest. There will be a small stream below the trail to your left 0.4 mile from the junction. The course continues to climb moderately, winding uphill through the old-growth forest that now contains some rather large Douglas firs.

The trail crosses a wooden bridge over a small stream, 1.5 miles from the junction with the Bumping Lake Trail. You will cross three more small streams, which may be dry by late summer, before reaching a talus slope at 4,610 feet elevation, 3.4 miles from the Swamp Lake Trailhead. The route crosses the talus, then climbs some more, crossing three more tiny streams (which may also be dry), and reaching 4,880 feet elevation, 4.1 miles into the hike. The route then flattens out and even descends a little for the next 0.2 mile to a creek crossing at the outlet of Swamp Lake. There are usually some logs available to make this crossing dry-footed.

Swamp Lake, at 4,795 feet elevation, is a fairly large lake, surrounded by good-size timber. There is a possible campsite next to the trail just before reaching the outlet crossing and more campsites after the crossing. Some of these campsites may be closed for restoration, and remember, camping is prohibited within 100 feet of the lake. From a campsite at Swamp Lake, it's only about a 2.5-mile hike to beautiful Cougar Lakes. Make the return trip by retracing your route back to the Swamp Lake Trailhead.

Miles and Directions

- **0.0** Swamp Lake Trailhead. GPS 46 49.925N 121 22.220W.
- **0.6** Bumping River ford. Cross river.
- **0.9** Junction with Bumping Lake Trail 971. GPS 46 49.773N 121 22.843W. Proceed straight ahead to the west.
- **4.3** Swamp Lake. Turnaround point.
- **8.6** Swamp Lake Trailhead.

Options: If the ford of the Bumping River is too intimidating, it is possible to access the Swamp Lake Trail at its junction with the Bumping Lake Trail. Using the Bumping Lake Trail will add 3.1 miles each way to your hike. To reach the Bumping Lake Trailhead, where the Bumping Lake Trail starts, drive back the way you came on FR 1800 for 6 miles to the Bumping Lake Dam. Turn left (northwest) and cross the dam. Once across the dam the road first turns right, then swings around to the left to follow the northwest shore of Bumping Lake. Continue along the shoreline road for 1.5 miles to its end at the trailhead. From the trailhead follow the Bumping Lake Trail for 4 miles southwest to the junction with the Swamp Lake Trail.

22 Fish Lake
Trails 971a, 971, and 2000

Hike through the old-growth forest along the Bumping River, passing large meadows that often host elk as you go. Then climb gently to Fish Lake near the crest of
the Cascades.

Start: Fish Lake Way Trailhead.
Type of hike: Out-and-back backpack or day
hike.
Total distance: 15.4 miles.
Difficulty: Moderate.
Maps: USDA Forest Service Norse Peak and
William O. Douglas Wilderness or Bumping
Lake and Cougar Lake USGS quads.

Permits and fees: Northwest Forest Pass and
William O. Douglas Wilderness permit.
Best months: Mid-July through October.
Special considerations: Bring sandals or ten-
nis shoes for crossing the Bumping River. If
you are making this hike before mid-July, the
crossing of the Bumping River could be difficult or even dangerous.

Finding the trailhead: To reach Fish Lake Way Trailhead from the **Seattle-Tacoma** area, drive
to Enumclaw. From Enumclaw follow State Route 410 for 41 miles east and south to Cayuse
Pass. From **Portland,** Oregon, drive north on Interstate 5 for 68 miles to the junction with U.S.
Highway 12. Then head east on US 12 for 71 miles (7 miles east of Packwood) to the junction
with State Route 123. Turn left off US 12 on SR 123 and drive north for 16.5 miles to Cayuse
Pass and the junction with SR 410.
 Turn right (left if coming from Seattle-Tacoma) on SR 410 and head east for 22.9 miles,
over Chinook Pass and down to the junction with Bumping Lake Road (Forest Road 1800). Turn
southwest on Bumping Lake Road (FR 1800) off SR 410. Drive 11 miles to Bumping Lake Dam.
Continue another 2.5 miles on FR 1800, leaving the pavement, to the junction with Forest Road
1808. Turn right, staying on FR 1800, and head west for 2.6 miles to Fish Lake Way Trailhead.
The trailhead is on the left side of FR 1800, at 3,850 feet elevation.
Parking and trailhead facilities: There is a new trailhead area on the right side of FR 1800 at
the trailhead, with restrooms, campsites, horse facilities, and ample parking.

The Hike

A sign next to the reader board at the trailhead states that it is 6 miles to the Pacific
Crest Trail and Fish Lake. Fish Lake Way Trail 971a descends gently to the southwest
through a mixed-age forest of lodgepole pine, Douglas and true fir, western white
pine, western red cedar, and tamarack as you leave the trailhead. Quickly the tread
flattens and then climbs, making a switchback to the left. The route is rough and
eroded as you climb. Soon the route flattens at 3,890 feet elevation. The trace crosses
a small wooden bridge over a wet area, next to a pond, 0.3 mile from the trailhead.
Soon you cross another small bridge, then climb slightly to cross a small, rounded
ridgeline at 3,920 feet elevation.

Meadows next to Fish Lake.

The trail then descends gently, and soon you'll pass beneath a talus slope, which is to the left. Pikas inhabit this rocky slope, and there is a good chance you will see one or at least hear their shrill voices warning the others of your presence. The route passes beneath the talus slopes for nearly 0.5 mile, then bears away, crossing a third small wooden bridge. Soon you will make two descending switchbacks. The trail is very rough and rocky here. Below the switchbacks the trail flattens and continues west to the Bumping River, at 3,610 feet elevation. There is no bridge here so you must ford the river. The ford is relatively easy at normal water levels but could be challenging when the water is high.

Once across the river the trail climbs the steep, loose riverbank and enters a mostly lodgepole pine forest. The route heads southwest for 0.2 mile to the junction with the Bumping Lake Trail 971. See the options below for an alternate route to reach this point if the Bumping River is too difficult and dangerous to ford. If you were to turn right on the Bumping Lake Trail here, it is only 0.5 mile to the junction with the Swamp Lake Trail and 4.5 miles to the Bumping Lake Trailhead along the northwest shore of Bumping Lake.

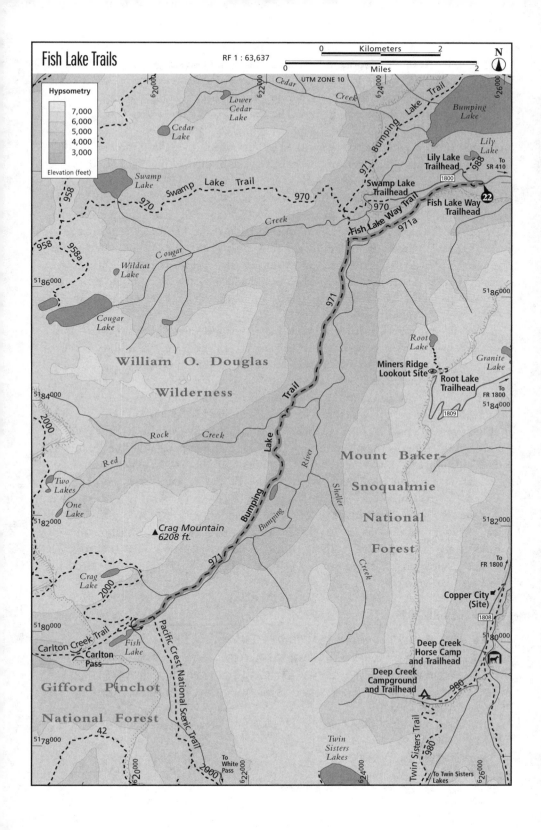

Fish Lake Trails

RF 1 : 63,637

Kilometers
0   2

Miles
0   2

N

UTM ZONE 10

Cedar   Creek

Lower
Cedar
Lake

Cedar
Lake

Bumping
Lake

Bumping Lake Trail

971

Lily
Lake

Lily Lake
Trailhead

Swamp
Lake

Swamp Lake Trail

970

958

970

Swamp Lake
Trailhead

1800

To
SR 410

6000

6200

6400

6600

22

Fish Lake Way
Trailhead

Creek

Fish Lake Way Trail

971a

970

958

958a

Cougar

Wildcat
Lake

Cougar
Lake

971

5186000

5186000

William O. Douglas

Wilderness

Root
Lake

Granite
Lake

Miners Ridge
Lookout Site

Root Lake
Trailhead

To
FR 1800

5184000

1809

5184000

Rock   Creek

Bumping   Lake   Trail

Red

Mount Baker–

Two
Lakes

One
Lake

Bumping

River

Sheller

Snoqualmie

National

5182000

2000

5182000

Crag Mountain
6208 ft.

Bumping

Creek

Forest

5182000

To
FR 1800

Crag
Lake

2000

971

Copper City
(Site)

1808

Carlton Creek Trail

Fish
Lake

Carlton
Pass

Pacific Crest National Scenic Trail

5180000

5180000

Gifford Pinchot

Deep Creek
Horse Camp
and Trailhead

National Forest

42

Deep Creek
Campground
and Trailhead

980

5178000

2000

6200

6400

Twin
Sisters
Lakes

Twin Sisters Trail

980

6600

To
White
Pass

To Twin Sisters
Lakes

Turn left at the junction and hike south along the Bumping Lake Trail. The trail quickly gets close to the Bumping River. The tread soon leaves the riverbank and crosses a creek 0.5 mile from the junction. Shortly after crossing the creek, there is a large meadow to the left of the trail. The route crosses a rocky area that appears to be an ancient lava flow 1.2 miles after accessing the Bumping Lake Trail. There is another large meadow to the left of the trail 0.4 mile farther along, after you cross a couple of tiny streams. If you are here early or late in the day, there is a good chance of seeing elk in this meadow.

Another 0.5 mile of hiking brings you to Rock Creek. There is no bridge over this rushing stream, but logs are usually available to make a dry-footed crossing. Rock Creek crossing is 3.9 miles from the trailhead, at 3,670 feet elevation. After crossing Rock Creek the trail climbs more steeply for the next 0.6 mile, then flattens out and even descends a little. The route remains relatively level for the next 0.4 mile, where you may notice a pond below and 150 yards to your left. The path again remains fairly flat for another 0.7 mile, then crosses a couple of tiny streams as it begins to climb gently.

You'll cross several small streams in the next mile, then the tread crosses three wooden bridges over wet areas. After crossing several more streams in the next 0.25 mile, there is a meadow to the right of the trail. If you look north across the meadow and up the mountainside above it, you can see a waterfall in the outlet stream from Crag Lake. The trail skirts the southeast side of the meadow, then crosses two more wooden bridges. Just past the bridges there is a pond with water lilies in a meadow to the right of the trail. After passing the pond there is a campsite on the right side of the trail, and a few yards farther is the junction with the Pacific Crest National Scenic Trail 2000. This junction, at 4,120 feet elevation, is 7.4 miles from the Fish Lake Way Trailhead.

At the junction turn right (west) on the PCT. The route stays north of the Bumping River (just a creek here) and enters a large meadow in about 0.2 mile. Another 0.1 mile of hiking brings you to the junction with the Carlton Creek Trail 22, near the east end of Fish Lake. This junction is at 4,120 feet elevation and 7.7 miles from Fish Lake Way Trailhead. Turn left on the Carlton Creek Trail to reach campsites along the northern shore of Fish Lake. Return by retracing your steps back to Fish Lake Way Trailhead.

Miles and Directions

- **0.0** Fish Lake Way Trailhead. 46 50.017N 121 21.095W.
- **1.6** Bumping River ford. GPS 46 49.558N 121 22.602W.
- **1.8** Junction with the Bumping Lake Trail 971. GPS 46 49.433N 121 22.852W. Turn left.
- **7.4** Junction with the Pacific Crest National Scenic Trail 2000. GPS 46 45.843N 121 25.559W. Turn right.
- **7.7** Junction with the Carlton Creek Trail 22 at Fish Lake. GPS 46 45.815N 121 25.731W. Turnaround point.
- **15.4** Fish Lake Way Trailhead.

Options: If you are making this hike early in the season when the Bumping River is high, you may want to consider a longer alternative that doesn't ford the river. Hiking this alternate route will add 2.7 miles each way to your hiking distance.

To reach the Bumping Lake Trailhead on the northwest side of Bumping Lake, where this alternate route begins, first backtrack on FR 1800 for 5.1 miles from the Fish Lake Way Trailhead. Then turn left on the road across the top of Bumping Lake Dam. Once across the dam the road first turns right, then swings around to the left to follow the northwest shore of Bumping Lake. Continue along the shoreline road for 1.5 miles to its end at the trailhead. The elevation at the trailhead is 3,460 feet. A sign at the trailhead reads SWAMP LAKE TRAIL 970 AND BUMPING LAKE TRAIL 971. There is parking for several cars at the trailhead but no other facilities.

From the trailhead hike southwest along the Bumping Lake Trail for 4 miles to the junction with the Swamp Lake Trail 970. Continue past the junction, staying on the Bumping Lake Trail for another 0.5 mile to the junction with the Fish Lake Way Trail. From here on, follow the route described in the "Hike" section above.

23 Lily Lake Trail 988

Take a short walk to a pretty little lake just south of Bumping Lake, where trout can be caught.

Start: Lily Lake Trailhead.
Type of hike: Out-and-back 1-hour hike.
Total distance: 0.4 mile round-trip.
Difficulty: Very easy.
Maps: Bumping Lake USGS quad. The USDA Forest Service William O. Douglas and Norse

Peak Wilderness map covers the area but doesn't show this trail.
Permits and fees: None.
Best months: Mid-June through October.
Special considerations: In late June and July, the mosquitoes can be thick along this trail.

Finding the trailhead: To reach the Lily Lake Trailhead from the **Seattle-Tacoma** area, drive to Enumclaw. From Enumclaw follow State Route 410 for 41 miles east and south to Cayuse Pass. If you are coming from **Portland,** Oregon, drive north on Interstate 5 for 68 miles to the junction with U.S. Highway 12. Then head east on US 12 for 71 miles (7 miles east of Packwood) to the junction with State Route 123. Turn left off US 12 on SR 123 and drive north for 16.5 miles to Cayuse Pass and the junction with SR 410.

Turn right (left if coming from the Seattle-Tacoma area) on SR 410 and head east for 22.9 miles over Chinook Pass and down to the junction with Bumping Lake Road (Forest Road 1800). Turn right (southwest) on Bumping Lake Road and follow it for 16.4 miles, passing Bumping Lake (where you leave the pavement) and bearing right at the junction with Forest Road 1808, to the Lily Lake Trailhead. The trailhead is on the right side of the road, at 3,860 feet elevation.
Parking and trailhead facilities: There is parking for three or four cars at the trailhead but no other facilities. There are campsites and horse facilities at Fish Creek Way Trailhead 0.3 mile east on FR 1800.

The Hike

From the trailhead the tread climbs very gently to the north through the hemlock, red cedar, white pine, fir, and tamarack forest. After less than 100 yards, the trail flattens and soon begins its gentle descent toward Lily Lake, which is reached 0.2 mile from the trailhead.

Lily Lake, at 3,850 feet elevation, has a use path encircling it and an island, which is often used as a campsite. It may be possible to reach the island via floating logs from the lake's north shore. There are trout—some of them good-size—to be caught in the lake.

Miles and Directions

0.0 Lily Lake Trailhead. GPS 46 50.138N 121 21.343W.

0.2 Lily Lake. GPS 46 50.225N 121 21.290W. Turnaround point.

0.4 Return to the trailhead.

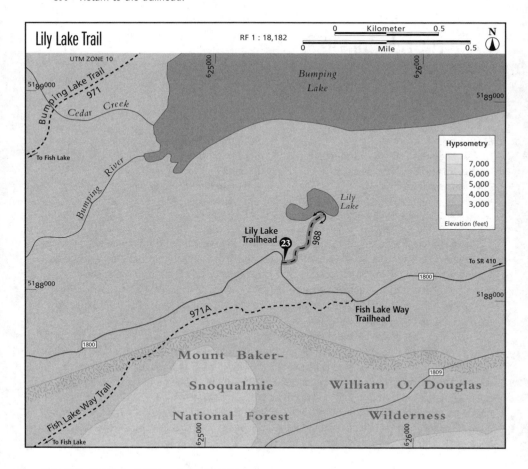

24 Root Lake

Hike from the subalpine ridgetop of Miners Ridge to Root Lake, which is nestled in deep hemlock forest, on the western side of Miners Ridge.

Start: Parking area 50 yards south of the abandoned Miners Ridge Lookout site.
Type of hike: Out-and-back day hike or backpack.
Total distance: 2 miles.
Difficulty: Strenuous but short.
Maps: USGS Bumping Lake quad. The USDA Forest Service William O. Douglas Wilderness map shows the location correctly but is cluttered up and difficult to read for this area.
Permits and fees: None.

Best months: July–September.
Special considerations: This seldom-maintained route requires considerable route-finding skills to follow. Steep snowdrifts may need to be crossed through mid-July. Ski poles may be helpful crossing these drifts. The alternate route mentioned in the options below, which is sometimes used to reach Root Lake, is extremely steep and can be dangerous. It is strongly advised that you not take it.

Finding the trailhead: To reach the abandoned Miners Ridge Lookout site from the **Seattle-Tacoma** area, drive to Enumclaw. From Enumclaw follow State Route 410 for 41 miles east and south to Cayuse Pass. From **Portland,** Oregon, drive north on Interstate 5 for 68 miles to the junction with U.S. Highway 12. Then head east on US 12 for 71 miles (7 miles east of Packwood) to the junction with State Route 123. Turn left on SR 123 and go north for 16.5 miles to Cayuse Pass and the junction with SR 410.

Turn right (left if coming from Seattle-Tacoma) on SR 410 and head east for 22.9 miles, over Chinook Pass and down to the junction with the Bumping Lake Road (Forest Road 1800). Turn southwest off SR 410 onto Bumping Lake Road (FR 1800) and drive 11 miles to Bumping Lake Dam. Continue another 2.5 miles on FR 1800, leaving the pavement, to the junction with Forest Road 1808. Turn right, staying on FR 1800, and head west for 0.7 mile to the junction with Forest Road 1809. Turn left on FR 1809 and drive 3.6 miles to Granite Lake Campground. Continue for another 1.8 miles on FR 1809 to the trailhead. The parking area is on the left side of the road at a switchback on top of the ridgeline. The road continues another 50 yards or so to an abandoned lookout site but is extremely steep. Don't drive up to the lookout site; turning around there can be difficult. FR 1809 is a rough rock road and requires a high-clearance, preferably four-wheel-drive vehicle to be driven safely. The elevation at the parking area is 6,040 feet.

Parking and trailhead facilities: There is parking for three or four vehicles at the parking area but no other facilities. Campsites are available at the Granite Lake Campground 1.8 miles back down FR 1809.

The Hike

From the parking area, walk about 50 yards back down the road the way you came, to a switchback. At the road switchback, there will be a vague path to your

Root Lake.

left (northeast). Take the path and traverse northeasterly along the slope. Soon you will reach and cross the ridgeline. Shortly after crossing the ridge, there is a fork in the path. This fork is at approximately 5,850 feet elevation and below a low point in the ridgeline.

Another option, more scenic but also requiring a bit more climbing, is to follow the roadbed from the parking area up to the abandoned lookout site, then walk down the ridgeline to the point where the path crosses it. Then descend the path to the fork. Either way it is only 0.2 mile to the fork.

Bear left at the fork and descend along the vague trail. Before mid-July there may be lingering and steep snowdrifts to cross along this section of the route. The sometimes hard-to-see trail makes ten switchbacks in 0.5 mile as it descends to about the 5,500-foot level. Then you wind generally northwesterly around, over, and in one case under the blow-downs, through the forest for another 0.3 mile to the shore of Root Lake, at 5,300 feet elevation.

Next to the lake you will find a campsite beneath the western hemlock trees. Both pink and white mountain heather bloom in July next to the lake. Root Lake

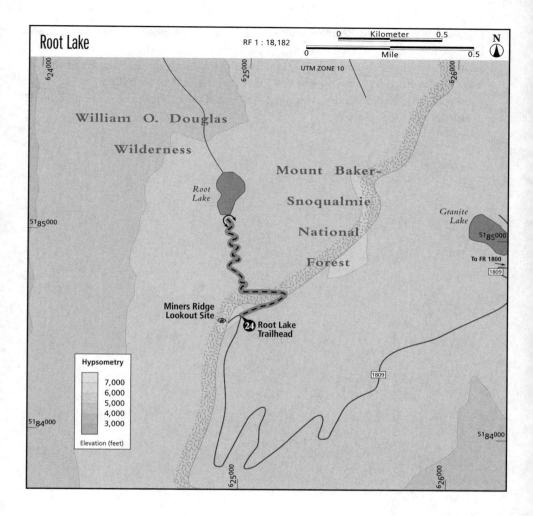

RF 1 : 18,182

0 Kilometer 0.5

0 Mile 0.5

N

UTM ZONE 10

William O. Douglas
Wilderness

Mount Baker-
Snoqualmie
National
Forest

Root
Lake

Granite
Lake

To FR 1800

1809

Miners Ridge
Lookout Site

24 Root Lake
Trailhead

1809

Hypsometry

	7,000
	6,000
	5,000
	4,000
	3,000

Elevation (feet)

got its name from Reuben Root, a miner who was active in the development of the Bumping Mining District in the late 1800s and early 1900s. Some of these mines were located only about 0.7 mile south of the Miners Ridge Lookout site. Return by retracing the route.

Miles and Directions

- **0.0** Parking area near the end of FR 1809. GPS 46 48.177N 121 21.777W.
- **0.2** Fork in route at 5,850 feet elevation. Bear left.
- **1.0** Root Lake. GPS 46 48.456N 121 21.779W. Turnaround point.
- **2.0** Parking area near the end of FR 1809.

Options: A very steep, difficult, and dangerous alternate route is often taken from the old lookout site directly down the semiopen ridge to the northwest. As you approach lake level, the route bears right (north) and heads through the forest to the lake. This route is included not because it is recommended but rather because it is specifically not recommended. It is much easier and safer to take the route described in the "Hike" section above.

Deep Creek Region

T he Deep Creek Region includes the country well south of Bumping Lake and east of Bumping Lake Road. Access is via Forest Roads 1800 and 1808. From Deep Creek Campground and Deep Creek Horse Camp, near the end of FR 1808, Hikes 25 through 29 climb onto a plateau that was once covered with ice. Hike 27, Tumac Mountain Trails, climbs to the summit of a volcano that postdates the ice cap, allowing for a 360-degree view of the lake-dotted

Mount Aix.

plateau. The short walk to Copper City (Hike 31) leads you to the site of a once-bustling mining camp.

On the east side of Deep Creek Road (FR 1808), Hike 33, Mount Aix Trail, takes you to the highest summit in the William O. Douglas Wilderness, where mountain goats are abundant. Hike 32, Richmond Lake via Richmond Mine Trail, climbs through marvelous alpine country, then descends to Richmond Lake, with the option of hiking to even more spectacular Bower Lake. Pear Butte Trail (Hike 30) climbs and traverses the high ridge between Copper Creek and Deep Creek southwest of Mount Aix. These ridges east of FR 1808 offer a much drier climate than the country to the west and are sometimes clear when the western part of the William O. Douglas Wilderness is shrouded in clouds and fog.

25 Twin Sisters Trail 980
Deep Creek Campground to Deep Creek Horse Camp

Hike downhill through highly diversified old-growth forest, checking out the elk tracks and looking for the abundant grouse, as well as other forest dwellers, as you stroll along.

Start: Deep Creek Campground and Trailhead.
Type of hike: Shuttle 1-hour hike.
Total distance: 0.9 mile.
Difficulty: Easy.
Maps: Bumping Lake USGS quad or USDA Forest Service William O. Douglas and Norse Peak Wilderness.

Permits and fees: Northwest Forest Pass.
Best months: Late June through October.
Special considerations: Even though this is a short, easy hike, good hiking boots are recommended.

Finding the trailhead: To reach the Deep Creek Campground and Trailhead from the **Seattle-Tacoma** area, drive to Enumclaw. From Enumclaw follow State Route 410 for 41 miles east and south to Cayuse Pass. From **Portland,** Oregon, drive north on Interstate 5 for 68 miles to the junction with U.S. Highway 12. Then head east on US 12 for 71 miles (7 miles east of Packwood) to the junction with State Route 123. Turn left off US 12 on SR 123 and drive north for 16.5 miles to Cayuse Pass and the junction with SR 410.

Turn right (left if coming from Seattle-Tacoma) on SR 410 and head east for 22.9 miles over Chinook Pass and down to the junction with Bumping Lake Road (Forest Road 1800). Turn right (southwest) on FR 1800 and follow it 13.5 miles (leaving the pavement at Bumping Lake Recreation Area) to the junction with Deep Creek Road (Forest Road 1808). Bear left on FR 1808 and follow it 7 miles to the Deep Creek Campground and Trailhead, where this hike begins. The elevation at this trailhead is 4,280 feet.

To get to Deep Creek Horse Camp, where this hike ends, first drive back down FR 1808 for 0.8 mile. Then turn right on the access road to Deep Creek Horse Camp and Trailhead. It's only a short distance to the parking area and trailhead. The elevation at this trailhead is 4,040 feet.
Parking and trailhead facilities: There is adequate parking, a campground, and a restroom at both trailheads. The Deep Creek Horse Camp also has stock facilities. Stock and stock trailers are prohibited at Deep Creek Campground.

The Hike

Twin Sisters Trail 980 crosses FR 1808 at the northeast end of Deep Creek Campground just before the road begins the campground loop. No sign marks the point where this section of the Twin Sisters Trail leaves the road. The point where the route begins is directly across FR 1808 from the trailhead sign and wilderness registration box. Behind the sign the Twin Sisters Trail leads southwest and south to Twin Sisters Lakes.

Pink wintergreen close to lower Twin Sisters Trail.

As you leave the road, at 4,280 feet elevation, the trail heads northeast. In a few yards the trail appears to fork. Bear left here, staying on the main trail. Alaska cedar, hemlock, true firs, and a few western white pines, of varying ages, line the route as you begin your gradual descent. Beneath the tall timber, huckleberry bushes, bear-grass and white-flowered rhododendrons add to the mix of flora.

If the trail is dusty or muddy, look at it carefully and notice the tracks. Elk tracks are most common, but there will also be deer tracks. Of course, if a party with horses has recently used the route, there will be only horse tracks. A little less than 0.2 mile into the hike, the tread crosses a small stream. Grouse are often seen close to this stream. By now you have lost about 100 feet of elevation. The course continues its

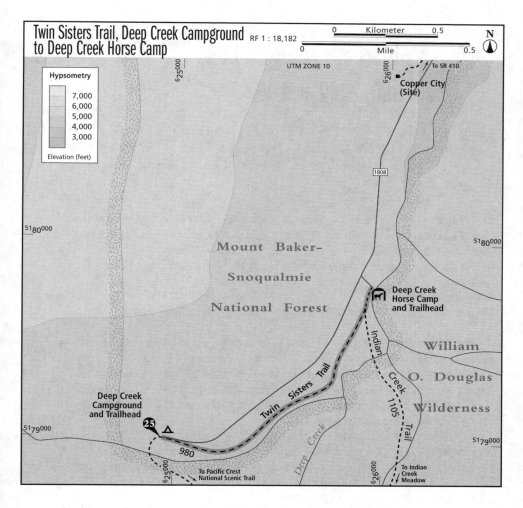

Twin Sisters Trail, Deep Creek Campground to Deep Creek Horse Camp RF 1 : 18,182

Kilometer 0 — 0.5
Mile 0 — 0.5

N

UTM ZONE 10

Hypsometry

7,000
6,000
5,000
4,000
3,000

Elevation (feet)

To SR 410

Copper City
(Site)

1808

Mount Baker–

Snoqualmie

National Forest

Deep Creek
Horse Camp
and Trailhead

Indian

William

O. Douglas

Creek

Twin Sisters Trail

1105

Wilderness

Deep Creek
Campground
and Trailhead

25

Trail

980

Deep Creek

To Pacific Crest
National Scenic Trail

To Indian
Creek
Meadow

gentle descent for about another 0.5 mile, then flattens out. At 0.8 mile from the trailhead, you will reach the junction with the Indian Creek Trail 1105. From here on to the horse camp trailhead, the two trails follow the same route. Several side trails leave the main trail in the next 0.1 mile. These trails lead to stock users' campsites. Follow the main trail to the Deep Creek Horse Camp and Trailhead, at 4,040 feet elevation, 0.9 mile from where you started.

Elk often use the meadow at the horse camp. If there are no parties camping here and you are here in the early morning or evening, you may catch sight of one or a group of these large animals.

Miles and Directions

0.0 Deep Creek Campground and Trailhead. GPS 46 45.156N 121 21.684W.

0.8 Junction with Indian Creek Trail 1105. Bear left.

0.9 Deep Creek Horse Camp and Trailhead. GPS 46 45.578N 121 21.061W.

26 Twin Sisters and Fryingpan Lakes
Trails 980, 2000, and 43

Climb from Deep Creek Trailhead to the plateau lands of the southwestern part of the William O. Douglas Wilderness. Then explore the lakes, meadows, and subalpine forest of the plateau as you watch and listen for the magnificent elk that abound in the area.

Start: Deep Creek Campground and Trailhead.
Type of hike: Out-and-back day hike or backpack, with a shuttle option.
Total distance: 11.6 miles round-trip to Little Snow Lake.
Difficulty: Moderate.
Maps: USDA Forest Service William O. Douglas

and Norse Peak Wilderness or Bumping Lake, Spiral Butte, and White Pass USGS quads.
Permits and fees: Northwest Forest Pass and William O. Douglas Wilderness permit.
Best months: July–September.
Special considerations: During July and early August, mosquitoes can be very bad.

Finding the trailhead: To reach the Deep Creek Campground and Trailhead, drive north from **Portland,** Oregon, on Interstate 5 for 68 miles to the junction with U.S. Highway 12. Then head east on US 12 for 71 miles (7 miles east of Packwood) to the junction with State Route 123. Turn north off US 12 on SR 123 and go 16.5 miles to Cayuse Pass and the junction with State Route 410. From the **Seattle-Tacoma** area, drive to Enumclaw. From Enumclaw follow SR 410 for 41 miles east and south to Cayuse Pass.

Turn left (right if coming from Portland) on SR 410 and head east for 22.9 miles over Chinook Pass and down to the junction with Bumping Lake Road (Forest Road 1800). Turn right (southwest) on FR 1800 and follow it 13.5 miles (leaving the pavement at Bumping Lake Recreation Area) to the junction with Deep Creek Road (Forest Road 1808). Bear left on FR 1808 and follow it 7 miles to the Deep Creek Campground and Trailhead.
Parking and trailhead facilities: Adequate parking, a campground, and a restroom are available at the trailhead.

The Hike

The Twin Sisters Trail leaves the Deep Creek Campground and Trailhead heading to the southwest. Shortly the trail crosses a wooden bridge over Deep Creek, at 4,280 feet elevation, where you enter the William O. Douglas Wilderness. After crossing the creek the route climbs to the southeast, through a mature forest of Douglas fir, cedar, hemlock, and true firs.

At about 1.6 miles into the hike, the route passes below a short cliff where Davidson's penstemons cling to the rocks above the trail. Alpine spiraea and white-flowered rhododendron grow from the rocky slope below the cliffs. Soon the trail turns west above a small canyon. The stream in the small canyon forms

Fryingpan Lake.

pools, which contain, and sometimes strand, trout. You will reach the junction with the Sand Ridge Trail 1104, next to Little Twin Sisters Lake, at 5,170 feet elevation and 1.8 miles from the trailhead. To the left the Sand Ridge Trail heads southeast, passing east of Tumac Mountain to a trailhead on US 12.

Turn right at the junction, staying on the Twin Sisters Trail. First you hike along the northwest shore of Little Twin Sisters Lake, where there are several campsites. Please camp at least 100 feet back from the shoreline. From Little Twin Sisters Lake, the trail continues west, getting close to Big Twin Sisters Lake 0.5 mile from the junction with Sand Ridge Trail. Soon you reach the junction with the Big Twin Trail 980b.

The Big Twin Trail turns to the right to reach campsites along the southwestern shore of Big Twin Sisters Lake. There are several campsites along the lake, but much of the area is closed for restoration. Please respect these restoration areas and don't enter them. As with Little Twin Sisters Lake (and all the lakes in the William O. Douglas Wilderness), regulations require that you camp at least 100 feet back from the lakeshore.

Twin Sisters and Fryingpan Lakes Trails; Tumac Mountain Trails

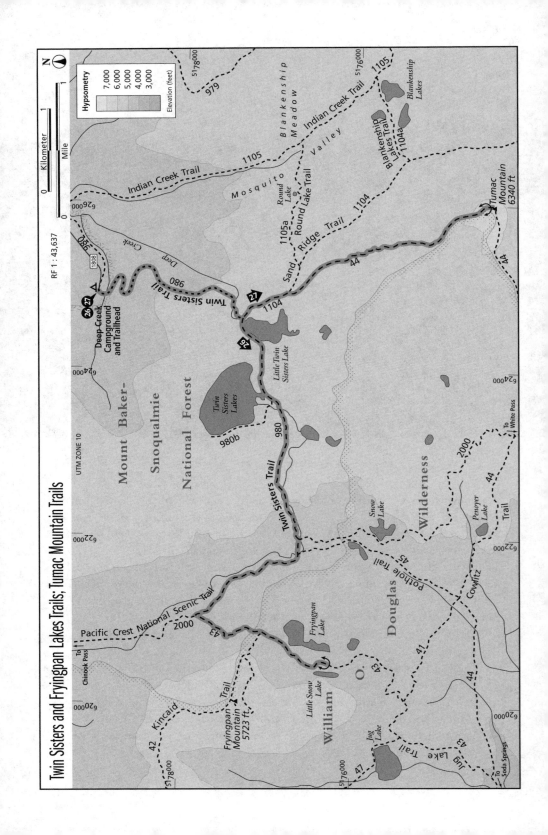

After passing the junction with the Big Twin Trail, the Twin Sisters Trail leads southwest for a little ways before turning west again. You will pass several small ponds as you begin the gradual descent toward the junction with the Pacific Crest National Scenic Trail 2000 (PCT). Before reaching the PCT the trail becomes braided and eroded in places. Just before getting to the junction, the course crosses a rocky streambed, which is often dry by July. You reach the junction with the PCT, at 4,870 feet elevation, 3.7 miles from the Deep Creek Campground and Trailhead. This junction is the end of the Twin Sisters Trail. At the junction the forest is somewhat larger and more mature than what you have been hiking through for the last couple of miles.

Turn right on the PCT and wind downhill for 0.1 mile to the junction with the Pothole Trail 45. The Pothole Trail turns left to head south for 2 miles to a junction with the Cowlitz Trail 44 near Penoyer Lake. As its name implies, the Pothole Trail passes many small ponds along the way. On the USGS White Pass quad map (1988 vintage), there is a trail shown turning right off the Pothole Trail a short distance south of this junction and heading west to Fryingpan Lake, thus making the distance to the lake much shorter. This trail has been abandoned and is very hard to follow. There are several elk trails in this area that are far more well used than is the trail shown on the map. If you are an expert at route finding and the use of a compass, it is possible to make your way through this route to Fryingpan Lake, but if you're not, getting lost could be very easy.

Bear right (straight ahead to the west), staying on the PCT as you leave the junction with the Pothole Trail. Soon the route turns north along the side of a meadow. The streambed that you crossed just before getting on the PCT runs down the middle of this meadow. Leaving the meadow the tread heads northwest, and 1 mile from the junction with the Pothole Trail, you will reach the junction with the Jug Lake Trail 43, at 4,670 feet elevation. There is no sign at this junction, just a weathered signpost.

At this junction the route to Fryingpan Lake leaves the PCT. Turn left and hike southwest from the junction on the Jug Lake Trail, through subalpine forest and small meadows. Lupine, huckleberry bushes, and beargrass line the tread as you climb gently. One-half mile from the junction, there will be a rather faint path to your right. This path is the Kincaid Trail 42, which leads west and south for about 9 miles to the Cowlitz Trailhead at the end of Forest Road 4510. There is no sign at this junction and it's fairly easy to miss. At the junction you have reached 4,810 feet elevation.

Continue southwest on the Jug Lake Trail and soon enter a meadow, where Fryingpan Lake comes into view ahead and to the left. As you get closer to the lake, there is a signpost next to the trail; the sign on it just says TRAIL. This is the west end of the now abandoned trail mentioned above that connected the Pothole Trail with Fryingpan Lake.

There are several campsites in the timbered areas around Fryingpan Lake.

Please don't camp in the meadows or too close to the shoreline. Most of the lake's western shore is meadowland. These meadows are heavily used by elk—be quiet and watch for them morning and evening. If you are here on a September evening, listen for bugling bull elk. Parties with stock also use these meadows for grazing, so at times they are closely cropped.

After passing the sign and abandoned trail, the Jug Lake Trail continues southwest through meadows and timber, staying well west of Fryingpan Lake. About a quarter mile from the junction with the abandoned trail, you will reach the shore of Little Snow Lake, where there is another possible campsite. Little Snow Lake is a shallow, long, and fairly slender pool. Lily pads grow in the shallows along its shores. The slope on the lake's western side is a good example of old-growth true-fir forest with some very large trees.

Fryingpan Lake and Little Snow Lake make excellent places to camp for a couple of days to explore the surrounding country. It's only a little over a mile from Little Snow Lake to Jug Lake via Trails 43 and 47, making it within easy hiking distance. Retrace your steps back to Deep Creek Campground and Trailhead or see the options below to make a one-way hike by continuing on the Jug Lake Trail.

Miles and Directions

0.0 Deep Creek Campground and Trailhead. GPS 46 45.157N 121 21.691W.

1.8 Junction with Sand Ridge Trail 1104 at Little Twin Sisters Lake. GPS 46 44.289N 121 22.144W. Turn right.

2.4 Junction with Big Twin Trail 980b next to Big Twin Sisters Lake. Bear left.

3.7 Junction with Pacific Crest National Scenic Trail 2000. 46 43.940N 121 24.192W. Turn right.

3.8 Junction with Pothole Trail 45. GPS 46 43.939N 121 24.312W. Proceed straight ahead.

4.8 Junction with Jug Lake Trail 43. GPS 46 44.604N 121 24.918W. Turn Left.

5.3 Junction with Kincaid Trail 42. Proceed straight ahead.

5.6 Fryingpan Lake.

5.8 Little Snow Lake. Turnaround point.

11.6 Deep Creek Campground and Trailhead.

Options: This out-and-back hike can easily be made into a one-way trip by continuing on the Jug Lake Trail for about 2.5 miles from Fryingpan Lake to the junction with Cowlitz Trail 44. Then turn right (west) and hike 2.3 miles to the Soda Springs Campground and Trailhead. This trip requires a car shuttle to Soda Springs Campground and Trailhead. The Jug Lake Trail bypasses Jug Lake. The lake is 0.1 mile to the right (northwest) of the Jug Lake Trail on the Judkin Trail 47, about 1 mile southwest from Little Snow Lake.

To reach Soda Springs Campground and Trailhead by car, drive back the way you came to SR 410. Turn left and drive 22.9 miles west to Cayuse Pass. Turn left and drive 16.5 miles south to the junction with US 12. Turn left and drive northeast for a little more than a mile to the junction with Forest Road 45. Turn left (north), on FR 45 and drive 0.3 mile, then bear left (northeast) on FR 4510. Follow FR 4510 for 4.1 miles to the junction with Forest Road 052, signed to Soda Springs Campground. Turn right (east) on FR 052 and go 0.6 mile to Soda Springs Trailhead, which is at the northeastern corner of the campground.

27 Tumac Mountain
Trails 980, 1104, and 44

Hike from Deep Creek Canyon to Twin Sisters Lakes. Then climb to the 6,340-foot-high summit of Tumac Mountain in the center of a lake-dotted plateau.

See map on page 132.
Start: Deep Creek Campground and Trailhead.
Type of hike: Out-and-back day hike with loop option.
Total distance: 8.2 miles to Tumac Mountain.
Difficulty: Moderate to strenuous.
Maps: USDA Forest Service William O. Doug-

las and Norse Peak Wilderness or Bumping Lake and Spiral Butte USGS quads.
Permits and fees: Northwest Forest Pass and William O. Douglas Wilderness permit.
Best months: Mid-July through September.
Special considerations: During July and early August, mosquitoes can be very bad.

Finding the trailhead: To reach the Deep Creek Campground and Trailhead, drive north from **Portland,** Oregon, on Interstate 5 for 68 miles to the junction with U.S. Highway 12. Then head east on US 12 for 71 miles (7 miles east of Packwood) to the junction with State Route 123. Turn north off US 12 on SR 123 and drive 16.5 miles to Cayuse Pass and the junction with State Route 410. From the **Seattle-Tacoma** area, drive to Enumclaw. From Enumclaw follow SR 410 for 41 miles east and south to Cayuse Pass.

Turn left (right if coming from Portland) on SR 410 and head east for 22.9 miles over Chinook Pass and down to the junction with Bumping Lake Road (Forest Road 1800). Turn right (southwest) on FR 1800 and follow it 13.5 miles (leaving the pavement at Bumping Lake Recreation Area) to the junction with Deep Creek Road (Forest Road 1808). Bear left on FR 1808 and follow it for 7 miles to the Deep Creek Campground and Trailhead.
Parking and trailhead facilities: Adequate parking, a campground, and a restroom are available at the trailhead.

The Hike

The first 1.8 miles of this hike follows the Twin Sisters Trail 980. The trail leads southwest from the trailhead. In 150 yards the route crosses a wooden bridge over Deep Creek, at 4,280 feet elevation. Once across the bridge the route enters the William O. Douglas Wilderness. Then the tread climbs to the southeast, through a mature forest of true firs, cedar, Douglas fir, and hemlock. As you cross a rocky slope that is

Mount Adams from the summit of Tumac Mountain.

mostly covered with brush 0.6 mile into the hike, note the two species of penstemon (woodland and small-flowered) growing almost side by side next to the trail.

A mile farther along, as the route passes below a short cliff, note a third species of penstemon (Davidson's) clinging to the rocks above the trail here. White-flowered rhododendron and alpine spiraea also grow from the rocky slope below these cliffs. Soon the trail turns west. Below and to your left here is a small canyon with a little stream in it. The stream forms pools as it descends through the canyon. These pools contain trout, which can sometimes be seen breaking the water's surface.

The course reaches the junction with the Sand Ridge Trail 1104, next to the smaller of the Twin Sisters Lakes, 1.8 miles from the trailhead. To the right from the junction, the Twin Sisters Trail heads west, passing the larger Twin Sisters Lake, to a junction with the Pacific Crest National Scenic Trail 2000.

Turn left at the junction to continue on toward Tumac Mountain. The route skirts the eastern side of the lake, passing several campsites. Then you'll traverse open subalpine woods and meadows to the junction with Trail 44. The opposite (western) end of Trail 44 is called the Cowlitz Trail, but the portion of it from here to the junction with the Pacific Crest Trail is more commonly known as the Tumac Mountain Trail. The trail sign at the junction just calls it "Trail 44." The junction with Trail 44 is at 5,220 feet elevation, 0.4 mile from where you left the Twin Sisters Trail and 2.2 miles from the trailhead.

Bear right at the junction, heading south-southeast on Trail 44. Shortly after leaving the junction, there is a sluggish stream to the right of the trail. Pink mountain heather, lupine, and beargrass complement the trail's sides between the stands of subalpine fir and hemlock as you climb gently but steadily toward Tumac Mountain. The route passes a tiny pond 0.4 mile from the junction, then crosses a streambed that will likely be dry. There will be another tiny pond to the right of the trail 0.3 mile farther along.

After passing this pond the trail begins to climb more steeply. A quarter mile past the pond, the tread makes a couple of switchbacks. As you climb between the clumps of both white and pink mountain heather, look to your right for a view of Nelson Ridge. The trail crosses a small cinder slope 0.4 mile above the switchbacks, and then you'll make a couple more switchbacks. Above these switchbacks the route enters a larger cinder slope, at about 6,100 feet elevation. The trail climbs this slope most of the rest of the way to the summit of Tumac Mountain, making three switchbacks along the way. Parts of this slope are covered with pink and white mountain heather and lupine. At the third switchback there is a path to the left that climbs along the ridgeline to the summit; stay on the trail—it's easier. You will reach the summit of Tumac Mountain 4.1 miles from the Deep Creek Campground and Trailhead.

Tumac Mountain is a postglacial volcano, probably less than 10,000 years old. It's a complex cone, built of both cinders and lava. The name "Tumac" is a poorly derived contraction of "Two Macs," possibly McCallister and McCall, who once ran sheep on this plateau.

The view from this 6,340-foot-high summit is wonderful in all directions; sit on one of the blocks that were once the foundation of the lookout that stood here and take it in. To the south are the craggy summits of Goat Rocks and the bulky rounded summit of Mount Adams, as well as the White Pass Ski Area. To the southwest, Mount St. Helens's blown-out crater lets out an occasional puff of steam and/or ash. To the west is the Tatoosh Range, and to its right (northwest) the glacier-covered slopes and jagged ridges of Mount Rainier dominate the scene. Far in the distance to the northeast is the rugged Stuart Range, crowned by Mount Stuart. Closer by, also to the northeast, are Nelson Ridge and Mount Aix, and south of Mount Aix is Bismarck Peak. To the southeast are Shellrock Peak and Ironstone Mountain. Return as you came or see the options below for an alternate return trip.

Miles and Directions

0.0 Deep Creek Campground and Trailhead. GPS 46 45.157N 121 21.691W.

1.8 Junction with Sand Ridge Trail 1104. GPS 46 44.289N 121 22.144W. Turn left.

Tumac Mountain Trail at the top of the cinder slope.

2.2 Junction with Trail 44. GPS 46 44.004N 121 21.887W. Bear right.

4.1 Summit of Tumac Mountain. GPS 46 42.735N 121 21.186W. Turnaround point.

8.2 Deep Creek Campground and Trailhead.

Options: If you wish to add 4.4 miles and make this a loop hike, continue on Trail 44 from the top of Tumac Mountain. Leaving the summit the route first makes a couple of descending switchbacks on the mountain's south slope. Then you hike southwest across the forested landscape to the junction with the Shellrock Trail 1142, 1.7 miles from the summit. Turn right, staying on Trail 44, and go 0.2 mile northwest to the junction with the Pacific Crest National Scenic Trail 2000 (PCT). Turn right on the PCT and hike northwest for 3 miles to the junction with the Twin Sisters Trail 980. Turn right on the Twin Sisters Trail and hike 1.9 miles east to the junction with the Sand Ridge Trail 1104. Turn left at the junction, staying on the Twin Sisters Trail, and descend the way you hiked in to the Deep Creek Campground and Trailhead.

28 Round Lake Trail 1105a

Hike through subalpine forest and meadows, passing tiny Round Lake, from the Indian Creek Trail to the Sand Ridge Trail.

Start: Junction with the Indian Creek Trail 2.4 miles south of the Deep Creek Horse Camp Trailhead.
Type of hike: Internal day hike.
Total distance: 1.1 miles on Round Lake Trail.
Difficulty: Easy.
Maps: USDA Forest Service William O. Douglas and Norse Peak Wilderness or Spiral Butte USGS quad.

Permits and fees: William O. Douglas Wilderness permit and a Northwest Forest Pass.
Best months: July–September.
Special considerations: Much of the Round Lake Trail is rough and eroded and is also braided in places. Mosquitoes can be very thick along this route in July.

Finding the trailhead: To reach the Deep Creek Horse Camp and Trailhead, drive north from **Portland,** Oregon, on Interstate 5 for 68 miles to the junction with U.S. Highway 12. Then head east on US 12 for 71 miles (7 miles east of Packwood) to the junction with State Route 123. Turn left off US 12 onto SR 123 and go north for 16.5 miles to Cayuse Pass and the junction with State Route 410. From the **Seattle-Tacoma** area, drive to Enumclaw. From Enumclaw follow SR 410 for 41 miles east and south to Cayuse Pass.

Turn right (left if coming from Seattle-Tacoma) on SR 410 and head east for 22.9 miles over Chinook Pass and down to the junction with Bumping Lake Road (Forest Road 1800). Turn right (southwest) on FR 1800 and follow it 13.5 miles (leaving the pavement at Bumping Lake Recreation Area) to the junction with Deep Creek Road (Forest Road 1808). Bear left on FR 1808 and follow it 6.2 miles to the Deep Creek Horse Camp and Trailhead, at 4,040 feet elevation. Then hike 2.4 miles south on the Indian Creek Trail to the junction with the Round Lake Trail, where this hike begins.

Parking and trailhead facilities: Adequate parking, restrooms, stock facilities, and campsites are available at the trailhead.

The Hike

The junction with Indian Creek Trail 1105, where this hike begins, is in beautiful Blankenship Meadow, at 5,150 feet elevation. There is a trail sign marking the junction, but the Round Lake Trail may not be visible on the ground here. To begin the hike along Round Lake Trail, head west across the meadow from the trail sign. In about 30 yards you will come to a rock cairn. Next to the cairn the path shows up as you continue west into the small subalpine timber. In a short distance the tread crosses a rough and rocky streambed that may or may not have water, depending on the season. To your left at the crossing, the sluggish stream forms a pool where common goldeneye ducks can often be seen.

Round Lake.

After crossing the rocky streambed, the course continues west through small meadows and timber. In slightly less than 0.25 mile, you will cross another streambed and shortly reach the southern shore of tiny Round Lake. At the lake you are 0.4 mile from the Indian Creek Trail and have dropped to 5,140 feet elevation. There are usually plentiful signs of elk around the lake; in fact, this entire trail offers a good possibility of seeing these magnificent creatures.

Just after passing Round Lake, the route crosses another streambed and begins to climb. The climb is gentle at first but soon steepens, gaining a couple of hundred feet of elevation in about 0.2 mile. After topping out at 5,350 feet elevation, the tread descends slightly to its end at a junction with the Sand Ridge Trail 1104, 1.1 miles from the Indian Creek Trail junction, at 5,310 feet elevation. Return the way you came or take the loop described in the options below.

Miles and Directions

0.0   Junction with Indian Creek Trail 1105. GPS 46 43.928N 121 20.454W. Turn right.

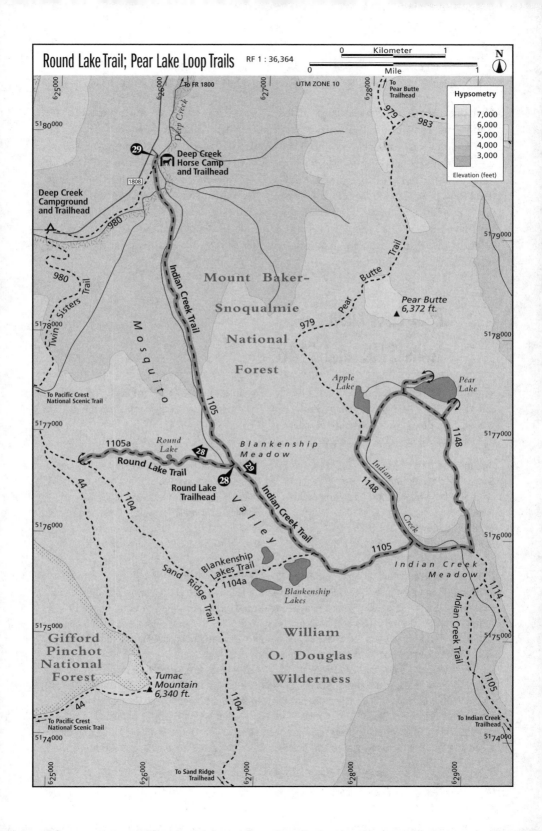

Round Lake Trail; Pear Lake Loop Trails

RF 1 : 36,364

Kilometer

Mile

UTM ZONE 10

N

Hypsometry

	7,000
	6,000
	5,000
	4,000
	3,000

Elevation (feet)

To FR 1800

To Pear Butte
Trailhead

979   983

Deep Creek

29

Deep Creek
Horse Camp
and Trailhead

1808

Deep Creek
Campground
and Trailhead

980

Pear Butte Trail

980

Twin Sisters Trail

Indian Creek Trail

Mount Baker–

Snoqualmie

National

Forest

Pear Butte
6,372 ft.

To Pacific Crest
National Scenic Trail

Mosquito

1105

979

Apple
Lake

Pear
Lake

1148

1105a

Round
Lake

Blankenship
Meadow

Round Lake Trail

28

29

Indian

1148

Creek

Round Lake
Trailhead

28

Valley

Indian Creek Trail

1105

Indian Creek
Meadow

44

1104

Sand Ridge Trail

Blankenship
Lakes Trail

1104a

Blankenship
Lakes

1114

Indian Creek Trail

Gifford
Pinchot
National
Forest

Tumac
Mountain
6,340 ft.

William

O. Douglas

Wilderness

1104

1105

44

To Pacific Crest
National Scenic Trail

To Indian Creek
Trailhead

To Sand Ridge
Trailhead

0.4 Round Lake.

1.1 Junction with Sand Ridge Trail 1104. GPS 46 43.942N 121 21.633W. Turnaround point.

Options: Make a 6.9-mile loop hike by combining this hike with parts of Sand Ridge and Twin Sisters Trails. To make the loop, first hike along Indian Creek Trail to the junction with the Round Lake Trail. Then take the Round Lake Trail as described above to the junction with the Sand Ridge Trail 1104. Turn right on the Sand Ridge Trail and follow it for 0.7 mile to the junction with the Twin Sisters Trail 980, at Little Twin Sisters Lake. Turn right on the Twin Sisters Trail and descend for 1.8 miles to Deep Creek Campground and Trailhead. Cross FR 1808 at the northern edge of the campground and continue to descend along the lower section of the Twin Sisters Trail for 0.9 mile to Deep Creek Horse Camp and Trailhead, where you started this hike.

29 Pear Lake Loop
Trails 1105 and 1148

Climb from the bottom of Deep Creek Canyon to beautiful Blankenship Meadow. Then traverse the plateau to sparkling Pear Lake before looping back through Indian Creek Meadows and returning to the trailhead.

See map on page 141.
Start: Deep Creek Horse Camp and Trailhead.
Type of hike: Lollipop-loop backpack or day hike.
Total distance: 10.7 miles.
Difficulty: Moderate.

Maps: USDA Forest Service Norse Peak and William O. Douglas Wilderness or Bumping Lake and Spiral Butte USGS quads.
Permits and fees: Northwest Forest Pass and William O. Douglas Wilderness permit.
Best months: July–September.

Finding the trailhead: To reach the Deep Creek Horse Camp and Trailhead, drive north from **Portland,** Oregon, on Interstate 5 for 68 miles to the junction with U.S. Highway 12. Then head east on US 12 for 71 miles (7 miles east of Packwood) to the junction with State Route 123. Turn left off US 12 on SR 123 and drive north for 16.5 miles to Cayuse Pass and the junction with State Route 410. From the **Seattle-Tacoma** area, drive to Enumclaw. From Enumclaw follow SR 410 for 41 miles east and south to Cayuse Pass.

Turn left (right if coming from Portland) on SR 410 and head east for 22.9 miles over Chinook Pass and down to the junction with Bumping Lake Road (Forest Road 1800). Turn right (southwest) on FR 1800 and follow it 13.5 miles (leaving the pavement at Bumping Lake Recreation Area) to the junction with Deep Creek Road (Forest Road 1808). Bear left on FR 1808 and follow it 6.2 miles to the Deep Creek Horse Camp and Trailhead entrance. Turn left, leaving FR 1808, and drive a short distance to the parking area and trailhead. The elevation at the trailhead is 4,040 feet.

Parking and trailhead facilities: Adequate parking, restrooms, stock facilities, and campsites are available at the trailhead.

The Hike

Fill out your wilderness permit then begin your hike along Indian Creek Trail 1105. Hike south, leaving the trailhead, and in 0.1 mile you will come to a junction. To the right is Twin Sisters Trail 980. Bear left at the junction, staying on the Indian Creek Trail. Soon the route crosses two streambeds that will probably be dry. Shortly after crossing the streambeds, the course enters the William O. Douglas Wilderness. There is a pond below the trail to your right 0.4 mile from the trailhead as the route begins to climb. Another 0.3 mile of hiking brings you to the crossing of a small stream. By midsummer this stream is usually intermittent or dry completely.

One mile from the trailhead, the tread crosses another small stream at 4,430 feet elevation. The route makes a switchback to the left at this crossing. This is the first of six switchbacks that allow you to climb about 100 feet of elevation in the next 0.1 mile. Shortly the track crosses another small stream, then makes a couple more switchbacks before crossing two more tiny streams. Many of these streams may be dry by late summer. You will cross a wooden bridge over yet another small stream 2.2 miles into the hike. Along the trail, pink mountain heather and lupine bloom in mid-July. After crossing the bridge the trail flattens out, and soon you'll enter Blankenship Meadow. The junction with the Round Lake Trail 1105a is reached at 5,150 feet elevation, 0.1 mile after entering the meadow. Round Lake Trail leads west, passing small Round Lake in 0.4 mile and reaching a junction with the Sand Ridge Trail 1104 in 1.1 miles.

From the junction with the Round Lake Trail, the Indian Creek Trail continues across the meadow to the southeast, then bears left into the timber. The trail has been rerouted here, slightly east of where it used to be. The old route is deeply eroded and braided and the trail was in need of rerouting. The highest point on this hike, 5,260 feet, is reached on this rerouted section. The Blankenship Lakes Trail 1104a turns to the right (west-southwest) 0.8 mile from the junction with the Round Lake Trail, after passing the rerouted section. See the options below for information about Blankenship Lakes.

Bear left at the junction, staying on the Indian Creek Trail, and descend gently to the southeast. In 0.2 mile the course crosses a tiny stream, and another 0.5 mile of hiking brings you to the junction with the Pear Lake Trail 1148. The junction with the Pear Lake Trail is at 4,970 feet elevation, 3.9 miles from the Deep Creek Horse Camp and Trailhead.

Turn left (north-northwest) at the junction, leaving the Indian Creek Trail. The Pear Lake Trail climbs very gently through subalpine forest and openings. The lupine, which nearly covers many of the openings, blooms in mid-July. Indian Creek is to your right as you hike toward the junction with the Pear Butte Trail 979, which is reached in 0.7 mile. At the junction with the Pear Butte Trail, turn

Pear Lake.

right, staying on the Pear Lake Trail, and quickly cross Indian Creek. Indian Creek is just a small stream here. After crossing the creek the trail heads northeast, staying south of Apple Lake and the large meadow that nearly surrounds it. In 0.4 mile there will be a path to your left.

The path descends a few feet to a bridge over the small stream that connects Apple and Pear Lakes. You can cross the bridge and follow the path east for a short distance to the northern shore of Pear Lake, at 5,060 feet elevation, where there are several good campsites. If you camp here, be sure to follow the wilderness regulations and camp at least 100 feet back from the water. There are lots of trout in Pear Lake, which is much deeper than the marshy Apple Lake.

After passing the path to the north shore of Pear Lake, the Pear Lake Trail heads southeast, skirting the lake through the timber. In 0.3 mile there is another path to the left that descends to the southeast corner of the lake. Past this path the Pear Lake Trail turns south and climbs slightly, reaching 5,170 feet elevation in 0.3 mile. Then the route descends for 0.8 mile to Indian Creek Meadows and another junction with the Indian Creek Trail. This junction is at 4,940 feet elevation and 6.4 miles into the hike.

Turn right (northwest) at the junction onto the Indian Creek Trail and cross the meadow and Indian Creek. After crossing the meadow, it is about 0.2 mile to the junction with the Pear Lake Trail, where you left Indian Creek Trail to make the loop. From the junction head west, then northwest, staying on the Indian Creek Trail for 3.9 miles back to the Deep Creek Horse Camp and Trailhead, where you started this hike.

Miles and Directions

0.0 Deep Creek Horse Camp and Trailhead. GPS 46 45.578N 121 21.061W.

2.4 Junction with Round Lake Trail 1105a. GPS 46 43.928N 121 20.454W. Proceed straight ahead.

3.2 Junction with Blankenship Lakes Trail 1104a. GPS 46 43.446N 121 19.868W. Bear left.

3.9 Junction with Pear Lake Trail 1148. GPS 46 43.477N 121 19.115W. Turn left.

4.6 Junction with Pear Butte Trail 979. GPS 46 44.035N 121 19.503W. Turn right.

5.0 Pear Lake.

6.4 Junction with Indian Creek Trail 1105. GPS 46 43.415N 121 18.632W. Turn right.

6.8 Junction with Pear Lake Trail, ending the loop. GPS 46 43.477N 121 19.115W. Bear left.

10.7 Deep Creek Horse Camp and Trailhead.

Options: From its junction with the Indian Creek Trail, it is only a short distance west on the Blankenship Lakes Trail 1104a to the easternmost of the Blankenship Lakes. In fact, the lake is just out of view from the Indian Creek Trail. The rocky shoreline of this lake makes it the most picturesque of the three Blankenship Lakes. At some points on the rocks surrounding the lake, glacial scratches can be observed. The movement of the ice cap that once covered this plateau caused these scratches. Many possible campsites exist around Blankenship Lakes, but be sure to camp back at least 100 feet from the shorelines.

30 Pear Butte Trail 979

Although this is not the easiest way to reach Pear Lake, it is much more scenic than the easier route. The views from the ridgeline between the Deep Creek and Copper Creek drainages rival anything to be found in the William O. Douglas Wilderness.

Start: Pear Butte Trailhead.
Type of hike: Out-and-back backpack with an easier shuttle-return option.
Total distance: 16.2 miles out and back to Pear Lake.
Difficulty: Strenuous.
Maps: USDA Forest Service William O. Douglas and Norse Peak Wilderness or Bumping Lake and Spiral Butte USGS quads.

Permits and fees: William O. Douglas Wilderness permit; a Northwest Forest Pass will be needed if you make the optional shuttle hike.
Best months: July–September.
Special considerations: There is no water for several miles along this ridge trail; carry all you will need.

Finding the trailhead: To reach the Pear Butte Trailhead from the **Seattle-Tacoma** area, drive to Enumclaw. From Enumclaw follow State Route 410 for 41 miles east and south to Cayuse Pass. If you are coming from **Portland,** Oregon, drive north on Interstate 5 for 68 miles to the junction with U.S. Highway 12. Then head east on US 12 for 71 miles (7 miles east of Packwood) to the junction with State Route 123. Turn left off US 12 on SR 123 and go north for 16.5 miles to Cayuse Pass and the junction with SR 410.

Turn right (left if coming from Seattle-Tacoma) on SR 410 and head east 3.7 miles to Chinook Pass. From Chinook Pass continue east on SR 410 for another 19.2 miles to the junction with Bumping Lake Road (Forest Road 1800). Turn right (southwest) on FR 1800 and follow it 13.5 miles (leaving the pavement at Bumping Lake Recreation Area) to the junction with Deep Creek Road (Forest Road 1808). Bear left on FR 1808 and follow it for another 1.8 miles to the Pear Butte Trail Trailhead. The trail leaves from the left side of FR 1808, but the trailhead sign and wilderness permits are on the right. The elevation at the trailhead is 3,660 feet.
Parking and trailhead facilities: Parking for several cars as well as a couple of rustic campsites are available at the trailhead.

The Hike

After getting your wilderness permit, cross FR 1808 and climb a few feet up the wide trail. The trail flattens for a short distance, then begins to climb again 0.2 mile from the trailhead. The route climbs up a small ridge. Then you cross a small draw and continue to climb through the forest of western white pine, lodgepole pine, firs, and hemlock. About 0.3 mile after crossing the small draw, the tread enters the William O. Douglas Wilderness. There is a small metal sign marking the wilderness boundary. Just after passing the wilderness boundary, the tread descends to cross another draw. Then you begin to climb again, with the rushing waters of Copper Creek far below to your left. Here, 0.6 mile from the trailhead, the trail appears to

Bismarck Peak from the Pear Butte Trail.

fork. Bear right; the left fork heads down into the creek bed to an abandoned mine. The route follows the ridgeline well above the creek for a ways, then bears right, heading south-southwest away from it.

One and eight-tenths miles into the hike, the route makes the first of eighteen switchbacks that take you up to the main ridgeline. In this fairly steep, sometimes rough and rocky, 0.6-mile-long set of switchbacks, the route gains over 500 feet of elevation. As you trudge up the switchbacks, the view of Nelson Ridge and Mount Aix opens up to the east. Above the switchbacks the trail turns left (south) to climb along the ridgeline. After climbing along the ridgeline for 0.4 mile, there is a viewpoint a few steep yards to your right. The timber, which now is mostly small Alaska cedar, white-bark pine, and subalpine fir, thins out to allow views in all directions. Far below to the north, Bumping Lake, surrounded by green forest, sparkles in the sunlight below American Ridge. The alpine peaks of Nelson Ridge make up the eastern skyline. Nearby to the south, sharp rock pinnacles rise from the top of the ridge you are climbing.

The trail soon bears off the left side of the ridgeline to traverse the talus slopes around the base of the pinnacles. You regain the ridge again at 5,390 feet elevation, in a little over 0.1 mile. The course soon climbs steeply, making a couple of small switchbacks before flattening out at 5,980 feet elevation, 3.8 miles from the trail-head. A short distance farther along there is a talus slope below to your right. From your vantage point, at the top of the talus, there is a fantastic view of Mount Rainier to the northwest. The route continues to climb, sometimes steeply along the ridge-line heading south, but there are no more long uphill grades. If you look behind you as you hike, you may be able to see Mount Stuart far in the distance to the north-northeast, and to your left Nelson Ridge is across the Copper Creek Canyon.

The trail reaches its highest point at 6,200 feet elevation, 4.7 miles from the trail-head. All along this ridge the views are wonderful, and if you are here in early sum-mer, the flowers are also great. From some places along the ridge, 12,276-foot-high Mount Adams can be seen to the south. The trail is a little vague in a couple of places along the ridge but it never disappears for long. Soon the tread begins a slow descent toward the junction with Bismarck Peak Trail 983. This junction, at 5,980 feet eleva-tion and 5.3 miles from the trailhead, is slightly left (east) of the ridgeline. The poorly maintained Bismarck Peak Trail follows a ridgeline for 3 miles east from the junction, to the summit of 7,585-foot-high Bismarck Peak.

The route quickly regains the ridgeline after leaving the junction. You follow the ridgeline for another 1.1 miles south. Take your time as you hike along the ridge: These views are the best on this trail. In a few places penstemon bloom between the rocks. If you need to make a cell phone call, the service is usually good along this ridge. About a mile from the junction with the Bismarck Peak Trail, the trail descends steeply, and in another 0.1 mile it turns right and leaves the ridgeline. At the point where the trail leaves the ridgeline, the summit of Pear Butte is close by to the southeast.

The route descends the forested slope, heading generally to the southwest for 0.9 mile. Then you make a couple of switchbacks before descending the last 100 feet of elevation to the edge of a large meadow, where the trail becomes very vague. Fol-low the right edge of the meadow, heading southeast for about 0.2 mile, and the trail will show up again close to Apple Lake. Apple Lake, which looks more like a marsh than a lake, is to your left. The trail then continues southeast for a little less than 0.2 mile to the junction with the Pear Lake Trail 1148. The junction with the Pear Lake Trail is 7.7 miles from the Pear Butte Trailhead, at 5,050 feet elevation.

This junction is the end of the Pear Butte Trail, but if you have come this far, you will want to continue to Pear Lake. Turn left (east) at the junction and quickly cross Indian Creek, which is but a small stream here. The route then heads north-east, staying south of Apple Lake and the large meadow that nearly surrounds it. In 0.4 mile there is a path on the left, which descends a few feet to a bridge over the small stream that connects Pear and Apple Lakes. Cross the bridge and follow the path east for a short distance to the shore of Pear Lake. Pear Lake is deeper than

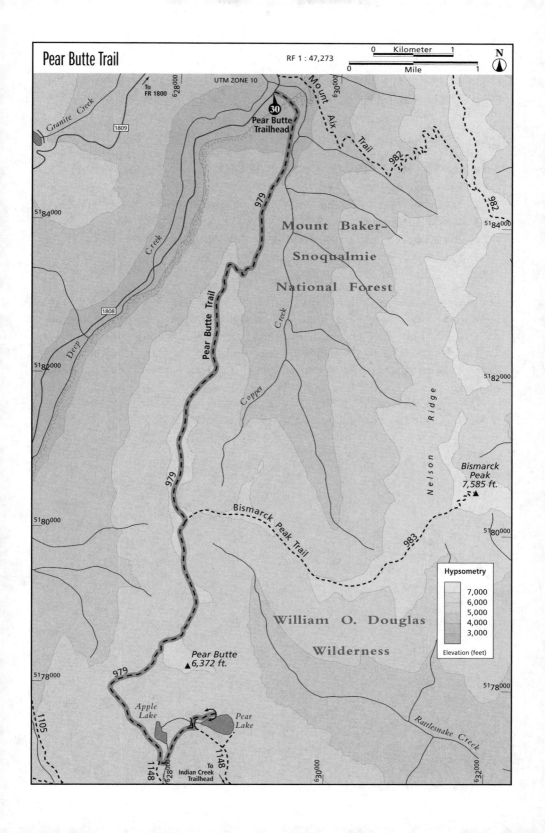

Apple Lake and seems to have a good trout population. There are several good campsites here, but be sure to camp at least 100 feet back from the water. Return the way you came, or see the options below for a shorter return trip that requires a short car shuttle.

Miles and Directions

0.0 Pear Butte Trailhead. GPS 46 48.741N 121 18.423W.

2.4 Trail reaches ridgeline.

5.3 Junction with the Bismarck Peak Trail 983. GPS 46 45.673N 121 19.337W. Bear right.

6.4 Trail leaves ridgeline near Pear Butte.

7.7 Junction with the Pear Lake Trail 1148. GPS 46 44.035N 121 19.503W. Turn left.

8.1 Pear Lake. Turnaround point.

16.2 Pear Butte Trailhead.

Options: An easier return hike for a total of 13.1 miles, requiring a car shuttle, can be made by following the Pear Lake Trail back the way you came to the junction with the Pear Butte Trail. Then turn south and hike 0.7 mile, following the Pear Lake Trail to the junction with the Indian Creek Trail 1105. Turn right on the Indian Creek Trail and hike 3.9 miles west and north to Deep Creek Horse Camp and Trailhead.

To get to the Deep Creek Horse Camp and Trailhead from the Pear Butte Trailhead, drive south on FR 1808 for 4.4 miles. Turn left off FR 1808 on the trailhead access road and go a short distance to the trailhead.

31 Copper City

Take this very short hike to the site of what was once a booming mining community. Then spend a little time imagining what it looked like in its heyday, more than half a century ago.

Start: Copper City Trailhead.
Type of hike: Out-and-back ½-hour hike.
Total distance: 0.4 mile.
Difficulty: Easy.
Maps: Bumping Lake USGS quad or USDA Forest Service William O. Douglas and Norse Peak Wilderness.

Permits and fees: None.
Best months: Mid-June through October.
Special considerations: Good hiking shoes or boots are recommended for this hike. Even though it is very short, the abandoned roadbed is rough and rocky. If you are going to continue past the town site, hiking boots are a must.

Finding the trailhead: To reach the Copper City Trailhead from the **Seattle-Tacoma** area, drive to Enumclaw. From Enumclaw follow State Route 410 for 41 miles east and south to Cayuse Pass. If you are coming from **Portland,** Oregon, drive north from Portland on Interstate 5 for 68 miles to the junction with U.S. Highway 12. Then head east on US 12 for 71 miles (7 miles east of Packwood) to the junction with State Route 123. Turn left off US 12 on SR 123 and go north for 16.5 miles to Cayuse Pass and the junction with SR 410.

Turn right (left if coming from Seattle-Tacoma) on SR 410 and head east, crossing Chinook Pass in 3.7 miles. Then continue on SR 410, heading east for another 19.2 miles to the junction with Bumping Lake Road (Forest Road 1800). Turn right (southwest) on FR 1800 and follow it 13.5 miles (leaving the pavement at Bumping Lake Recreation Area) to the junction with Deep Creek Road (Forest Road 1808). Bear left on FR 1808 and follow it 5.5 miles to the Copper City Trailhead. The trailhead is on the right side of FR 1808.

Parking and trailhead facilities: There is roadside parking for several cars but no other facilities at the trailhead.

The Hike

A sign at the trailhead states that it is "1/8" mile to Copper City. The trail is actually an abandoned roadbed that is now closed to motorized travel. The route climbs southwest up the eroded and rocky roadbed. In 0.1 mile the course crosses a large culvert, and shortly you'll reach the run-down remains of what was once a bunkhouse. The old building, which is now protected by the Antiquities Act of 1906 and the Archeological Resources Act of 1979, is just to the left of the roadbed. At the building the road (trail) forks; bear left (south) and cross the meadow to the mill ruins. Most of the buildings and all of the machinery are no longer here, but in several spots the flattened-out sites where buildings once stood are evident.

Late in the ninteenth century, James (Cap) Simmons found signs of copper in the area of Deep Creek and filed a mining claim near the present site of Copper

Bunkhouse at Copper City.

City. In 1899 he turned the claim over to his son Bud, who sold the claim in 1905 to Reuben Root. Root Lake, near the top of Miners Ridge about 2.5 miles north of Copper City, is named for Reuben Root. Root had other mining claims in the area and was very interested in the development of the mining district and Copper City. This interest was possibly at least partly fueled by rumors that a railroad was going to be built up the Bumping River Canyon to access coal deposits near the headwaters of the Bumping River.

Root sold shares in the claims so that he would have the capital to buy machinery to develop Copper City and the mines. A sawmill was built at Copper City in 1907 to provide lumber for the development. The Copper City area had more than forty active mining claims between 1907 and 1942, most of them high on Miners Ridge above the town. The minerals here included silver, tungsten trioxide, and a tiny amount of gold as well as copper. But transportation was difficult and the railroad never came. In 1948 all the machinery was moved to other mining areas.

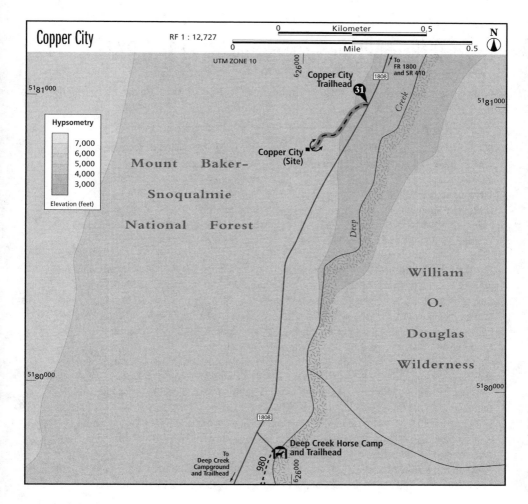

Miles and Directions

0.0 Copper City Trailhead. GPS 46 46.220N 121 20.827W.

0.2 Copper City.

0.4 Copper City Trailhead.

Options: If you are an ambitious hiker, you can continue up the eroded roadbed for another 3.2 miles, nearly reaching the top of Miners Ridge and passing abandoned cabin sites and mines along the way. This route climbs 1,600 vertical feet with an average grade of about 10.5 percent, making it a fairly strenuous hike. The upper end of the roadbed and the mines can also be reached via a short cross-country hike from the now abandoned Miners Ridge Lookout site near the end of Forest Road 1809. The lookout site is also the start of the Root Lake Trail. From the last switchback on FR 1809, just below the lookout site, hike south along the ridgeline of Miners Ridge to reach the mines. The way is mostly open and in view.

32 Richmond Lake via Richmond Mine Trail 973

Climb into the subalpine terrain high above the Bumping River Canyon, then descend a short distance to the shore of Richmond Lake.

Start: Richmond Mine Trailhead.
Type of hike: Out-and-back day hike or backpack.
Total distance: 10.8 miles.
Difficulty: Strenuous.
Maps: Goose Prairie, Bumping Lake, and Timberwolf Mountain USGS quads or USDA

Forest Service William O. Douglas and Norse Peak Wilderness.
Permits and fees: William O. Douglas Wilderness permit.
Best months: Mid-July through September.
Special considerations: The trail is very rough and eroded in places.

Finding the trailhead: To reach the Richmond Mine Trailhead from the **Seattle-Tacoma** area, drive to Enumclaw. From Enumclaw follow State Route 410 for 41 miles east and south to Cayuse Pass. If you are coming from **Portland,** Oregon, drive north on Interstate 5 for 68 miles to the junction with U.S. Highway 12. Then head east on US 12 for 71 miles (7 miles east of Packwood) to the junction with State Route 123. Turn left off US 12 on SR 123 and drive for 16.5 miles to Cayuse Pass and the junction with SR 410.

Turn right (left if coming from Seattle-Tacoma) on SR 410 and head east for 22.9 miles over Chinook Pass and down to the junction with Bumping Lake Road (Forest Road 1800). Follow FR 1800 for 9.8 miles to the junction with Forest Road 391, which is across FR 1800 from Bumping Crossing Campground. Turn left (east) on FR 391 and drive 0.2 mile to the Richmond Mine Trailhead. FR 391 may be rough, so unless you have a high-clearance vehicle, you may want to park in the Bumping Crossing Campground and walk the last 0.2 mile to the trailhead. The elevation at the trailhead is 3,380 feet.

Parking and trailhead facilities: There is adequate parking but no other facilities at the trailhead. Campsites are available at Bumping Crossing Campground 0.2 mile to the west.

The Hike

The wide, gentle trail leaves the trailhead through a forest of mostly lodgepole pine and Douglas fir with a scattering of tamarack and western white pine mixed in. Lodgepole pine and western white pine can easily be told apart by looking at their needles. The needles on a lodgepole pine are in bundles of two, and on the western white pine the bundles contain five needles.

About 0.25 mile into the hike, the route steepens as you climb to cross Thunder Creek, at 3,570 feet elevation, 0.5 mile from the trailhead. There are usually logs available to cross above the creek, but they are often very slippery. One hundred yards after crossing Thunder Creek, the route enters the William O. Douglas Wilderness. Prince's pine, huckleberry bushes, and an occasional leopard lily line the rough and rocky path as you climb. The tread climbs steeply in places and makes a hard turn to the right at 3,900 feet elevation. Soon columbine, vanilla leaf, tall bluebells,

Bower Lake.

and queen's cup join the array of flowers along the trail. One and one-half miles into the hike, as you pass some large Douglas fir trees, the view of the surrounding mountains begins to open up. Beside the trail in shady places, white-flowered rhododendrons grow in profusion, and in the openings where it can get plenty of sun, Rocky Mountain maple forms the understory.

The course crosses a small stream 2.2 miles from the trailhead, at 4,590 feet elevation. Both sides of the stream crossing are steep and often muddy. Lewis monkey flowers bloom beside the stream near the crossing. Once across the stream the tread climbs steeply, making several switchbacks. The trail passes a small spring 0.3 mile from the stream and quickly crosses another small stream on a wooden bridge. Then you recross Thunder Creek and continue climbing on the now rough, steep, rocky, and deeply eroded path. About 0.5 mile after recrossing Thunder Creek, the trail crosses a talus slope and flattens as you enter a semiopen basin. Watch for pikas in the rocks above the trail. Pink mountain heather grows between the groves of subalpine fir and Alaska cedar and boulders. There is a good campsite to the left of the trail in this basin, just before you cross Thunder Creek for the third time.

The route crosses Thunder Creek for the third time at 5,330 feet elevation and quickly begins to climb a rocky slope. Trailside phlox, asters, and Indian paintbrush bloom in late July. A couple hundred yards after crossing the creek, you may notice an old 3-mile marker on a tree to the right of the trail. The trail has been realigned since this marker was placed here, and you are now 3.5 miles from the trailhead. The tread climbs fairly steeply along the slope, crossing several tiny streams. The route makes the first of a series of switchbacks, at 5,790 feet elevation, 0.5 mile after passing the old 3-mile marker. Then the course winds and switchbacks, climbing steeply, for another 0.5 mile. Here the trail appears to fork. Bear left at the fork—the right fork is a section of old and now abandoned trail. Above the fork the route makes one more switchback as you climb the last 100 feet to a pass on the ridgeline. This pass, at 6,160 feet elevation, is the highest point on this hike. See the options below for a side trip to Bower Lake from the pass.

After crossing the pass the trail descends through the timber for 0.3 mile to the shoreline of Richmond Lake, at 5,950 feet elevation. There is a good campsite between the trail and the lake. The lake is surrounded by timber, but the view across it makes for a pretty camping spot. Return the way you came.

Beyond Richmond Lake the trail descends steeply for about 1.5 miles through the timber to the junction with the Nelson Ridge Trail 984, near the bottom of the North Fork Rattlesnake Creek Canyon. This section of trail is not very scenic, but it is not eroded as badly as the parts you have already covered.

Miles and Directions

0.0 Richmond Mine Trailhead. GPS 46 52.855N 121 16.647W.
5.1 Pass. GPS 46 50.959N 121 14.656W. Optional side trip to the right.
5.4 Richmond Lake. GPS 46 50.826N 121 14.695W. Turnaround point.
10.8 Richmond Mine Trailhead.

Options: The side trip to Bower Lake is far more scenic than anything along the Richmond Mine Trail. In fact, Bower Lake makes an excellent destination for a hike up the Richmond Mine Trail. It is slightly less than 1 mile from the pass on the Richmond Mine Trail to Bower Lake, making it about 6 miles from the trailhead. The route to the lake, while a little vague, is no more difficult than what you have already climbed to reach the pass. Bower Lake is shown on the Bumping Lake USGS quad map but is not named. Bower is a local rather than an official name for this lake.

From the pass at 6,160 feet elevation, the vague route to Bower Lake leaves the Richmond Mine Trail, heading southwest along the ridgeline. The route climbs quickly through the thinning timber and ridgetop meadows. The vague path goes around the left side of a rock outcropping, where rock penstemon abound, showing their brilliant pink-purple blooms in late July. You then climb back to the ridgeline and ascend to about 6,550 feet elevation. If you need to use your cell phone, serv-

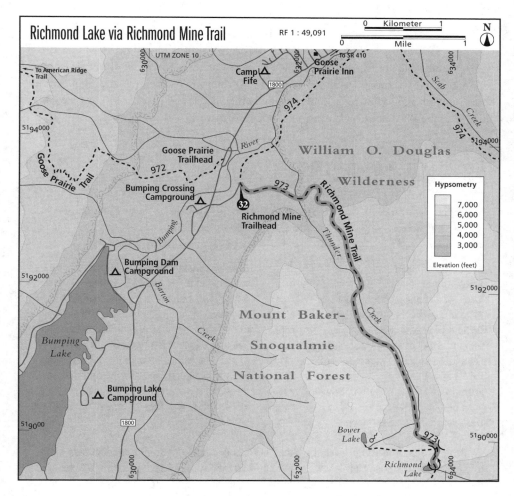

RF 1 : 49,091

0   Kilometer   1

0   Mile   1

N

UTM ZONE 10

To American Ridge Trail

To SR 410

Camp Fife

Goose Prairie Inn

1800

974

Goose Prairie Trailhead

River

William O. Douglas

Wilderness

Goose Prairie Trail

972

Bumping Crossing Campground

973

Richmond Mine Trail

32

Richmond Mine Trailhead

Bumping

Thunder

Hypsometry

7,000
6,000
5,000
4,000
3,000

Elevation (feet)

Bumping Dam Campground

Barron

Mount Baker–

Creek

Creek

Bumping Lake

Snoqualmie

National Forest

Bumping Lake Campground

1800

Bower Lake

973

Richmond Lake

ice can generally be had from this ridge. As you climb, Richmond Lake is in view below to your left (east). Then the path makes a descending traverse off the right (northwest) side of the ridge. You descend a couple hundred feet and enter the lower end of a hanging subalpine valley. As you enter the valley, there will be a large spring to your right. This spring is one of the main tributaries of Thunder Creek. Past the spring there is no path; head west-southwest, climbing gently. In about 0.1 mile you will pass a pond, which is on your left. A short distance farther along, you'll reach the shore of Bower Lake, at 6,530 feet elevation. The GPS coordinates on the north shore of the lake are 46 50.840 N 121 15.440W.

The lake is nestled at the head of this beautiful valley, surrounded by meadowland that blooms with a variety of wildflowers. You may notice the many trails crossing the hillsides above the lake; both elk and mountain goats, which are common here, use these paths. When I hiked this route, I encountered a mountain goat along the ridge shortly after leaving the Richmond Mine Trail.

There are a few groves of stunted alpine trees a short distance north of the lake, making for possible campsites. Please don't camp in the alpine meadows, the damage caused by camping here would take years to recover. If you tread lightly on the land, this makes a wonderful place to camp for a couple of nights and explore the magnificent high country around and above the lake. There is also another pretty little pond, nestled in a bowl, a short distance northwest of Bower Lake.

33 Mount Aix Trail 982

Hike and scramble to the highest summit in the William O. Douglas Wilderness, where the view is outrageous and mountain goats are abundant.

Start: Mount Aix Trailhead.
Type of hike: Long out-and-back day hike or 2- or 3-day backpack.
Total distance: 13.8 miles.
Difficulty: Strenuous.
Maps: USDA Forest Service William O. Douglas and Norse Peak Wilderness or Bumping Lake USGS quad.
Permits and fees: William O. Douglas Wilderness permit.
Best months: July–September.

Special considerations: Water sources are very limited along this trail, so take along all you will need unless you plan to camp and melt snow near the summit. The last 0.3 mile to the very summit of Mount Aix as described below is a rock scramble and may be difficult or even dangerous for all but experienced hikers and climbers. Following the return route to the summit isn't much better. Be sure of your ability before you attempt to reach the highest point.

Finding the trailhead: To reach the Mount Aix Trailhead from the **Seattle-Tacoma** area, drive to Enumclaw. From Enumclaw follow State Route 410 for 41 miles east and south to Cayuse Pass. If you are coming from **Portland,** Oregon, drive north on Interstate 5 for 68 miles to the junction with U.S. Highway 12. Then head east on US 12 for 71 miles (7 miles east of Packwood) to the junction with State Route 123. Turn left off US 12 onto SR 123 and go north for 16.5 miles to Cayuse Pass and the junction with SR 410.
  Turn right (left if coming from Seattle-Tacoma) on SR 410, heading east over Chinook Pass, and drive 22.9 miles to the junction with Bumping Lake Road (Forest Road 1800). Turn right and follow FR 1800 southwest for 13.5 miles (leaving the pavement at Bumping Lake Recreation Area) to the junction with Deep Creek Road (Forest Road 1808). Bear left on FR 1808 and follow it for another 1.6 miles to the Mount Aix access road, where there is a sign at the turnoff. Turn left (east) on the access road and go 0.1 mile to the trailhead, at 3,680 feet elevation. The access road may be very rough so you may want to park close to FR 1808 and walk 0.1 mile to the trailhead.
Parking and trailhead facilities: There is adequate parking for several cars at the trailhead but no other facilities.

Lunch on the summit of Mount Aix.

The Hike

The Mount Aix Trail leads east from the trailhead through a semiopen forest of lodgepole pine, western white pine, tamarack, and Douglas and true firs. Beneath the trees on the forest floor grows kinnikinnick, and gray jays coast between the trees looking for handouts. For the first 0.1 mile the route follows an abandoned roadbed. At 0.25 mile the trail crosses a creek at 3,870 feet elevation, then shortly crosses another tiny stream. The tread, which is rough and rocky in places, makes its first two switchbacks 0.4 mile into the hike. In the next 0.4 mile, you'll cross four small talus slopes near their tops. Watch for pikas between the rocks and boulders.

Shortly the course begins to climb a series of seventeen switchbacks, taking you up to 4,870 feet elevation, 1.7 miles from the trailhead. At a couple of these switchbacks, the trail is relatively close to a fork of Copper Creek, but well above it. Trying to get water at these spots is very difficult and possibly dangerous. These switchbacks are the steepest part of the route between the trailhead and the junction with the Nelson Ridge Trail.

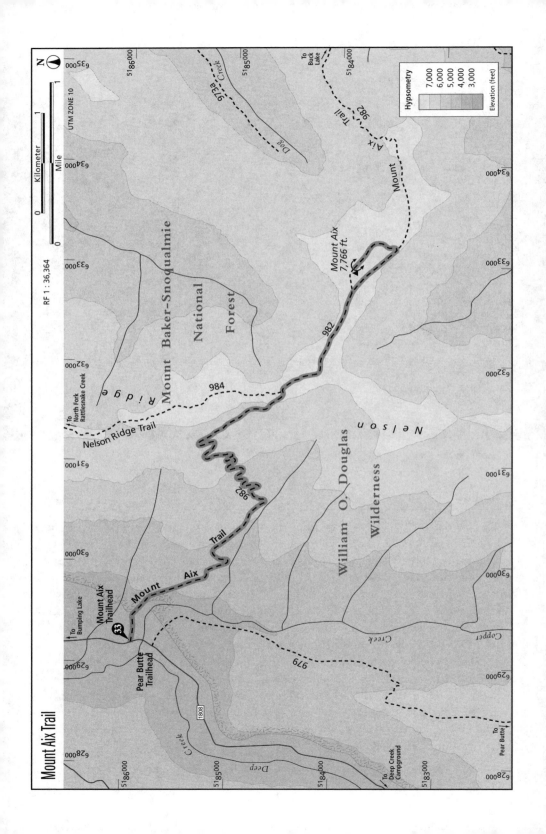

Mount Aix Trail

Above the switchbacks the tread makes an ascending traverse to the southeast along a steep slope. Rocky Mountain maple grows in the openings and a few woodland penstemons sprout beside the trail. The ascending traverse lasts for about 0.4 mile, crossing a tiny stream, which may be dry by late summer. You then make a switchback to the left at 5,160 feet elevation. By now the composition of the forest has changed—there are some fairly large Douglas firs, hemlocks, and noble firs.

At about 2.5 miles from the trailhead and 5,400 feet elevation, after passing a flattened-out but very small campsite close to a tiny spring, the whole character of the woods begins to change. White-flowered rhododendron begins to show up beside the trail beneath the increasingly subalpine forest.

The course soon begins another series of fourteen switchbacks, taking you up to 6,600 feet elevation and a very nice but dry campsite 4.3 miles from the trailhead. By the time you reach the campsite, which is on the left side of the trail at a switchback, the timber has thinned considerably. There are now sloping meadows between the increasingly stunted subalpine firs, hemlocks, and white-bark pines. Views have now opened up in all directions. The massive, ice-shrouded cone of 14,408-foot-high Mount Rainier dominates the view to the west. To the south is the very old, extinct, and highly eroded Goat Rocks volcano. Far to the southwest, the sometimes active volcanic cone of Mount St. Helens can be seen through the haze.

Past the campsite the tread continues to climb, making seven more switchbacks before reaching the junction with the Nelson Ridge Trail 984, at 7,160 feet elevation. This junction is 5.1 miles from the Mount Aix Trailhead and very close to a saddle on Nelson Ridge. See the options below for more information about the Nelson Ridge Trail.

Mountain goats are often seen from this saddle and elk can sometimes be seen in the meadows far below. If you are here in late August or September, the bull elk may be bugling. At the last switchback, a few yards before reaching the junction, there is a flattened campsite a few feet to the left of the trail. This is a dry camp if there is no snow available to melt. This tiny campsite is sheltered from the prevailing southwest wind by a thick grove of scrubby alpine trees.

To continue to the summit of Mount Aix, bear right at the junction with the Nelson Ridge Trail, staying on the Mount Aix Trail. The route first climbs through the stunted subalpine trees, then emerges on an open slope, where Mount Adams comes into view to the south. The trail appears to fork 0.25 mile from the junction. Bear left; the right fork goes 50 yards to a viewpoint overlooking the head of Hindoo Creek. Mountain goats are regularly observed below the viewpoint and elk can also sometimes be seen.

After passing the fork the route rounds a ridgeline and descends about 170 feet on a semiopen scree slope. You will make a couple of switchbacks before reaching a saddle at 7,150 feet elevation. A few feet to the left of the trail, in the saddle, a viewpoint overlooks the North Fork Rattlesnake Creek. In the distance to the north, the Stuart Range, capped by 9,415-foot-high Mount Stuart, rises above the hazy intervening hills. Leaving the saddle the route climbs an open ridge 0.5 mile before beginning a traverse across the south slope of Mount Aix.

As the trail begins its traverse, there is a very vague path to the left leaving the trail at 7,450 feet elevation. This path is one of the routes to the summit of Mount Aix. *Caution:* This route is steep and there is a considerable amount of loose and easily dislodged rock. If you are an experienced mountain climber, it will be easy, but for the average hiker it is difficult and somewhat dangerous. This is the place to end your hike if you are not sure of your abilities. The Mount Aix Trail ahead, on the traverse, is in very poor condition and is dangerous, especially for stock. The other route to the summit, described as the return trip below, is only slightly easier than the path to your left.

If you're sure of your abilities and want to climb to the summit, turn left and start up the path. The route first climbs a shallow gully, and then you must scramble over the rock to the northeast to the summit of Mount Aix, at 7,766 feet elevation, 0.3 mile from the main Mount Aix Trail.

From the summit the view is superb in all directions, as this is the highest point for some distance around. To the west over Nelson Ridge is Mount Rainier. To the south, Mount Adams's icy, humped form is just to the left of Goat Rocks, and far to the southwest is Mount St. Helens. On the small but flat summit is a rock cairn in which there is a plastic pipe with end caps that serves as a summit register, should you want to record your climb. Mount Aix was once the site of a lookout, and evidence of this can be seen scattered around the summit area.

After you have taken in the view, start your return by descending the rock steps east from the summit. These steps are part of an old trail to the lookout. This trail is somewhat easier, especially when descending, than the ascending route. This is the route we recommend for the ascent if you don't want to climb up the steep gully and scramble over the rocks. Ascending the peak via this trail will add about 0.7 mile in distance to your climb. Below the steps the tread switchbacks down to a small ridge at the base of a snowfield. There are several campsites close to the trail here, and water can usually be obtained in late summer from the base of the snowfield. At other times you may have to melt snow for water. Either way, be sure to treat, filter, or boil your drinking water.

Past the snowfield the trail climbs to the top of a rise to the southeast. At the top of the rise, the trail becomes very vague. The route traverses south around the ridgeline and passes through a tiny notch. Then you must scramble down a gully for a few feet. Below the gully, descend southeast to meet the main Mount Aix Trail in another notch, at 7,470 feet elevation, 0.5 mile from the summit.

Turn right (northwest) on the Mount Aix Trail and traverse a rough 0.6 mile back to the point where you left it on your ascent. This section of the Mount Aix Trail is marked "dangerous section" on some maps. For an experienced hiker or mountain climber, this section of trail should not be too difficult. But it may scare some less experienced travelers and could be dangerous under some conditions. Once across the traverse, return to the Mount Aix Trailhead the way you came.

Miles and Directions

0.0   Mount Aix Trailhead. GPS 46 48.846N 121 18.328W.

5.1   Junction with Nelson Ridge Trail 984. GPS 46 48.053N 121 16.419W. Turn right.

6.2   First rough path to Mount Aix Summit. GPS 46 47.701N 121 15.491W. Turn left.

6.5   Mount Aix Summit. GPS 46 47.702N 121 15.349W.

7.0   Rejoin Mount Aix Trail. GPS 46 47.540N 121 15.188W. Turn right.

7.6   Junction with first rough path. GPS46 47.701N 121 15.491W. Go straight ahead.

8.7   Junction with Nelson Ridge Trail. GPS 46 48.053N 121 16.419W. Bear left.

13.8   Mount Aix Trailhead.

Options: Hiking north along Nelson Ridge is a very rewarding side trip for a party camped near the junction of the Nelson Ridge and Mount Aix Trails. Nelson Ridge is named for Jack Nelson, the first gatekeeper at the Bumping Lake Dam, which was built about 1910. Jack ran the operation until his retirement in 1946.

To make the trip along Nelson Ridge, turn left at the junction with the Mount Aix Trail, 5.1 miles from the Mount Aix Trailhead. The route heads north, closely following the ridgeline and climbing to about 7,300 feet elevation before losing 100 feet at a saddle. Along the ridge, stunted subalpine firs and white-bark pines cling to the rocks. On the moister slopes to the right of the ridgeline, a few mountain hemlocks and groves of shrubby Alaska cedar fight for life in this harsh alpine location. The beautiful alpine basin to the right of the ridgeline is the headwaters of the North Fork Rattlesnake Creek. It's best to check out this basin with binoculars; mountain goats are nearly always present and elk can also occasionally be seen.

The route passes just west of the highest point on Nelson Ridge (7,537 feet), 0.5 mile from the junction with the Mount Aix Trail. Then the route begins its 5-mile descent to a junction with Richmond Mine Trail 973, deep in the North Fork Rattlesnake Creek Canyon.

Eastern Region

This region generally encompasses the Rattlesnake Creek and Indian Creek drainages along the eastern boundary of the William O. Douglas Wilderness. The eastern region has the driest climate in the wilderness. In the lower reaches of the area, orange–barked ponderosa pine dominates the forest, and, yes, there may be a few rattlesnakes, although I have yet to see one here. Three main access roads service the area, State Route 410 on the north, Forest Road 1500 on the east, and U.S. Highway 12 on the south.

Hike 35, Boulder Cave National Recreation Trail, is an easy and fairly short lol-lipop loop that takes you through a cave. Reader boards along the trail provide plenty of information about the sights you are seeing. Rattlesnake Trail (Hike 37) is

Shellrock Peak.

a challenging route with many creek crossings. Farther south, Hike 39, Ironstone Mountain Trails, traverses a subalpine ridgeline. All the land along Ironstone Mountain Trail is view property. Southwest of Ironstone Mountain, the Indian Creek Trail (Hike 40) leads into the heart of the wilderness to connect with many of the trails in the southwest, northwest, Bumping River, and Deep Creek regions. A bit farther west, the Spiral Butte Trail (Hike 44) climbs to 5,860 elevation near the summit of Spiral Butte, where you can look down on the White Pass Ski Area.

34 Soda Springs Loop
Trails 975 and 975a

Climb high on the slope of the Bumping River Canyon, then descend to Soda Springs.

Start: Soda Springs Campground and Trailhead next to the Bumping River.
Type of hike: 2-hour loop hike.
Total distance: 2.2 miles.
Difficulty: Moderate to strenuous.
Maps: The USDA Forest Service William O. Douglas and Norse Peak Wilderness map shows these trails correctly but the scale is quite small. Old Scab Mountain USGS quad covers the area but shows these trails somewhat incorrectly.
Permits and fees: William O. Douglas Wilderness permit.
Best months: May–October.
Special considerations: It is very easy to miss the path to the left, 0.15 mile into the hike.

Finding the trailhead: To reach Soda Springs Campground and Trailhead from the **Seattle-Tacoma** area, drive to Enumclaw. From Enumclaw follow State Route 410 for 41 miles east and south to Cayuse Pass. From **Portland,** Oregon, drive north on Interstate 5 for 68 miles to the junction with U.S. Highway 12. Then head east on US 12 for 71 miles (7 miles east of Packwood) to the junction with State Route 123. Turn left off US 12 on SR 123 and go north for 16.5 miles to Cayuse Pass and the junction with SR 410.

Turn right (left if coming from Seattle) on SR 410 and drive 22.9 miles east to the junction with Bumping Lake Road (Forest Road 1800). Turn right (southwest) on FR 1800 and follow it 5.1 miles to Soda Springs Campground and Trailhead. The campground is on the left side of FR 1800. The trailhead parking area is at the west end of the bridge over the Bumping River in the campground, at 3,020 feet elevation.

Parking and trailhead facilities: Parking for several cars, restrooms, and a campground are available at the trailhead. A concessionaire operates Soda Springs Campground. Campsite fees are $15 a day at present, with premium sites slightly more.

The Hike

Head east from the parking area, crossing the footbridge over the sparkling Bumping River. Most people take a minute in the middle of the bridge to gaze up- and downriver. Just past the bridge is a trail junction and a wilderness registration box; get your wilderness permit here.

To make the loop, turn right at the junction on Trail 975 and head upriver. Western red cedar, grand fir, Engelmann spruce, and ponderosa pine make up the forest canopy along the riverbank. Beneath the tall trees grow wild rose and Oregon grape, and on the ground vanilla leaf grabs the open spaces. If you watch the river carefully, you may see a dipper. The American dipper feeds mostly on the bottoms of swift streams; it has the ability to fly underwater and climb into the air without miss-

Bridge over the Bumping River.

ing a beat. Dippers are always very close to or over water.

The route follows the river for about 0.1 mile, where there is a steep path to your left. The river trail continues on up the river for another 0.2 mile but becomes very rough. The Old Scab Mountain USGS quad map shows the trail continuing up the river here, but the map is incorrect.

Turn left on the path and climb steeply to the southeast. In a short distance the tread makes a switchback to the left. Another 0.4 mile of climbing brings you to a wooden bridge over an often dry streambed, at 3,360 feet elevation. Three hundred yards farther along, the track crosses another wooden bridge over a wet area. Shortly after crossing the bridge over the wet area, the course turns to the right and then makes two switchbacks before reaching the junction with Trail 975a, at 3,640 feet elevation, 1 mile from the trailhead. See the options below to continue on Trail 975.

Turn left at the junction and hike north on Trail 975a. The route climbs for a little less than 0.2 mile, to the north, reaching 3,750 feet elevation, then begins to descend. About 0.25 mile from the junction, the tread makes a switchback to the right. A short path to your left at the switchback leads to a viewpoint overlooking

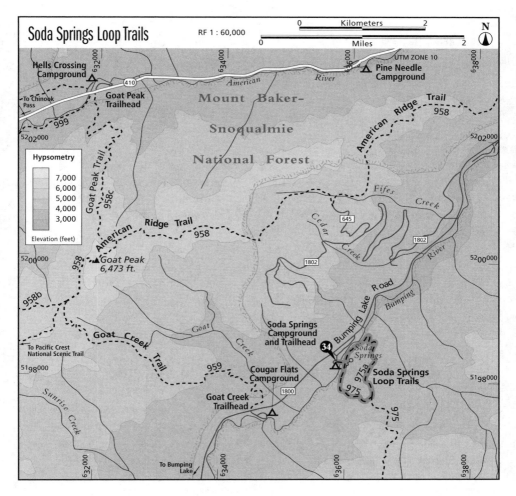

Soda Springs Loop Trails   RF 1 : 60,000

Hypsometry

7,000
6,000
5,000
4,000
3,000

Elevation (feet)

the Bumping River Canyon. The trail, which is steep in places, continues its descent through the forest, which here includes western hemlock and western white pine.

The route follows the top of a small ridge for a short distance 0.7 mile from the junction. By now you have descended to 3,250 feet elevation. Leaving the ridge in a tiny saddle, the trace begins a series of four switchbacks that take you down to below 3,100 feet elevation. Then the route flattens out and soon crosses a wooden bridge over a sluggish stream that has skunk cabbage growing along its banks. Soon the Bumping River becomes visible on your right.

You reach Soda Springs a little less than 0.1 mile after crossing the sluggish stream. There are two springs here, both of which have been surrounded with rock rims, forming basins. The minerals in the water make the springs a bright orange color. Past the springs the trail continues southwest for about 100 yards to the junction with Trail 975. Turn right at the junction and cross the bridge over the Bumping River back to the trailhead.

Miles and Directions

0.0 Soda Springs Trailhead. GPS 46 55.442N 121 12.920W.

0.05 First junction with Trail 975a. Turn right.

0.15 Path to the left. Turn left.

1.0 Second junction with Trail 975a. GPS 46 55.158N 121 12.545W. Turn left.

2.1 Soda Springs.

2.2 Soda Springs Trailhead.

Options: From the junction with Trail 975a, 1 mile into the hike, Trail 975 continues to climb to the southeast. The route reaches a trailhead on Forest Road 1600 near Flat Iron Lake in about 5.5 miles. FR 1600 is a rough and steep road, which is not suitable for passenger cars.

If you just want to see the springs and not make the loop hike, turn left at the first junction with Trail 975a, just after crossing the bridge over the Bumping River. Then walk the 100 yards to Soda Springs. The sign states that it's 500 feet to the springs, but it is really a much shorter distance than that. The springs are on the right side of the trail.

35 Boulder Cave National Recreation Trail 962

Hike through the east-side transition-zone forest to the upper entrance of Boulder Cave. Then descend through a short but very interesting cavern to its mouth.

Start: Boulder Cave parking area and trailhead.
Type of hike: 2-hour lollipop loop.
Total distance: 1.3 miles.
Difficulty: Easy.

Maps: Cliffdell USGS quad or just use the map in this book.
Permits and fees: $5 parking fee.
Best months: April–October.
Special considerations: A good light source is needed for the cave section of this hike.

Finding the trailhead: To reach Boulder Caves from the **Seattle-Tacoma** area, drive to Enumclaw. From Enumclaw follow State Route 410 for 41 miles east and south to Cayuse Pass. From **Portland,** Oregon, drive north on Interstate 5 for 68 miles to the junction with U.S. Highway 12. Then head east on US 12 for 71 miles (7 miles east of Packwood) to the junction with State Route 123. Turn left off US 12 on SR 123 and go north for 16.5 miles to Cayuse Pass and the junction with SR 410.

Turn right (left if coming from Seattle-Tacoma) on SR 410 and head east for 30 miles, over Chinook Pass and down to the junction with the Boulder Cave Access Road. There is a large sign at this junction. Turn right and cross the bridge over the Naches River, then bear right again, fol-

Exiting Boulder Cave. ▶

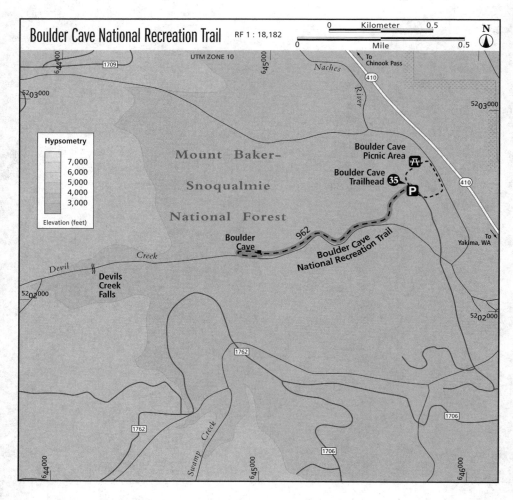

Boulder Cave National Recreation Trail

RF 1 : 18,182

0   Kilometer   0.5

0   Mile   0.5

N

UTM ZONE 10

1709

To Chinook Pass

Naches

410

Boulder Cave Picnic Area

Boulder Cave Trailhead 35

P

410

Hypsometry

7,000
6,000
5,000
4,000
3,000

Elevation (feet)

Mount Baker-

Snoqualmie

National Forest

962

Boulder Cave National Recreation Trail

Boulder Cave

To Yakima, WA

Creek

Devil

Devils Creek Falls

1762

1762

Swamp Creek

1706

1706

lowing the signs, and drive about a mile to the Boulder Cave parking area and trailhead.
Parking and trailhead facilities: Adequate parking, restrooms, and a picnic area are available
at the trailhead.

The Hike

Spend a few minutes reading the reader boards at the trailhead before beginning
your hike. From the trailhead the route climbs gently southwest, through open ponderosa pine, Douglas fir, tamarack (western larch), and grand fir forest. In 0.2 mile
you will pass a reader board describing these trees, and on a short spur trail to the
right is another reader board that discusses fire scars. A few yards farther along, there
is a path to the left that goes to a platform and viewpoint overlooking the nearly
vertical cliffs of Devils Creek Canyon. Another reader board on the platform helps
you identify some of the native plants of this area.

Back on the main trail, another couple hundred yards of hiking brings you to another reader board. This one talks about another cave that is in its formation stage. This forming cave can be seen across Devils Creek Canyon. Shortly ahead the trail forks at its high point, 210 feet above the trailhead. Bear left at the fork and follow the main trail for a short distance to another reader board and another fork in the trail. Bear right at this fork and descend, making a switchback to the upper entrance of Boulder Cave.

Boulder Cave is the largest of its kind in the Northwest. It is not a lava-tube cave as are most of the caves in the Washington Cascades. Boulder Cave was formed from the alternating layers of volcanic debris and basalt lava that covered the area over millions of years. The basalt covered this softer layer of debris, then cooled, forming a hard layer. Water in the form of Devils Creek worked its way through the basalt in places and eroded out the softer debris layer below it over thousands of years. The stream cut a deep, wide channel beneath the harder basalt roof. About 25,000 years ago the undercutting became too much for the basalt to remain suspended above it. The layer of basalt collapsed, forming the cave much as we see it today.

Stop near the entrance and read the reader boards about the cave, the restoration of this trail, and the big-eared bats that inhabit it. Boulder Cave is the only known home of Pacific western big-eared bats in Washington. A population of about fifty of these bats uses this cave during the winter. These bats are not tolerant of human activities. Thousands of the bats once used the cave during the summer. To lessen the disturbance caused by people, Boulder Cave and the trail leading to it are closed to entry from November 1 to April 1.

Turn on your light and hike through the cave, staying on the trail. Devils Creek splashes along to your right as you pass through the dark, broad, but not very high cave. In about 300 feet the trail exits the cave on a boardwalk. The route passes over another boardwalk, then reaches a viewing platform. The tread makes a switchback to the right 25 yards farther along. On the viewing platform next to the trail, at the switchback, is a reader board discussing moss and lichens. The course then crosses another boardwalk and makes a couple of switchbacks before reaching the junction with the inbound trail. Turn right at the junction and retrace your steps for 0.5 mile back to the trailhead and parking area.

Miles and Directions

0.0 Boulder Cave parking area and trailhead. GPS 46 57.650N 121 05.142W.
0.5 Trail forks at beginning of loop. GPS 56 57.473N 121 05.643W. Bear right.
0.6 Boulder Cave. Turn on lights.
0.8 End of loop. GPS 56 57.473N 121 05.643W. Turn right.
1.3 Boulder Cave parking area and trailhead.

Options: A pleasant addition to hiking to Boulder Cave is the 0.4-mile-long River Trail Loop, which leaves from the same trailhead. The paved trail leaves from the northwest end of the trailhead parking area. Soon you turn right and head toward the Naches River. As you leave the picnic area, the route passes a shelter and a reader board discussing riparian plants. The trail also crosses a wooden bridge here as you enter the mixed forest of Engelmann spruce, Douglas fir, grand fir, ponderosa pine, and black cottonwood. Soon the route turns right, close to the river, where stonecrop and cardinal flower sprout between the rocks at the sides of the path. A quarter mile into the hike, there is a short path to bench in the rose and alder bushes.

The tread crosses another wooden bridge to another reader board that will give you information about the Yakima Basin spring chinook salmon. Shortly you will reach another short path to the left. At the end of this path is another bench, where you can sit and watch the river flow by. The route then turns right, away from the river, and crosses the entrance road to the Boulder Cave Trailhead. Buckwheat, yarrow, leopard lilies, and sweet peas grow in the openings close to the road. A few more steps bring you back to the Boulder Cave Trailhead.

36 Buck Lake via Mount Aix Trail 982

Hike the relatively easy section of the Mount Aix Trail from East Mount Aix Trailhead, passing Buck Lake, to a campsite on Dog Creek.

Start: East Mount Aix Trailhead.
Type of hike: Out-and-back day hike or backpack to the eastern base camp for a climb of Mount Aix.
Total distance: 6.8 miles round-trip to Dog Creek.

Difficulty: Easy to moderate.
Maps: Timberwolf Mountain USGS quad.
Permits and fees: William O. Douglas Wilderness permit.
Best months: Mid-June through September.

Finding the trailhead: To reach East Mount Aix Trailhead from **Portland,** Oregon, drive north on Interstate 5 for 68 miles to the junction with U.S. Highway 12. Then head east on US 12 for 71 miles (7 miles east of Packwood) to the junction with State Route 123. Turn left off US 12 on SR 123 and drive 16.5 miles north to Cayuse Pass and the junction with State Route 410. From the **Seattle-Tacoma** area, drive to Enumclaw. From Enumclaw follow SR 410 for 41 miles east and south to Cayuse Pass.

Turn left (right if coming from Portland) on SR 410 and head east for 3.7 miles to Chinook Pass. From Chinook Pass continue east on SR 410 for 39 miles to the junction with Nile Road at Eagle Rock Country Junction. This junction is about 12 miles west of Naches. Turn right (southwest) on Nile Road and follow it for 1.3 miles to the junction with Bethel Ridge Road (Forest Road 1500). Turn left (southwest) on FR 1500 and drive 7.4 miles to the junction with Forest Road 1502. Turn right on FR 1502 and drive west for 8.1 miles to the point where the road forks. There are no signs or road-number markers at this fork. Bear right at the fork and go 0.3 mile to the trailhead. The elevation at the trailhead is 4,520 feet.

Hiker at the viewpoint between Buck Lake and Dog Creek.

Parking and trailhead facilities: There is parking for several vehicles, a stock-loading and -unloading ramp, and a couple of hitching rails at the trailhead. A couple of primitive campsites are located close by. Please do not park where you will block the stock ramp.

The Hike

Two trails appear to start from the East Mount Aix Trailhead: The one you want heads southwest on the left side of the signboard. There is a MT. AIX TRAIL sign on a tree to the left of this trail. The route leaves the trailhead heading southwest but soon turns west along a poorly defined ridgeline. The USGS quad map (Timberwolf Mountain) shows the other trail to be the correct route, but the trail has been rerouted. Along the trailside, ponderosa pine and grand fir are the predominant trees, with a few Douglas firs mixed in. Along the ridgeline, mats of kinnikinnick cover sections of the sandy ground.

There is a path to the right 0.6 mile from the trailhead. This path was once the main trail. If you had taken the trail to the right of the signboard at the trailhead, you would have come out here. The trail you took was the better and shorter route. Just past the path there is a wooden William O. Douglas Wilderness boundary sign. You may have noticed a metal wilderness-boundary sign a couple tenths of a mile back. The trail very closely parallels the boundary here, and the metal sign is actually at the point where you first enter the wilderness. The wooden sign would have been the wilderness boundary if you had started on the older route, shown on the quad map.

Past the wooden wilderness boundary sign, the course soon begins to contour along the left side of the ridge, with the ridgeline getting farther and farther away. Soon the route bears to the southwest, crossing a tiny stream, a dry streambed, and another tiny stream in quick succession. Then the tread traverses a small bench for a short distance. Near the end of the bench, there is a vague path to your left. This path leads 50 yards to a viewpoint overlooking Rattlesnake Creek Canyon, with 6,391-foot-high Timberwolf Mountain rising out of the depths on its far side.

Another 0.3 mile of hiking brings you to Buck Lake. The tread crosses the lake's outlet stream, then turns right to reach the shoreline. The lake really has two outlet streams, but this is the only one that flows during the drier parts of the year. Shallow Buck Lake, at 4,730 feet elevation, has a few dead snags standing in it, and groves of shrubby alder hug its shore. Stately orange-barked ponderosa pines stand around the shore above the high-water line. Above the lake to the north, bare stratified rock cliffs reach to the skyline. There are a couple of possible campsites to the right of the trail next to the lake.

The course follows the shoreline for only a short distance, then crosses a small wooden bridge over the lake's other outlet. This stream is usually dry by midsummer. Then the trail climbs slightly as you head west. Soon the tread flattens out and you pass a small marsh at 4,800 feet elevation. Past the marsh the route soon bears south to contour along a slope. Green rock cliffs and outcrops rise above the trail as you traverse the slope. Shortly the track makes a hard turn to the right. A few feet to your left at this turn is a viewpoint with an excellent view of rugged Timberwolf Mountain. The trail crosses a small rounded ridgeline 0.25 mile farther along and shortly enters a small sloping meadow.

Across the meadow the route makes a turn to the right. If you climb a few yards to your left from this turn to the top of a rocky outcrop, you will reach another very spectacular viewpoint. This viewpoint, marked 4,692 (4,692 is the elevation) on the quad map, overlooks Dog Creek Canyon, as well as Rattlesnake Canyon. After you have taken in the view, get back on the trail and make a couple of short descending switchbacks. Below the switchbacks the route descends to the northwest along a semiopen slope for a little over 0.1 mile. Then you make two more switchbacks and continue to descend for another 0.2 mile. By now you have dropped to slightly below 4,500 feet elevation and the grade flattens out. The trail becomes very rough and eroded 0.5 mile farther along as you climb up the bottom of a gully. The rough stretch lasts only a short distance, however. Then you reach the junction with the Richmond Mine Trail 973, just before the route crosses Dog Creek. This junction, at 4,430 feet elevation, is 3.4 miles from the East Mount Aix Trailhead. There is a

Buck Lake via Mount Aix Trail; Rattlesnake Trail

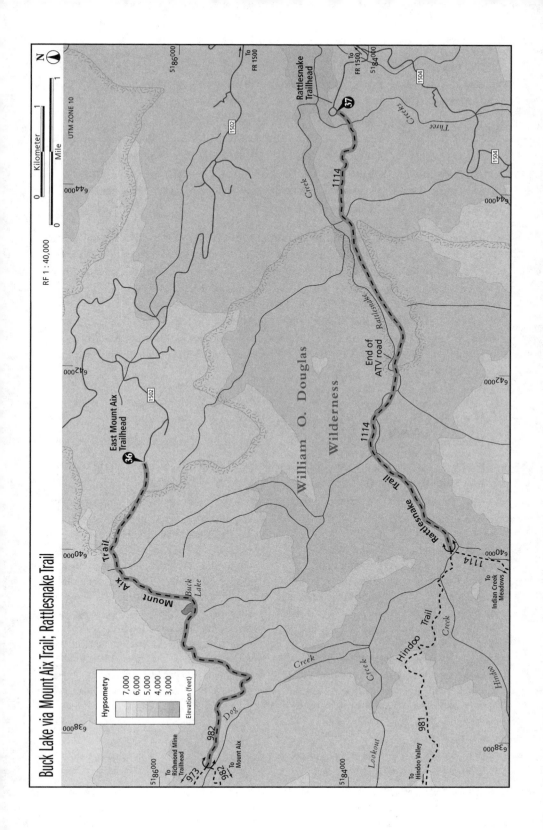

RF 1 : 40,000

UTM ZONE 10

N

Kilometer

Mile

Hypsometry

7,000
6,000
5,000
4,000
3,000

Elevation (feet)

East Mount Aix Trailhead

36

1502

Mount Aix Trail

Buck Lake

973
982
To Richmond Mine Trailhead

982
To Mount Aix

Dog Creek

Creek

Creek

Lookout Creek

Hindoo Trail

981
To Hindoo Valley

To Indian Creek Meadows

Hindoo Creek

1114

Rattlesnake Trail

William O. Douglas Wilderness

1114

End of ATV road

Rattlesnake

Creek

1114

37

Rattlesnake Trailhead

To FR 1500

1502

5186000

5184000

To FR 1500

1504

Three Creeks

1504

5186000
6440000
6442000
6444000
6440000
6442000
6444000
5184000
5184000

good campsite to the left of the trail next to the junction. If this is a day hike, this is the place to turn around, but if you brought your camping gear with you, check out the options below.

Miles and Directions

0.0   East Mount Aix Trailhead. 46 48.875N 121 09.057W. Head southwest.

1.7   Buck Lake. 46 48.606N 121 10.331W.

3.4   Junction with Richmond Mine Trail 973. 46 48.497N 121 11.710W. Turnaround point.

6.8   East Mount Aix Trailhead.

Options: The campsite next to the junction of the Mount Aix and Richmond Mine Trails makes a good base camp for parties that wish to climb Mount Aix from the east. Water can be obtained a short distance ahead where the Mount Aix Trail crosses Dog Creek. From the campsite it is about 5 miles and nearly 3,400 vertical feet along the Mount Aix Trail to the summit of Mount Aix.

If you bear right at the junction and take the Richmond Mine Trail, you continue up Dog Creek Canyon for a little less than 1.5 miles. Then the trail climbs over the ridge southwest of Nelson Butte before descending into the North Fork Rattlesnake Canyon.

37 Rattlesnake Trail 1114

Hike into a lightly used portion of the William O. Douglas Wilderness, along the very scenic Rattlesnake Canyon, beneath the rugged cliffs of Timberwolf Mountain.

See map on page 177.
Start: Rattlesnake Trailhead.
Type of hike: Out-and-back day hike or a backpack to the campsite at the junction of the Rattlesnake and Hindoo Trails.
Total distance: 7.4 miles to the junction with the Hindoo Trail.
Difficulty: Moderate for the first 1.9 miles, strenuous above there.
Maps: USDA Forest Service William O. Douglas and Norse Peak Wilderness or Meeks Table and Timberwolf Mountain USGS quads.
Permits and fees: William O. Douglas Wilderness permit.

Best months: August–September.
Special considerations: Although the weather and lack of snow in spring and early summer seem to make this an inviting route for that time of year, the creek crossings can be very difficult and dangerous. This route is very rough in places, so good hiking boots are a necessity. You must cross Rattlesnake Creek several times, making sandals or some other type of water shoes very useful. Though not very common, rattlesnakes are present along this trail, so be aware of the possibility of encountering one.

Finding the trailhead: To reach Rattlesnake Trailhead from the **Seattle-Tacoma** area, drive to Enumclaw. From Enumclaw follow State Route 410 for 41 miles east and south to Cayuse Pass. If you are coming from **Portland,** Oregon, drive north on Interstate 5 for 68 miles to the junction with U.S. Highway 12. Then head east on US 12 for 71 miles (7 miles east of Packwood) to the junction with State Route 123. Turn left off US 12 on SR 123 and head north for 16.5 miles to Cayuse Pass and the junction with SR 410.

Turn right (left if coming from Seattle) on SR 410 and head east for 3.7 miles to Chinook Pass. From Chinook Pass continue east on SR 410 for 39 miles to the junction with Nile Road at Eagle Rock Country Junction. This junction is about 12 miles west of Naches. Turn right (southwest) on Nile Road and follow it for 1.3 miles to the junction with Bethel Ridge Road (Forest Road 1500). Turn left (southwest) on FR 1500 and drive 8.3 miles to the junction with Forest Road 1504. The Wenatchee National Forest map has 1504 and 1500 mixed up in this area. Follow the road numbers on the signs. Turn right (west) and follow FR 1504 for 1.8 miles to the junction with Forest Road 1504-185. Turn right on FR 1504-185 and go 0.7 mile to its end at Rattlesnake Trailhead. About halfway along FR 1504-185, the ATV road, which the route follows for most of the first 2 miles of this hike, leaves the road and climbs over the hill to your left.
Parking and trailhead facilities: There is a circle drive at the trailhead with a horse ramp, hitching rails, possible primitive campsites, and a small pond.

The Hike

The hike begins at 3,080 feet elevation, in a mixed forest of ponderosa pine, Douglas fir, tamarack (western larch), and grand fir typical of the east slope of the Cascades. The route heads southwest leaving the trailhead and joins a 4WD-ATV road in about 200 yards. After joining the ATV road, the track crosses Three Creeks on a narrow wooden bridge.

Once across the bridge the route climbs steeply for 0.1 mile, gaining about 200 feet of elevation, then levels out. The track undulates, never gaining or losing much elevation for slightly over 0.3 mile, then descends another 0.3 mile to the level of Rattlesnake Creek. The course then follows Rattlesnake Creek, heading southwest, for a little over 1 mile to the large campsite at the end of the ATV road. The route passes several campsites along the way. The altitude at the end of the ATV road is 3,050 feet and you are 1.9 miles from the trailhead. The end of the ATV road is a good place to take a break. To your right and slightly upstream, Rattlesnake Creek forms a beautiful pool as it flows through a solid rock formation.

If you have access to an ATV, you could drive to this point easily, but with a larger 4WD, it would be a slow trip. The route has some very rough places with stumps in the road, so it is not a good idea to attempt it with a low-clearance 4WD. For most of us it is much better to hike from the Rattlesnake Trailhead.

The trail climbs over a small ridge, through snowbrush and ocean spray bushes, as you leave the end of the ATV road. Then you enter the William O. Douglas Wilderness and descend to the first crossing of Rattlesnake Creek. This crossing is only 0.1 mile from the end of the ATV road. Just before reaching the crossing, there is a great campsite on the right side of the trail.

Pools in Rattlesnake Creek.

This first crossing is the most difficult of the creek crossings up to the junction with the Hindoo Trail. In September when the water is low, it is still knee-deep. The round rocks on the bottom are unstable and slick with a thin layer of algae. As you approach the far shore, you leave the round rocks and cross solid rock for a few feet. This solid rock can also be very slippery. A hiking staff or poles will give you a welcome advantage at this crossing as well as the ones farther upstream. Earlier in the season when the water is higher, this crossing is very intimidating and can be dangerous. Be sure of your river-crossing ability before attempting this crossing.

The trail climbs the creek bank on the far side of the crossing, then follows the north bank of Rattlesnake Creek for 0.2 mile to the next crossing. A rock cliff rising from the north side of the creek here blocks further progress up the stream bank on this side, so the crossing must be made. The last few feet down to this crossing are steep and rough. Below the cliff the creek forms a clear, deep pool where fish can often be seen. Cross the creek below the pool, then turn right on the far side and walk over the cobbles for a few yards upstream. Look to your left to pick up the trail as it heads into the brush and trees.

Now that you are on the south side of Rattlesnake Creek again, the tread continues upstream. This area abounds with wild rose bushes that can scratch an unwary hiker's legs. The route is also somewhat rough and rocky. You reach the third crossing of Rattlesnake Creek 0.2 mile past the second crossing. This is generally a fairly easy crossing.

After making the third crossing the trail heads on upstream, shortly crossing a tiny side stream. About 0.25 mile from the third crossing, the route crosses a usually dry creek bed. In another 150 yards there is a vague path to the right that leads a short distance to another good campsite. The trail makes a switchback to the right 0.5 mile past the third crossing of Rattlesnake Creek. Climb the switchback and quickly make a turn to the left to head upstream well above the creek. The USGS quad map (Timberwolf Mountain) shows the trail incorrectly for the next 0.4 mile. The tread contours along the slope, winding in and out of side draws and undulating slightly. Then the route crosses a small stream and traverses the top of a small bench for about 150 yards. Leaving the bench, the track again descends to Rattlesnake Creek and another crossing.

Here you have a choice. You can ford the stream and stay on the other side for about 50 yards before recrossing it. Or you can skirt along the tiny rock ledges just above the water for about 50 feet, then walk along a bar on the cobblestones for 150 yards to find the trail again as it enters the woods. If you're an agile hiker with some rock-climbing ability, following the ledges will be easy. If you are not, this can be a difficult and scary place. The water level must be very low in order for a hiker to follow the tiny ledge.

Whether you made the two crossings or skirted the rocks above the water, you'll then hike along the bar, watching to your right for the point where the trail enters the timber. A little over 0.2 mile after leaving the bar, there will be another campsite on your right. A few yards farther along, you'll reach the junction with the Hindoo Trail 981. The junction with the Hindoo Trail is 3.7 miles from the Rattlesnake Trailhead, at 3,230 feet elevation.

There is a good campsite a few yards to your left at the junction. This is a good place to end your hike up the Rattlesnake Trail. A short distance above here, a rock slide has completely covered the trail for about 100 yards. The rock slide can be crossed, but the trail is rough and vague above it and there are several more creek crossings. The MJB Trail, although it requires considerable climbing on the return trip, is a better way to access the upper part of Rattlesnake Canyon. Return by hiking back to the Rattlesnake Trailhead the way you came.

Miles and Directions

0.0   Rattlesnake Trailhead. GPS 46 47.729N 121 06.058W. Head southwest.

1.9   ATV road ends. GPS 46 47.415N 121 08.198W. Head southwest.

3.7   Junction with Hindoo Trail 981. GPS 46 47.102N 121 09.838W. Turnaround point.

7.4   Rattlesnake Trailhead.

Options: Set up your camp at the junction of the Rattlesnake and Hindoo Trails and explore the country to the west along the Hindoo Trail. The Hindoo Trail soon becomes a ridge route as you climb toward Mount Aix.

38 MJB Trail 1101

Hike into Rattlesnake Canyon from high on a ridge just east of the O. Douglas Wilderness. The MJB Trail was once used as a stock driveway. It got its name because a sheepherder marked its starting point with an MJB coffee can so he wouldn't miss it as he had before. The MJB Trail is the best access route into the middle portion of Rattlesnake Canyon.

Start: MJB Trailhead.
Type of hike: Out-and-back day hike or backpack.
Total distance: 8.6 miles round-trip to Rattlesnake Creek.
Difficulty: Moderate to strenuous.
Maps: USDA Forest Service William O. Douglas and Norse Peak Wilderness or Rimrock Lake and Timberwolf Mountain USGS quads.

Permits and fees: William O. Douglas Wilderness permit.
Best months: July–September.
Special considerations: This trail becomes much steeper below about 4,100 feet elevation. There is no water along the route above Rattlesnake Creek at 4.3 miles, so be sure to carry enough to make the climb back up.

Finding the trailhead: To reach the MJB Trailhead from the **Seattle-Tacoma** area, drive to Enumclaw. From Enumclaw follow State Route 410 for 41 miles east and south to Cayuse Pass. Turn left on SR 410 and head east for 3.7 miles to Chinook Pass. From Chinook Pass continue east on SR 410 for 39 miles to the junction with Nile Road at Eagle Rock Country Junction. This junction is about 12 miles west of Naches. Turn right (southwest) on Nile Road and follow it for 1.3 miles to the junction with Bethel Ridge Road (Forest Road 1500). Turn left (southwest) on FR 1500 and drive 21.3 miles to the MJB Trailhead. The Wenatchee National Forest map has 1504 and 1500 mixed up in this area. Follow the road numbers on the signs. The trailhead is on the left side of FR 1500. FR 1500 is gravel much of the way, but it is usually in good condition except for some washboard sections.

If you are coming from **Portland,** Oregon, drive north on Interstate 5 for 68 miles to the junction with U.S. Highway 12. Then head east on US 12 for 102 miles over White Pass and down to the junction with Bethel Ridge Road (FR 1500). Turn north (left) off US 12 on Bethel Ridge Road and follow it for 8.8 miles to the MJB Trailhead. The road is gravel all the way from US 12 but is in generally good condition. The trailhead is on the right (east) side of FR 1500. The elevation at the MJB Trailhead is 5,280 feet.

Parking and trailhead facilities: There is adequate parking and a stock-loading ramp at the trailhead but no other facilities.

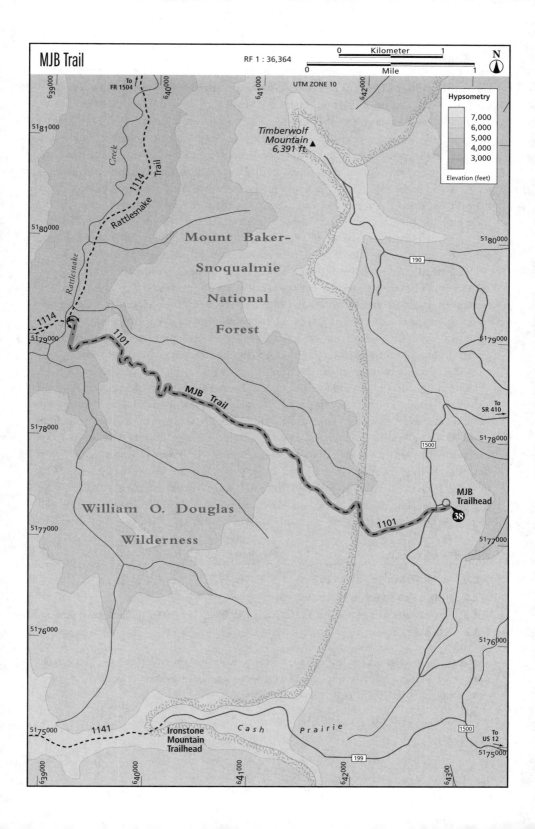

The Hike

From the trailhead the trail heads west-southwest through a clear-cut. In about 50 yards the route crosses FR 1500. There is a small sign on a tree on the west side of the road at the crossing. You then head to the southwest, shortly leaving the logged area, entering a mature forest of Douglas fir, western hemlock, tamarack, and a few western white pines. The tread climbs very gently, and in 0.2 mile you reach an unsigned junction with an abandoned path. Bear right at the junction and traverse west. As you make this gently descending traverse along the north-facing slope, Timberwolf Mountain comes into view to the north through the trees. Seven-tenths mile into the hike, the trail enters the William O. Douglas Wilderness, at 5,220 feet elevation, as you descend a small spur ridge. Soon you bear left off the small spur ridge to continue your descending traverse of the north-facing slope.

The tread crosses a ridgeline and a small talus slope 0.7 mile after entering the wilderness. The trail generally follows this ridge for the next 0.8 mile, heading northwest and descending to about 5,000 feet elevation. The views improve in the more open spots along the ridge. In places snowbrush and kinnikinnick cover the ground between the trees and a few beautiful ponderosa pines show up. Watch for elk tracks along the trail—there is a good possibility of seeing these magnificent animals if you are here early in the morning.

The ridge and the trail become steeper 2.2 miles from the trailhead. You descend around a point on the ridgeline and begin a series of switchbacks. Twenty-one switchbacks and 1.4 miles farther along, you come to a viewpoint on the ridgeline, at 4,090 feet elevation. Below and east of the viewpoint, scattered pines grow from the unstable volcanic slope. Below the viewpoint the course continues its steep descent, making six more switchbacks before reaching the junction with the Rattlesnake Trail 1114, at 3,580 feet elevation, 4.3 miles from the MJB Trailhead. There is a good campsite next to the junction. Rattlesnake Trail crosses Rattlesnake Creek just a few yards from the junction.

Miles and Directions

0.0 MJB Trailhead. GPS 46 44.076N 121 07.834W.
2.2 Ridge steepens and switchbacks begin.
4.3 Junction with Rattlesnake Trail 1114. GPS 46 45.060N 121 10.661W. Turnaround point.
8.6 MJB Trailhead.

Options: The MJB Trail is a good access route into the upper reaches of Rattlesnake Canyon. It's only about 3 miles southwest along the Rattlesnake Trail from its junction with the MJB Trail to Rattlesnake Meadows.

39 Ironstone Mountain
Trails 1141, 1111, and 1110

Hike along an alpine ridgeline, passing over or close to several peaks, taking in some of the best views in the William O. Douglas Wilderness and watching for mountain goats and elk along the way.

Start: Ironstone Mountain Trailhead.
Type of hike: Shuttle backpack or long day hike to Andy Creek Trailhead or an optional out-and-back day hike or backpack to Shellrock Peak.
Total distance: 10.1 miles one-way to Andy Creek Trailhead.
Difficulty: Moderate to Andy Creek Trailhead, strenuous to Shellrock Peak.
Maps: USDA Forest Service William O. Douglas and Norse Peak Wilderness or Rimrock Lake and Spiral Butte USGS quads.

Permits and fees: William O. Douglas Wilderness permit.
Best months: July–September.
Special considerations: Water is very limited along this trail, so take along all that you will need. Much of this trail is not shaded, so put on your sunscreen. The optional route to Shellrock Peak requires good route-finding skills and a little scrambling.

Finding the trailhead: To reach the Ironstone Mountain Trailhead from the **Seattle-Tacoma** area, drive to Enumclaw. Then take State Route 410 east and south for 41 miles to Cayuse Pass. Turn left at Cayuse Pass, staying on SR 410, and drive east for 43 miles to the junction with Nile Road at Eagle Rock Country Junction, about 12 miles west of Naches. Turn right (southwest) on Nile Road and follow it for 1.3 miles to the junction with Bethel Ridge Road (Forest Road 1500). Turn left (southwest) on FR 1500 and drive 23.6 miles to the junction with Forest Road 199. The Wenatchee National Forest map has 1504 and 1500 mixed up in this area. Follow the road numbers on the signs. Turn right on FR 199 and follow it for 2 miles, passing Cash Prairie, to its end at the Ironstone Mountain Trailhead. The elevation at the trailhead is 6,320 feet. The road is gravel all the way from Nile Road but is in generally good condition.

From **Portland,** Oregon, drive north on I-5 to exit 68 (68 miles north of the Interstate Bridge), then follow U.S. Highway 12 east for 85 miles to White Pass. From White Pass continue east on US 12 for 17.5 miles to the junction with Bethel Ridge Road (FR 1500). Turn north off US 12 on Bethel Ridge Road and follow it for 6.6 miles to the junction with FR 199, signed to Cash Prairie. Turn left on FR 199 and follow it for 2 miles to its end at the Ironstone Mountain Trailhead.

To reach Andy Creek Trailhead, where this hike ends, drive back the way you came to FR 1500. Turn right on FR 1500 and go 6.6 miles to the junction with US 12. Turn right on US 12 and drive 8.5 miles west to the junction with Indian Creek Road (Forest Road 1308). This junction is 0.6 mile west of milepost 160. Turn right on FR 1308 and go 0.8 mile to the junction with Forest Road 1382. Turn right on FR 1382 and follow it for 3.8 miles to the access road for Andy Creek Trailhead. Turn right on the access road and follow it to the turnaround at its end (about 0.2 mile). The forest service roads are all gravel after leaving US 12, and the 0.2-mile-long access road to the trailhead can be very rough. If you don't have a high-clearance vehicle, you may want to park on FR 1382 and walk the last 0.2 mile to the trailhead.

Flowers along the Ironstone Mountain Trail near Burnt Mountain.

Parking and trailhead facilities: There is a parking area about 50 yards before reaching the Ironstone Mountain Trailhead, with parking for several cars. There are no stock facilities or water at this trailhead. The last 50 yards of FR 199 before reaching the trailhead is an unimproved dirt road, however, there are a couple of campsites along it. There are also several primitive campsites before reaching the parking area along FR 199. At Andy Creek Trailhead, there is parking for several vehicles but no other facilities.

The Hike

Get your wilderness permit at the trailhead, then descend very slightly through a mature subalpine forest typical of the east slopes of the Cascade Mountains. Hemlock is the dominant species of tree, with white-bark and lodgepole pine mixed in, along with subalpine fir and Alaska cedar. A few yards into the hike, you'll pass the William O. Douglas Wilderness boundary. Past the wilderness boundary the tread climbs slightly. To your left a short path leads to a viewpoint, where mountain goats are sometimes seen.

A little farther along, the tread begins to descend. To the right the north-facing slope is forested, but to the left the drier south-facing slope is mostly open. This allows for a fantastic view of Mount Adams and Goat Rocks to the south and south-west. If the air is clear enough, you can see just the tip of Mount Hood in Oregon, slightly to the left of Mount Adams. In a few more yards the huge ice-covered bulk of Mount Rainier comes into view to the west–northwest. To the north on a very clear day, Glacier Peak, 95 miles away, can also be seen, as well as the Stuart Range to the north–northeast; Bismarck Peak and Mount Aix are close by to the northwest.

Soon the tread makes a turn to the right, temporarily leaving the ridgeline and descending a forested slope. The route makes three switchbacks and drops to 6,120 feet elevation, 0.7 mile from the trailhead. Soon you will climb back to the ridgeline and continue on more open slopes, covered with sagebrush and flowers, to the junc-tion with the Burnt Mountain Trail 1140. At the junction your elevation is 6,270 feet and you are 1.2 miles from the trailhead. Burnt Mountain Trail turns to the right and heads north. There is generally good cell phone service at the junction.

Past the junction with the Burnt Mountain Trail, the Ironstone Mountain Trail heads southwest, quickly crossing a small spur ridge. Then you traverse back to the semi-open ridgeline, where the route descends gently. In 0.5 mile you will have dropped to 6,090 feet elevation in a poorly defined saddle. From the saddle the tread climbs for 0.4 mile, then flattens and passes a campsite, which is a few yards to the left of the trail. After passing the campsite the course climbs, making a couple of tiny switchbacks, then trav-erses left of the ridgeline on an open slope. You then ascend to cross a spur ridge just south of the summit of Burnt Mountain. The trail crosses the spur ridge, at 6,440 feet elevation, 2.4 miles from the trailhead. As you cross the spur ridge, a vague path lead-ing to the summit of Burnt Mountain turns to the right (north–northwest). The short side trip to the 6,536-foot-high summit is well worth the time it takes.

After passing the path to the summit of Burnt Mountain, the Ironstone Moun-tain Trail makes a descending traverse to the northwest for 0.25 mile, back to the main ridgeline. Then you continue your gradual descent along the ridge, heading west–southwest for 0.75 mile to a semiopen saddle at 5,840 feet elevation. Leaving the saddle the trail climbs in and out of the timber, sometimes steeply, for 0.9 mile to the junction with the Shellrock Peak Trail 1132. This junction, 4.4 miles from the trailhead, is at 6,280 feet elevation. The Shellrock Peak Trail turns to the right (north) at the signed junction.

The Shellrock Peak Trail descends to Rattlesnake Creek and does not go to Shellrock Peak. To reach the route to the Shellrock Peak summit, continue west–southwest on the Ironstone Mountain Trail for another 200 yards. See the options below for a description of the route to the summit of Shellrock Peak.

After passing the obscure route to Shellrock Peak, the trail continues southwest for a little more than 0.1 mile, then turns south. If you make this turn to the south, you have passed the route to Shellrock Peak. As you make the turn, Ironstone Mountain is in view to the southwest.

If you have decided to continue on the Ironstone Mountain Trail, turn the cor-ner and continue south along the ridgeline. In about 0.6 mile, just after passing Peak

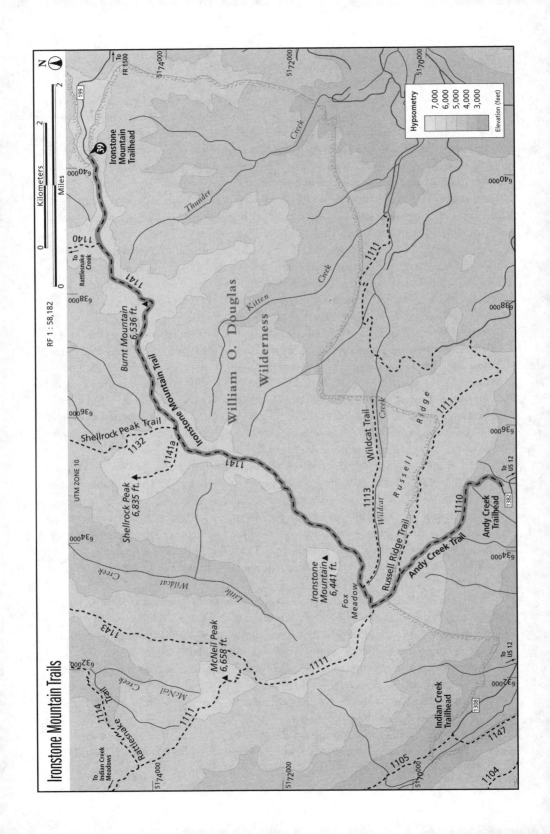

Ironstone Mountain Trails

RF 1 : 58,182

6,264, the route descends to a small open saddle, then bears off the left side of the ridgeline. The route generally stays below and on the left side of the ridgeline from here to the junction with the Wildcat Trail 1113. One and six tenths miles after you leave the ridgeline, the tread passes beneath the southeastern slope of 6,441-foot-high Ironstone Mountain, at 5,780 feet elevation. Fox Meadow and the junction with the Wildcat Trail are reached 7.5 miles from the Ironstone Mountain Trailhead, at 5,700 feet elevation.

Bear right (nearly straight ahead to the southwest) at the junction, and you'll soon begin to climb toward Russell Ridge. The route shortly becomes steep and eroded. As you near the junction with the Russell Ridge Trail, the tread disappears—the groove in the ground that was the trail has been filled with logs and sticks. Stay just on the left side of the obliterated trail, heading southwest, and in about 100 yards you will reach the Russell Ridge Trail 1111, at 5,980 feet elevation. There are no signs at the junction and it is very hard to spot when hiking along the Russell Ridge Trail. To the right the Russell Ridge Trail heads northwest for about 4 miles, over McNeil Peak to a junction with the Rattlesnake Trail 1114.

Turn left on the Russell Ridge Trail and climb slightly for 0.1 mile before beginning to descend. As you begin your descent, look to your right (southwest): The oddly shaped Bootjack Rock is close by and slightly below the trail on the upper slope of Indian Creek Canyon. In another 0.4 mile the trail crosses a small, old burn area, where there is a good view of Goat Rocks to the southwest. The route leaves the burned area and in 0.1 mile reaches the junction with the Andy Creek Trail 1110, at 5,690 feet elevation. Here you leave the William O. Douglas Wilderness.

Turn right on the Andy Creek Trail and begin to head down toward Andy Creek Trailhead. Much of the route between here and the Andy Creek Trailhead is shown incorrectly on the USGS Rimrock Lake quad map. As you descend, the timber becomes less alpine. From the grass-covered openings, Goat Rocks are still in view. The route passes through an alder thicket 0.6 mile from the junction, at 5,250 feet elevation. The openings around the thicket may be nearly covered with lupine, larkspur, and phlox blooms in early summer. In the thicket the trail crosses a tiny stream. You'll cross another tiny stream, which may be dry by late summer, 0.2 mile farther along. Another 0.2 mile of hiking through thick timber and across open slopes brings you to Andy Creek. The path crosses Andy Creek, which is but a small stream here, at 4,950 feet elevation. Shortly the trail crosses another tiny stream that may be dry, then makes a right turn to head southwest and down. Near this stream crossing you enter an area that was logged many years ago. The route descends to the southwest for a couple hundred yards, then turns left to head southeast. In about another 0.2 mile, the grade steepens as the route makes a sweeping right turn. After making the turn you descend a long-abandoned roadbed for 300 yards to the Andy Creek Trailhead. There are actually two roadbeds that make this descent—the one on the right is the easier of the two. The elevation at Andy Creek Trailhead is 4,530 feet.

Miles and Directions

0.0   Ironstone Mountain Trailhead. GPS 46 42.944N 121 09.913W.

1.2   Junction with Burnt Mountain Trail 1140. GPS 46 42.841N 121 10.931W. Proceed straight ahead.

2.4   Burnt Mountain (just south of the summit).

4.4   Junction with Shellrock Peak Trail 1132. GPS 46 42.149N 121 13.415W. Proceed straight ahead.

4.5   Route to Shellrock Peak. Proceed straight ahead or optional turn to right.

7.5   Junction with the Wildcat Trail 1113. Bear right.

8.0   Junction with the Russell Ridge Trail 1111. GPS 46 40.581N 121 15.641W. Turn left.

8.6   Junction with Andy Creek Trail 1110. GPS 46 40.347N 121 15.042W. Turn right.

10.1   Andy Creek Trailhead. GPS 46 39.517N 121 14.131W.

Options: To reach Shellrock Peak on what was once Trail 1141a, turn right (north-west) off the Ironstone Mountain Trail 200 yards southwest of the junction with the Shellrock Peak Trail 1132, and climb gently to the west-northwest through the woods. In a short distance you will reach a rounded ridgeline. Follow the rounded ridgeline, still heading west-northwest, for another couple hundred yards. Here the timber will open up and your objective will come into full view. The route drops a few feet to cross a small saddle, then turns north-northwest and begins to climb steeply. As you begin to climb, the sketchy remains of Trail 1141a are visible, but the route remains vague all the way to the summit. The route bears around to the left as you reach the second rock outcropping on the boulder-strewn ridge. You regain the ridgeline above the outcropping at a little over 6,400 feet elevation. From here on, the route generally follows the ridgeline north to the summit of Shellrock Peak, at 6,835 feet elevation, about 0.8 mile from the Ironstone Mountain Trail. The total distance from the trailhead is 10.6 miles out and back.

40 Indian Creek Trail 1105

Hike completely across the southern part of the William O. Douglas Wilderness on a generally well-maintained route.

Start: Indian Creek Trailhead.
Type of hike: Shuttle backpack, with a loop option.
Total distance: 9.8 miles.
Difficulty: Moderate.
Maps: USDA Forest Service Norse Peak and William O. Douglas Wilderness or Spiral Butte and Bumping Lake USGS quads.

Permits and fees: Northwest Forest Pass and William O. Douglas Wilderness permit.
Best months: July–September for the entire trail. Mid-June through October up to the falls in Indian Creek.
Special considerations: The first crossing of Indian Creek can be difficult early in the season. Mosquitoes are thick in places during July.

Finding the trailhead: To reach the Indian Creek Trailhead, where this hike begins, drive north from **Portland,** Oregon, on Interstate 5 to exit 68 (68 miles north of the Interstate Bridge). Then follow U.S. Highway 12 east for 92 miles, crossing White Pass to the junction with Indian Creek Road (Forest Road 1308). From the **Seattle-Tacoma** area, drive to Enumclaw. From Enumclaw take State Route 410 for 41 miles east and south to Cayuse Pass and the junction with State Route 123. Turn right (nearly straight ahead) on SR 123 and follow it for 16.5 miles to the junction with US 12. Turn left (east) on US 12 and go 21 miles over White Pass and down to the junction with Indian Creek Road (FR 1308).

Turn left (north) on FR 1308 and follow it northwest for 2.6 miles to its end at Indian Creek Trailhead. The elevation at the trailhead is 3,370 feet.

To reach the Deep Creek Horse Camp and Trailhead, where this hike ends, from Indian Creek Trailhead, drive back to US 12 and turn right (west). Follow US 12 west for 21 miles to the junction with SR 123. Turn right (north) off US 12 on SR 123 and drive 16.5 miles to Cayuse Pass and the junction with SR 410. Turn right on SR 410 and head east for 22.9 miles, over Chinook Pass and down to the junction with the Bumping Lake Road (Forest Road 1800). Turn right (southwest) on FR 1800 and follow it 13.5 miles (leaving the pavement at Bumping Lake Recreation Area) to the junction with Deep Creek Road (Forest Road 1808). Bear left on FR 1808 and follow it 6.2 miles to the Deep Creek Horse Camp and Trailhead entrance. Turn left off FR 1808 and drive a short distance to the parking area and trailhead.

Parking and trailhead facilities: Adequate parking, restrooms, stock facilities, and campsites are available at or very near both trailheads.

The Hike

Heading northwest from the trailhead, the Indian Creek Trail passes through a semi-open forest of ponderosa pine and fir atop the alluvial debris along the bottom of Indian Creek Canyon. The course, which is a long-abandoned roadbed that allowed access to the Indian Creek Mine, climbs very gently. In the first 0.5 mile, to the boundary of the William O. Douglas Wilderness, you gain only 130 feet of eleva-

Entering Indian Creek Meadow.

tion. Past the wilderness boundary the forest composition changes slightly, with Douglas fir and grand fir making up the bulk of the timber.

Slightly less than 1 mile from the trailhead, the tread crosses a small stream. You leave the roadbed and make a switchback to the right 0.6 mile farther along. This is the first of five switchbacks that take you up to 3,950 feet elevation. Then the trail drops slightly to cross a creek bed, which is usually dry. Shortly after crossing the creek bed, the route rejoins the roadbed. The route follows the roadbed for another 0.8 mile. Then the roadbed makes a hard right turn and becomes Trail 1105b. Trail 1105b climbs to the east for a little over a mile to the abandoned mine site. The Indian Creek Trail bears to the left, leaving the roadbed for good. This junction, at 4,200 feet elevation and 2.5 miles from Indian Creek Trailhead, has a possible campsite next to it.

Bear left (north) where the roadbed turns to the right, staying on the Indian Creek Trail, and descend steeply, making three switchbacks to the rushing waters of Indian Creek. There was once a bridge across Indian Creek here, as shown on the USGS Spiral Butte quad map, but it has been washed out, so you must ford the stream. The crossing is easy except during times of high water.

The trail passes another possible campsite a few yards after making the creek crossing. Then the route climbs steeply. Wooden steps that also serve as water bars ease the ascent. The trail makes six switchbacks in the next 0.3 mile, climbing to 4,350 feet elevation. Then the grade moderates, although the tread is very rough, rocky, and eroded for a short distance. A little less than 0.3 mile past the last switchback, there is a viewpoint to the right of the trail. The path to the viewpoint, which is only a few yards off the trail, is very vague, but the sound of the waterfall that the viewpoint overlooks is easy to hear. The junction with the McCallister Trail is reached a little less than 0.2 mile after passing the falls. The junction with the McCallister Trail 1109 is 3.3 miles from the trailhead, at 4,500 feet elevation.

The Indian Creek Trail turns right at the junction, crosses a small stream, and then crosses Indian Creek. The course climbs along the east side of Indian Creek for the next 1.4 miles, then recrosses the stream. At this stream crossing, meadows start to show up next to Indian Creek. The route stays on the west side of Indian Creek for another 0.6 mile, then crosses it again in the southern end of Indian Creek Meadow. Lodgepole pines line the sides of the meadow; in fact, they seem to be encroaching on it. Shortly after crossing Indian Creek, you come to the junction with the Rattlesnake Trail 1114. This junction, at 4,920 feet elevation, is 5.4 miles from the Indian Creek Trailhead. Rattlesnake Trail turns to the right, climbs over a rise, and then descends along Rattlesnake Creek to a trailhead at the end of Forest Road 1504-185. There are several possible campsites in the edge of the timber along the sides of Indian Creek Meadow.

From the junction with the Rattlesnake Trail, the Indian Creek Trail continues north across the meadow for 0.1 mile to the junction with the Pear Lake Trail 1148. Pear Lake Trail turns right (north-northwest) and makes a loop, passing Pear and Apple Lakes before rejoining the Indian Creek Trail 0.4 mile ahead.

Bear left at the junction with the Pear Lake Trail and cross the meadow, heading northwest. Shortly the trail crosses Indian Creek for the last time, then leaves Indian Creek Meadow. You will reach the upper junction with the Pear Lake Trail 0.2 mile after leaving the meadow. Bear left (west) at the junction and begin to climb. For the next 0.7 mile to the junction with the Blankenship Lakes Trail 1104a, the route is mostly in the timber. Blankenship Lakes Trail turns left (west-southwest), reaching the first of the Blankenship Lakes in 0.1 mile. At the junction with the Blankenship Lakes Trail, you are 6.6 miles from the Indian Creek Trailhead, at 5,240 feet elevation.

The Indian Creek Trail heads northwest from the junction with the Blankenship Lakes Trail. Shortly after leaving the junction, you may notice that the trail has been rerouted to the right (east) of where it once went. The need for this rerouting is obvious, as the older route is deeply rutted and braided. Leaving the rerouted section, the trail enters Blankenship Meadow. As you enter the meadow, Mount Rainier comes into full view to the northwest. The junction with the Round Lake Trail 1105a is reached 0.8 mile from the junction with the Blankenship Lakes Trail, in the center of the meadow. At the signed junction the Round Lake Trail is often not vis-

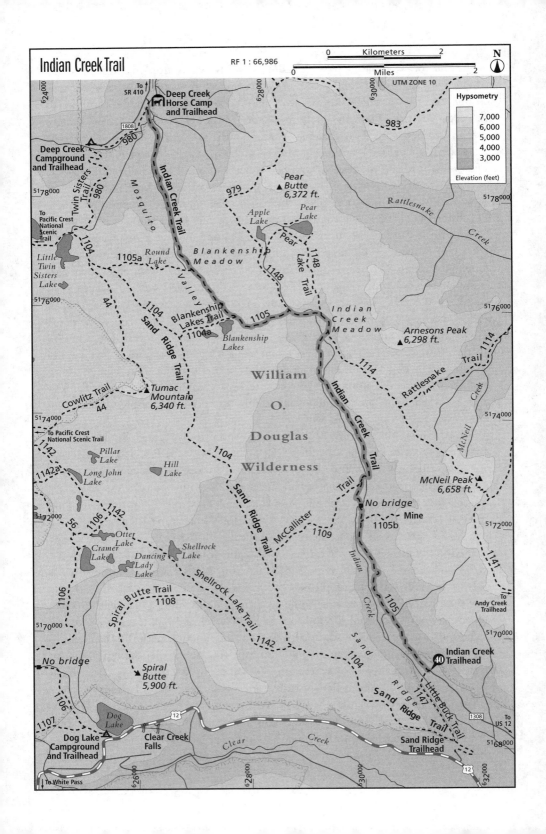

ible on the ground, but if you head west across the meadow, it soon shows up as you enter the small timber.

Soon after passing the junction with the Round Lake Trail, the Indian Creek Trail leaves Blankenship Meadow. In the openings in the timber, pink mountain heather and lupine line the route. The tread crosses a wooden bridge over a small stream 0.2 mile from the junction, then begins to descend. In the next 0.9 mile, the course crosses several tiny streams, most of which may be dry by late summer. Then the route descends, making eight switchbacks and crossing a couple more small streams in the next 0.25 mile. Below the switchbacks you cross yet a couple more tiny streams. Two miles from the junction with the Round Lake Trail, there is a pond with lily pads below the trail to the left. Just after passing the pond, the trail leaves the William O. Douglas Wilderness. Another 0.3 mile of hiking brings you to the junction with the Twin Sisters Trail 980. Bear right at the junction and walk the last 0.1 mile to the Deep Creek Horse Camp and Trailhead. The Deep Creek Horse Camp and Trailhead is 9.8 miles from the Indian Creek Trailhead, at 4,040 feet elevation.

Miles and Directions

- **0.0** Indian Creek Trailhead. GPS 46 39.889N 121 17.120W.
- **2.5** Junction with Trail 1105b. Bear left.
- **3.3** Junction with the McCallister Trail 1109. GPS 46 41.844N 121 18.148W. Bear right.
- **5.4** Junction with the Rattlesnake Trail 1114. GPS 46 43.289N 121 18.592W. Proceed straight ahead.
- **5.5** Lower junction with Pear Lake Trail 1148. GPS 46 43.415N 121 18.632W. Bear left.
- **5.9** Upper junction with Pear Lake Trail 1148. GPS 46 43.477N 121 19.115W. Bear left.
- **6.6** Junction with Blankenship Lakes Trail 1104a. GPS 46 43.446N 121 19.868W. Proceed straight ahead.
- **7.4** Junction with Round Lake Trail. GPS 46 43.928N 121 20.454W. Proceed straight ahead.
- **9.8** Deep Creek Horse Camp. GPS 46 45.578N 121 21.061W.

Options: To make a 9.3-mile loop hike starting and ending at Indian Creek Trailhead, first hike up the Indian Creek Trail for 3.3 miles to the junction with the McCallister Trail 1109. Turn left on the McCallister Trail and follow it for 1.9 miles southeast to the junction with the Sand Ridge Trail 1104. Turn left on the Sand Ridge Trail and hike southeast for 3.2 miles to the junction with the Little Buck Trail 1147. Turn left on the Little Buck Trail and descend for 0.9 mile to the Indian Creek Trailhead.

It's a good idea to walk 0.1 mile south on the Little Buck Trail from the Indian Creek Trailhead to check out the ford of Indian Creek before hiking this loop. Check the water level in Indian Creek to be sure it's low enough to make a safe ford, as you must cross Indian Creek here to complete the loop.

41 Little Buck Trail 1147

Hike across the flower-covered streambed of Indian Creek, then climb to the top of Sand Ridge.

Start: Indian Creek Trailhead.
Type of hike: Out-and-back 1½-hour hike with a shuttle option.
Total distance: 1.8 miles round-trip.
Difficulty: Moderate.
Maps: USDA Forest Service William O. Douglas and Norse Peak Wilderness or Spiral Butte USGS quad.

Permits and fees: Northwest Forest Pass and William O. Douglas Wilderness permit.
Best months: Mid-July through October.
Special considerations: Sandals or other water shoes may be needed to cross Indian Creek. This crossing can be difficult and even dangerous at times of high water.

Finding the trailhead: To reach the Indian Creek Trailhead, drive north from **Portland,** Oregon, on Interstate 5 to exit 68 (68 miles north of the Interstate Bridge). Then follow U.S. Highway 12 east for 92 miles, crossing White Pass to the junction with Indian Creek Road (Forest Road 1308). From the **Seattle-Tacoma** area, drive to Enumclaw. Then take State Route 410 east and south for 41 miles to Cayuse Pass and the junction with State Route 123. Bear right on SR 123 and go 16.5 miles south to the junction with US 12. Turn left (east) on US 12 and drive 21 miles to the junction with Indian Creek Road (FR 1308).

Turn left (north) on FR 1308 and follow it northwest for 2.6 miles to its end at Indian Creek Trailhead. The elevation at the trailhead is 3,370 feet.
Parking and trailhead facilities: Adequate parking and stock facilities are available at the trailhead. Primitive campsites are located nearby, along FR 1308.

The Hike

There are two trails that leave from Indian Creek Trailhead; Indian Creek Trail 1105 and Little Buck Trail 1147. To hike the Little Buck Trail first, fill out your wilderness permit. Then head south on the left side of the trailhead signboard, through the Douglas and grand fir forest. Where it can get enough direct sunlight, Rocky Mountain maple forms the forest understory. In 150 yards the route enters the rocky streambed of Indian Creek, where it becomes vague. Lupine, penstemon, and skyrockets grow between the rocks beside the route as you cross the 30 yards of streambed to Indian Creek. There is no bridge here so the creek must be forded. By midsummer this ford is usually easy, but earlier in the season it can be difficult.

After crossing Indian Creek you'll cross a few more yards of rocky streambed, then cross two much smaller side channels. Both Lewis and yellow monkey flowers sprout from the gravel on this side of Indian Creek, and alders hug the shores of the small channels. After crossing the side channels the route becomes more obvious, and you quickly enter the William O. Douglas Wilderness. The course turns to the left and begins to climb below a talus slope. Soon the track crosses two smaller talus

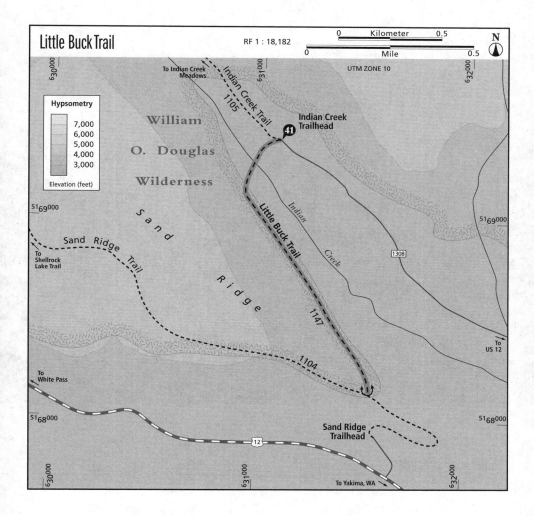

Little Buck Trail

RF 1 : 18,182

Kilometer
Mile

UTM ZONE 10

N

Hypsometry

7,000
6,000
5,000
4,000
3,000

Elevation (feet)

To Indian Creek
Meadows

Indian Creek Trail
1105

Indian Creek
Trailhead

41

William

O. Douglas

Wilderness

Sand Ridge Trail

To
Shellrock
Lake Trail

Little Buck Trail

Indian

Creek

1308

Sand

Ridge

1147

1104

To
US 12

To
White Pass

12

Sand Ridge
Trailhead

To Yakima, WA

slopes. Watch and listen for pikas on these rock-strewn slopes. They are common here and often whistle to announce your presence. Past the talus the course continues to climb along the northeast-facing slope through the timber. Beneath the trees Oregon grape nearly covers the ground in places. Through the openings in the trees to your left, look across the Indian Creek Canyon for a glimpse of Bootjack Rock, sitting high on Russell Ridge. You will reach the junction with the Sand Ridge Trail 1104 0.9 mile from the Indian Creek Trailhead. The junction is on the ridgeline of Sand Ridge at 3,680 feet elevation. Little Buck Trail is often used as an alternate access route for the Sand Ridge Trail. To the right (west-northwest) the Sand Ridge Trail leads 8.4 miles to Twin Sisters Lakes. Return as you came or see the options below for an alternate hike, requiring a car shuttle.

Bootjack Rock.

Miles and Directions

0.0   Indian Creek Trailhead. GPS 46 39.889N 121 17.120W. Hike south.

0.9   Junction with Sand Ridge Trail. GPS 46 39.221N 121 16.862W. Turnaround point.

1.8   Indian Creek Trailhead.

Options: If you can arrange a car shuttle, you can turn left on the Sand Ridge Trail and descend for 0.9 mile to the Sand Ridge Trailhead. To reach the Sand Ridge Trailhead by car, drive back the way you came on FR 1308 to US 12. Turn right on US 12 and go 1.8 miles to the access road for the Sand Ridge Trailhead. There is a small sign marking this road. Turn right onto the access road and drive a short distance to its end at the Sand Ridge Trailhead.

42 McCallister Trail 1109

Traverse out of Indian Creek Canyon, then hike across the gently rolling terrain through old-growth forest to a junction with the Sand Ridge Trail.

Start: Junction of McCallister and Indian Creek Trails, 3.3 miles northwest of Indian Creek Trailhead.
Type of hike: Internal day hike.
Total distance: 1.9 miles.
Difficulty: Easy.
Maps: USDA Forest Service William O. Doug-las and Norse Peak Wilderness or Spiral Butte USGS quad.
Permits and fees: William O. Douglas Wilderness permit and Northwest Forest Pass.
Best months: July–September.
Special considerations: Mosquitoes can be abundant along this trail in July.

Finding the trailhead: To reach the Indian Creek Trailhead, drive north from **Portland,** Oregon, on Interstate 5 to exit 68 (68 miles north of the Interstate Bridge). Then follow U.S. Highway 12 east for 92 miles, crossing White Pass to the junction with Indian Creek Road (Forest Road 1308). From the **Seattle-Tacoma** area, drive to Enumclaw. Then take State Route 410 east and south for 41 miles to Cayuse Pass and the junction with State Route 123. Bear right on SR 123 and go 16.5 miles south to the junction with US 12. Turn left (east) on US 12 and drive 21 miles to the junction with Indian Creek Road (FR 1308).

Turn left (north) on FR 1308 and follow it northwest for 2.6 miles to its end at Indian Creek Trailhead. The elevation at the trailhead is 3,370 feet. Then hike 3.3 miles northwest along Indian Creek Trail to the junction with the McCallister Trail, where this hike starts. The elevation at the junction is 4,500 feet.

Parking and trailhead facilities: Adequate parking and stock facilities are available at the Indian Creek Trailhead. Primitive campsites are located nearby, along FR 1308.

The Hike

The McCallister Trail leaves the junction with the Indian Creek Trail heading southwest. The forest here is typical for the elevation, with Douglas fir, true firs, western red cedar, and hemlock, with a few western white pines mixed in. In the openings beneath the trees, white-flowered rhododendron blooms in July. The course crosses a couple of streams in the first mile. Walk quietly and listen and you may hear a grouse drumming. Elk are also common along this route—in September you might hear a bull bugling. Bugling is the shrill call a bull elk makes during the rut to challenge other bulls.

The trail crosses a couple more small streams and reaches a swampy meadow 1.3 miles from the Indian Creek Trail. Early in the season the trail may be very muddy hear. A few Alaska cedars grow beside another small stream that you cross leaving the swampy meadow. The tread crosses a muddy streambed 0.1 mile farther along, then climbs a short, rough, rocky spot. Soon you pass a small pond, which may be

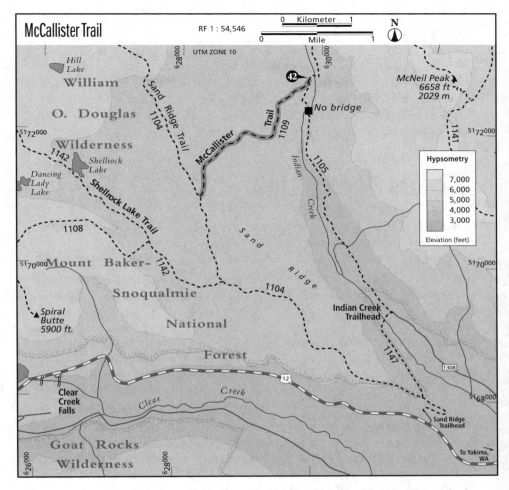

McCallister Trail

RF 1 : 54,546

Hill Lake

William

Sand Ridge Trail 1104

O. Douglas

5172000

Wilderness

1142

Shellrock Lake

Dancing Lady Lake

Shellrock Lake Trail

1108

Mount Baker-

1142

Snoqualmie

Spiral Butte 5900 ft.

National

Forest

McCallister

Trail 1109

No bridge

McNeil Peak 6658 ft 2029 m

1141

5172000

Indian Creek

1105

Sand Ridge

1104

Indian Creek Trailhead

1147

1308

Hypsometry

	Elevation (feet)
	7,000
	6,000
	5,000
	4,000
	3,000

5170000

5170000

Clear Creek Falls

Clear Creek

12

Sand Ridge Trailhead

To Yakima, WA

Goat Rocks

Wilderness

5168000

dry, then climb steeply again for a short distance. You reach the junction with the Sand Ridge Trail 1104 1.9 miles from the Indian Creek Trail, at 4,720 feet elevation.

Miles and Directions

0.0   Junction with the Indian Creek Trail 1105. GPS 46 41.844N 121 18.148W. Turn left.

1.3   Meadow.

1.9   Junction with the Sand Ridge Trail 1104. GPS 46 40.817N 121 19.472W.

Options: The McCallister Trail is best used as part of a 9.3-mile loop hike that includes the Sand Ridge and Little Buck Trails. To make this loop, first hike up the Indian Creek Trail to the junction with the McCallister Trail. Then follow the McCallister Trail as described above to the junction with the Sand Ridge Trail. Turn

◀ *Indian Creek Falls.*

left on the Sand Ridge Trail and hike 3.2 miles southeast to the junction with the Little Buck Trail 1147. Turn left on the Little Buck Trail and descend for 0.9 mile north-northwest to the Indian Creek Trailhead.

Before making this loop, it is a good idea to walk 0.1 mile south on the Little Buck Trail from the Indian Creek Trailhead to check the ford of Indian Creek. Check the water level in Indian Creek to be sure it's low enough to make a safe ford, as you must cross Indian Creek here to complete the loop.

43 Sand Ridge Trail 1104

Hike nearly all the way across the William O. Douglas Wilderness to a beautiful subalpine lake, enjoying the diverse flora and fauna as you go.

Start: Sand Ridge Trailhead.
Type of hike: Out-and-back backpack with loop, alternate destination, and shuttle options.
Total distance: 18.6 miles round-trip to Little Twin Sisters Lake.
Difficulty: Moderate.

Maps: USDA Forest Service William O. Douglas and Norse Peak Wilderness or Spiral Butte USGS quad.
Permits and fees: Northwest Forest Pass and William O. Douglas Wilderness permit.
Best months: July–September.
Special considerations: Much of this route passes through damp areas, so mosquitoes can be a problem, especially in July.

Finding the trailhead: To reach Sand Ridge Trailhead from the **Seattle-Tacoma** area, drive to Enumclaw. From Enumclaw take State Route 410 for 41 miles east and south to Cayuse Pass and the junction with State Route 123. Turn right (nearly straight ahead) on SR 123 and follow it for 16.5 miles south to the junction with U.S. Highway 12. Turn left (east) on US 12 and drive 13 miles east to White Pass. From **Portland,** Oregon, drive north on Interstate 5 to exit 68 (68 miles north of the Interstate Bridge), then follow US 12 east for 85 miles to White Pass.

From White Pass continue east on US 12 for 6.2 miles to the poorly marked entrance to the Sand Ridge Trailhead, which is on the left (north) side of the highway. The trailhead is at the northwest corner of the parking area next to a signboard, at 3,390 feet elevation.
Parking and trailhead facilities: Adequate parking and restrooms are available at the trailhead, but there are no other facilities.

The Hike

At the trailhead the trail appears to fork: Take the right fork and pass a TRAIL sign. From the trailhead at 3,390 feet elevation, the wide trail climbs north through medium-age fir and tamarack forest. In about 100 yards you will come to a junction. Turn left (northwest); the trail to the right descends back to the parking area

Pink mountain heather.

but nearly fades out before reaching it. In a short distance the tread makes a switch-back to the right, then climbs easterly to the rounded ridgeline of lower Sand Ridge, at just under 3,600 feet elevation.

The course makes a turn to the left to follow Sand Ridge as it climbs to the northwest, passing some large ponderosa pines. Oregon grape bushes and straw-berries cover much of the ground on the ridgeline. You will pass the William O. Douglas Wilderness boundary 0.8 mile from the trailhead and reach the junction with Little Buck Trail 1147 0.1 mile farther along, at 3,680 feet elevation. Little Buck Trail turns to the right at the signed junction and descends 0.9 mile to the Indian Creek Trailhead.

Past the junction with the Little Buck Trail, the Sand Ridge Trail heads on up the ridgeline to the northwest for about 0.2 mile. Then the route bears slightly left of the ridge, continuing to climb. The trail ascends the slope on the left side of the ridgeline for 1.3 miles, climbing to about 4,550 feet elevation. Then the trace regains the ridgeline and flattens out some. Now you generally follow the ridgeline for 0.8 mile to the junction with the Shellrock Lake Trail 1142, at 4,590 feet elevation.

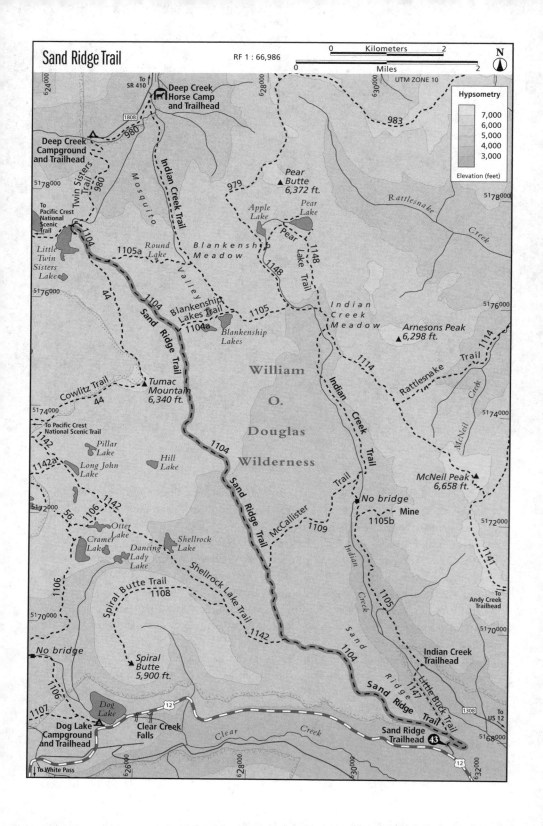

Along the ridge the forest is more open and the views are much better. When I hiked this trail, there was a bear near this junction.

At the junction with the Shellrock Lake Trail, the Sand Ridge Trail bears to the right, leaving the ridgeline. Before long you will cross the first of several open, nearly flat areas that are very wet early in the season. In fact, for a time shortly after the snow melts, the trail may be under water in places. From the junction with the Shellrock Lake Trail, the Sand Ridge Trail ungulates some but generally climbs slightly for 0.9 mile to the junction with the McCallister Trail 1109. At this junction you have reached 4,720 feet elevation and are 4.1 miles from the Sand Ridge Trailhead. From the junction the McCallister Trail heads northeast to join the Indian Creek Trail in 1.9 miles.

Bear left (really straight ahead) to the northwest to continue along the Sand Ridge Trail. The route continues to climb gently, passing beneath the east slope of Tumac Mountain in about 2 miles. As you hike along, the timber becomes smaller and more alpine in character. By the time you reach the junction with the Blankenship Lakes Trail 1104a, you have climbed to 5,400 feet elevation and are 7.3 miles from the Sand Ridge Trailhead. Watch for elk all along this route; they are abundant on this plateau. Like the McCallister Trail, the Blankenship Lakes Trail turns to the right to connect with the Indian Creek Trail near Blankenship Lakes. See the options below for a description of the Blankenship Lakes Trail.

Bear left (really straight ahead) at the junction and hike northwest. In slightly over 0.5 mile, the Sand Ridge Trail will cross a meadow with a pond. The route may be vague as you cross the meadow but quickly shows up again on the far side. The path continues to ungulate, never gaining or losing more than a few feet. Some of the dips in the trail may be wet and muddy early in the season. In mid-July pink mountain heather and lupine grace the trailside with their beautiful blooms. The trace reaches the junction with Round Lake Trail 1105a 1.3 miles after passing the junction with Blankenship Lakes Trail. At this junction you are 8.6 miles into the hike, at 5,320 feet elevation. Round Lake Trail, like McCallister Trail and Blankenship Lakes Trail, heads east to join Indian Creek Trail.

To continue on the Sand Ridge Trail, bear left (really almost straight ahead) at the junction and head west-northwest. Three-tenths mile more of hiking across this beautiful subalpine plateau will bring you to the junction with Trail 44. When you reach the junction with Trail 44, you have descended to 5,220 feet elevation. Trail 44 is called the Cowlitz Trail at its western end, but here it is more often referred to as the Tumac Mountain Trail. Trail 44 leads south directly over the top of Tumac Mountain, then descends west, crossing the Pacific Crest Trail, to Soda Springs Campground and Trailhead and Forest Road 4510. See the options below for an alternate return hike over Tumac Mountain.

Turn right at the junction and hike northwest, through the small meadows and passing a couple of tiny ponds. In 0.4 mile you will come to the junction with the Twin Sisters Lakes Trail 980, next to Little Twin Sisters Lake. This junction, at 5,160 feet elevation and 9.3 miles from the Sand Ridge Trailhead, is the end of the Sand Ridge Trail.

There are several great campsites at Twin Sisters Lakes and fish to be caught. Be sure to follow the wilderness regulations and camp at least 100 feet from the shoreline. Return the way you came or try one of the options below.

Miles and Directions

0.0 Sand Ridge Trailhead. GPS 46 39.041N 121 16.760W.

0.9 Junction with Little Buck Trail 1147. GPS 46 39.221N 121 16.862W. Proceed straight ahead.

3.2 Junction with Shellrock Lake Trail 1142. GPS 46 40.058N 121 18.779W. Turn right.

4.1 Junction with McCallister Trail 1109. GPS 46 40.817N 121 19.472W. Bear left.

7.3 Junction with Blankenship Lakes Trail 1104a. GPS 46 43.148N 121 20.591W. Bear left.

8.6 Junction with Round Lake Trail 1105a. GPS 46 43.942N 121 21.633W. Bear left.

8.9 Junction with Trail 44. GPS 46 44.004N 121 21.887W. Turn right.

9.3 Junction with Twin Sisters Lakes Trail 980 at Little Twin Sisters Lake. GPS 46 44.289N 121 22.144W. Turnaround point.

18.6 Sand Ridge Trailhead.

Options: If you have arranged for a car shuttle, it is only a couple of miles north from Little Twin Sisters Lake, along Twin Sisters Trail, to Deep Creek Campground and Trailhead at the end of Forest Road 1808, south of Bumping Lake.

Choosing Blankenship Lakes as your destination rather than Twin Sisters Lakes will shorten your round-trip hike by about 2 miles. To reach Blankenship Lakes, turn right off the Sand Ridge Trail 7.3 miles from the Sand Ridge Trailhead on the Blankenship Lakes Trail 1104a. Heading east-northeast from the junction, the Blankenship Lakes Trail descends gently through the mostly hemlock forest. In 0.5 mile you will be close to the southern shore of the northernmost of the three Blankenship Lakes. Side paths lead to the lakeshore. The lake is mostly surrounded with subalpine fir and hemlock timber. In the openings between the groves of trees are patches of white-flowered rhododendron, lupine, and a few alpine spiraea bushes.

Leaving the first lake, the trail crosses a meadow, and in a short distance the easternmost of the lakes comes into view to your right. The rocky shoreline of this lake makes it more picturesque than the first one. At some points on the rocks surrounding the lake, glacial scratches can be observed. The movement of the ice cap that once covered this plateau caused these scratches. Many possible campsites exist around Blankenship Lakes, but be sure to camp back at least 100 feet from the shoreline. Once you have passed the easternmost lake, it is just a short distance to the junction with the Indian Creek Trail 1105.

A more strenuous but rewarding loop can be made by returning from Twin Sisters Lakes over Tumac Mountain and then following the Shellrock Lake Trail back to a junction with the Sand Ridge Trail 3.2 miles from the Sand Ridge Trailhead. Making this loop adds 2.5 miles to the hike and about 1,500 feet of elevation gain.

To make this loop, first hike back to the southeast on the Sand Ridge Trail for 0.4

mile to the junction with Trail 44. Bear right on Trail 44 and follow it to the summit of Tumac Mountain. From the summit the route first makes a couple of descending switchbacks. Then you hike southwest across the forested landscape to the junction with the Shellrock Lake Trail, 1.7 miles from the summit of Tumac Mountain.

Turn left on the Shellrock Lake Trail and hike southeast, passing Long John Lake and the junction with the Cramer Lake Trail, to Shellrock Lake. Shellrock Lake is at 4,930 feet elevation and about 2.5 miles from the junction with Trail 44. The trail skirts the southwestern shore of the lake, passing some campsites.

Continuing southeast from Shellrock Lake, you pass the junction with the Spiral Butte Trail 1108 and reach the junction with the Sand Ridge Trail in about 2 miles. From here retrace your route along the Sand Ridge Trail for 3.2 miles to Sand Ridge Trailhead.

44 Spiral Butte
Trails 1106, 1142, and 1108

Hike to the top of Spiral Butte for great views of the White Pass and Goat Rocks area.

Start: Dog Lake Campground and Trailhead.
Type of hike: Out-and-back long day hike or backpack.
Total distance: 18 miles.
Difficulty: Strenuous with some route-finding skills required.
Maps: USDA Forest Service William O. Douglas and Norse Peak Wilderness or Spiral Butte and White Pass USGS quads.
Permits and fees: William O. Douglas Wilderness permit. A Northwest Forest Pass is required

at Dog Lake Campground and Trailhead.
Best months: July–September.
Special considerations: Mosquitoes can be a problem, especially between Cramer Lake and the Shellrock Lake Trail, in July and August. Much of the section of the Shellrock Lake Trail, which this route traverses, can be very muddy early in the season. There is no water available between the junction of the Spiral Butte Trail and the viewpoint near the summit of Spiral Butte.

Finding the trailhead: To reach Dog Lake Campground and Trailhead from the **Seattle-Tacoma** area, drive to Enumclaw. From Enumclaw take State Route 410 for 41 miles east and south to Cayuse Pass and the junction with State Route 123. Turn right (nearly straight ahead) on SR 123 and follow it for 16.5 miles south to the junction with U.S. Highway 12. Turn left (east) on US 12 and drive 15 miles east over White Pass to the Dog Lake Campground and Trailhead. From **Portland,** Oregon, drive north on Interstate 5 to exit 68 (68 miles north of the Interstate Bridge), then follow US 12 east for 87 miles to the Dog Lake Campground. Dog Lake Campground is 2.1 miles east of White Pass. Turn left into the campground and go to its western edge to reach the Dog Lake Trailhead, at 4,290 feet elevation.
Parking and trailhead facilities: Campsites, a boat launch, restrooms, and limited parking are available at the trailhead.

Dog Lake and White Pass Ski Area from Spiral Butte.

The Hike

This hike begins on the Cramer Lake Trail 1106. Get your wilderness permit at the trailhead, then climb gently to the northwest. In 0.1 mile you will reach the junction with the Dark Meadow Trail 1107. The Dark Meadow Trail heads west for 1.8 miles to connect with the Pacific Crest Trail. Hike straight ahead at the junction, heading northwest. Soon you will pass the William O. Douglas Wilderness boundary. The trail is nearly level for the next 0.8 mile as you walk through the old-growth forest, crossing a small wooden bridge along the way. The route then turns west and you climb for 0.2 mile, along the north fork of Clear Creek, before fording the stream. The crossing is generally easy but could be difficult during times of high water. The crossing is 1.3 miles from the trailhead, at 4,350 feet elevation.

The trail climbs gently to the northwest after crossing the creek. After slightly less than 0.3 mile, the route makes a sweeping turn to the right and you begin to climb along a south-facing slope heading northeast. At about 4,800 feet elevation, the trail turns north on gentler ground. A little over 2 miles after crossing the north fork of Clear Creek, Cramer Lake can be spotted to the northeast through the timber. The course then descends gently for 0.3 mile to the junction with the path to Cramer Lake. The path to Cramer Lake turns to the right 3.7 miles from the Dog Lake Trailhead, at 5,030 feet elevation. To continue on toward Spiral Butte, turn left (northwest), following the main trail, and skirt the meadow to the junction with the Dumbbell Trail 56. The Dumbbell Trail heads northwest from the junction, passing Dumbbell Lake and reaching the Pacific Crest National Scenic Trail 2000 in 1.4 miles.

Bear right (east) at the junction and climb to 5,090 feet elevation as you cross a small, poorly defined ridge. After crossing the ridge the tread makes a switchback and quickly crosses a small, sluggish stream. Soon the route passes Otter Lake, which is a little difficult to spot through the timber. The course passes a couple more ponds as you hike through the now smaller and thinner subalpine timber. Between the groves of trees are small meadows, where elk can sometimes be observed. The route reaches the junction with the Shellrock Lake Trail 1142 in a meadow, 4.6 miles from the trailhead, at 5,060 feet elevation.

Turn right on the Shellrock Lake Trail and hike southeast across the meadow, which is dotted with mountain heather and lupine. Around the groves of subalpine timber grow a bounty of huckleberries. The route passes several ponds, then descends to the shore of Shellrock Lake at 4,930 feet elevation, 0.8 mile from the junction. Early in the season, much of this section of the trail can be muddy. The trail skirts the southwestern shore of the lake, passing some campsites.

Continuing southeast from Shellrock Lake, the route passes a couple of ponds, then travels between the bottom of a talus slope on the right and a small lake on the left. You will reach the junction with the Spiral Butte Trail 1108 0.5 mile after leaving the talus slope. This junction, at 4,800 feet elevation, is 6.6 miles from the Dog Lake Trailhead.

Turn right at the junction on the Spiral Butte Trail. The route climbs steeply at first, then flattens out for 100 yards before continuing its steep ascent. The first mile of the Spiral Butte Trail is shown incorrectly on the USGS Spiral Butte quad map and on all other maps I have seen. The tread climbs steeply west-southwest for 0.7 mile, gaining nearly 500 feet of elevation. Then the trail bears right to head northwest along a poorly defined ridgeline. For the next 0.6 mile, the route ungulates, not gaining or losing much elevation.

Then the course begins to climb fairly steeply again. Beargrass, lupine, and huckleberries line the route as you progress through the now smaller timber. The steep route becomes somewhat overgrown with brush about 2.1 miles from the junction with the Shellrock Lake Trail. If you look behind here, to the north, you may catch a glimpse of Nelson Ridge and Mount Aix. To the northwest between the trees and brush, Mount Rainier is nearby. Soon the view ahead begins to open up as you pass through some larger hemlock trees. The trail ends at a viewpoint 2.4 miles from the junction with the Shellrock Lake Trail, at 5,860 feet above sea level. From the view-

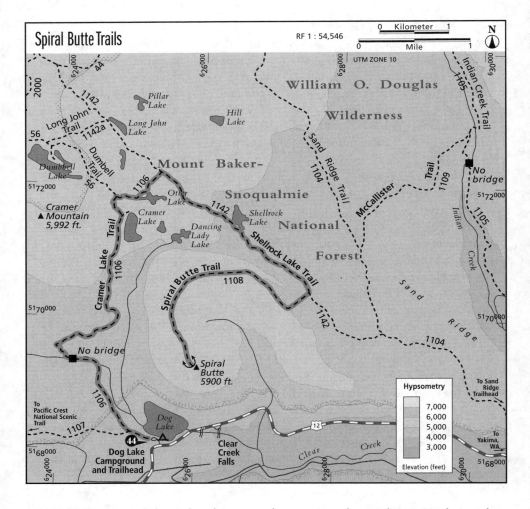

RF 1 : 54,546

UTM ZONE 10

N

0   Kilometer   1

0   Mile   1

William O. Douglas
Wilderness

Pillar
Lake

Hill
Lake

Indian Creek Trail
1105

Long John
Trail
1142

1142a

Long John
Lake

56

Dumbbell
Trail

2000

44

56

Dumbbell
Lake

5172000

1106

Otter
Lake

Mount Baker-

Snoqualmie

National

Forest

Cramer
▲ Mountain
5,992 ft.

Cramer
Lake

1142

Dancing
Lady
Lake

Shellrock
Lake

Sand Ridge Trail
1104

McCallister Trail

1109

No
bridge

5172000

Indian   Creek

1105

Cramer Lake Trail

1106

Shellrock Lake Trail

Spiral Butte Trail

1108

Sand

1142

Ridge

1104

5170000

5170000

No bridge

1106

Spiral
Butte
5900 ft.

To Sand
Ridge
Trailhead

To
Pacific Crest
National Scenic
Trail

1107

Dog
Lake

12

Clear   Creek

Hypsometry

7,000
6,000
5,000
4,000
3,000

Elevation (feet)

To
Yakima,
WA

5168000

44

Dog Lake
Campground
and Trailhead

Clear
Creek
Falls

5168000

point, White Pass and Leech Lake are in clear view to the southwest. To the south are the rugged peaks of Goat Rocks. Below and nearby is Dog Lake, next to where you started this hike. Resist the temptation to return to Dog Lake by descending the scree and talus slopes below the viewpoint, as they are unstable and very dangerous. Return the way you came.

Miles and Directions

0.0   Dog Lake Trailhead. GPS 46 39.278N 121 21.696W.

0.1   Junction with Dark Meadow Trail 1107. Bear right.

1.3   Cross North Fork Clear Creek.

3.7   Junction with path to Cramer Lake. GPS 46 41.135N 121 22.069W. Turn left.

3.9   Junction with Dumbbell Trail 56. GPS 46 41.261N 121 22.144W. Turn right.

4.6   Junction with Shellrock Lake Trail 1142. GPS 46 41.461N 121 21.619W. Turn right.

6.6 Junction with Spiral Butte Trail 1108. GPS 46 40.360N 121 19.868W. Turn right.

9.0 Spiral Butte viewpoint. GPS 46 39.869N 121 21.301W. Turnaround point.

18.0 Dog Lake Trailhead.

Options: An optional return trip, requiring a car shuttle, can be made via the Shellrock Lake Trail and the Sand Ridge Trail to Sand Ridge Trailhead. To return this way, descend back to the junction with the Shellrock Lake Trail and turn right (southeast). Follow the Shellrock Lake Trail for 1.1 miles to the junction with the Sand Ridge Trail. Bear right (east–southeast) at the junction and hike 3.2 more miles to the Sand Ridge Trailhead.

To reach the Sand Ridge Trailhead by car, get back on US 12 and head east for 4.1 miles to the access road for the Sand Ridge Trailhead. Turn left and drive a short distance to the trailhead.

Glossary

ant pile Same as anthill. The river bottoms along the American and Bumping Rivers have many huge ant piles.

ATV All-terrain vehicle.

blacktail deer A subspecies of mule deer that inhabits the coastal areas of southern Alaska, western Canada, Washington, Oregon, and Northern California.

blaze A mark on a tree made by cutting away a small section of bark with an axe or hatchet. A blaze may consist of one or two marks. Blazes can usually be seen for some distance ahead while hiking.

blow-downs Trees that have fallen or been blown by the wind. If there are many blow-downs across a trail, the travel will be slow.

BM (bench mark) A USGS survey marker. Bench marks and their elevations are shown on USGS quad maps.

braided trail A section of trail formed by two or more interconnecting paths.

bundles—needle bundles The needles on pine trees grow from the twig in a very short stem. Anywhere from one to five needles sprout from this short stem. If the stem sprouts five needles, as is the case with the western white pine and the white-bark pine, it is called a five-needle bundle, and the western white pine is classed as a five-needle pine. The lodgepole pine is a two-needle pine as it sprouts two needles from the stem, and the ponderosa pine is a three-needle pine as it sprouts three.

cairn A stack or pile of rocks that marks the trail or route.

cirque A bowl-shaped area where a glacier has eaten its way into a mountain slope, then melted. A cirque is formed at the head of a glacier.

cinder cone A volcanic vent from which little or no liquid lava has erupted. Cinder cones are typically fairly steep, smooth-sided, and made up of fragments of volcanic rock.

cinder slope The loose, unstable slope of a cinder cone.

clear-cut An area that has been logged of all or nearly all its timber.

cross deer A cross between a blacktail deer and a mule deer.

elk trail A route that is heavily used by elk and/or other big game. Heavily used elk trails can easily be mistaken for hiking trails.

exposure In climbing, the amount of exposure refers to the possibility of falling farther than just to the ground at your feet. In a highly exposed spot, it would be possible to fall several tens to several thousands of feet.

fire scars Charred bark, and in some cases wood, on the trunks of living trees, generally caused by a long-ago forest fire.

forest duff Needles, leaves, and other organic debris that accumulate on the forest floor.

FR Forest Road.

GPS Global positioning system.

intermittent stream A stream, usually small, that at least part of the time flows beneath ground level. Many small, steep streams become intermittent in the late summer and fall.

internal trail A trail that begins and/or ends at a junction with another trail. Internal trails do not reach any trailhead.

lava flow A stream of molten rock flowing from a volcano, or a stream of rock after it has cooled and hardened.

mixed forest/mixed woods A forest made up of several species of trees.

mule deer A large-eared deer of the western United States, southwestern Canada, and northern Mexico.

NWFP Northwest Forest Pass.

old-growth forest Forest that has never been logged and has not been burned in a fire hot enough to kill the mature trees in the last 100 years.

ORV Off-road vehicle.

outcrop or outcropping Bedrock that protrudes through the surface of the ground. An outcrop may reach high above ground level or be nearly level with the surrounding terrain.

PCT Pacific Crest National Scenic Trail.

Peak # or Point # Found mostly on maps but occasionally in the text, these are unnamed peaks or points that have been surveyed; their elevation is on the quad maps.

pika A small mammal that lives in steep, rocky areas or talus slopes. Pikas are related to rabbits and do not hibernate.

pumice The solidified froth of volcanic rock. Pumice is a light-colored rock that is light enough to float.

saddle A low point on a ridge, usually with a gentle slope. A saddle is larger than a notch.

scree or scree slope Small, loose rock on a slope. The sizes of the rocks are smaller than on a talus slope. Scree is very tiring to climb.

second-growth forest Regrown forest that has been logged or burned in the last 100 years.

signed junction A junction with a sign next to it indicating direction to a particular point and or the mileage to a point.

spur ridge A smaller ridge on the side of a main ridge. Spur ridges may be very steep.

spur trail A short side trail.

SR State Route.

switchback A sharp turn in a trail, usually on a steep slope. Switchbacks allow a trail to ascend a steep slope more easily.

talus or talus slope A slope covered with large rocks or boulders.

traverse The crossing of a slope, climbing or descending but usually in nearly a straight line. The term is also used to describe a route that follows a fairly flat ridge-line.

true fir Conifers of the genus *Abies*. In the William O. Douglas Wilderness, this includes grand fir, noble fir, subalpine fir, and Pacific silver fir. Douglas fir is not a true fir.

understory Plants, brush, and short trees beneath the canopy of a mature forest.

USDA United States Department of Agriculture.

USGS United States Geological Survey.

USGS quads United States Department of the Interior Geological Survey 7.5-minute quadrangle maps.

water bar A bar (may be made of wood, rock, soil, or even used highway guardrail) that drains water off a trail to prevent erosion.

Index

About the Author

A native of the Northwest, Fred Barstad has spent a large part of the last 40 years hiking, climbing, skiing, and snowshoeing in the region's mountains, deserts, and canyons. He has climbed most of the Cascades' volcanoes as well as Mount McKinley in Alaska, Popocatepetl, Iztaccihuatl, and El Pico de Orizaba in Mexico, and Aconcagua in Argentina.

Despite climbing Mount Rainier, just across the Cowlitz River Canyon from the William O. Douglas Wilderness, seven times and writing the FalconGuide *Hiking Washington's Goat Rocks Country,* Fred had never set foot in this wilderness before the spring of 2004. This quickly changed and Barstad personally hiked the trails described in this book in the summers of 2004 and 2005. This is Fred's ninth FalconGuide, all of them covering areas in Washington, Oregon, or Idaho.

Fred lives in Enterprise, Oregon, at the base of the Wallowa Mountains, where he continues to enjoy his passion for the outdoors.